"The editors and contributors of this volume have done a fine job of defining crucial issues that will shape the future of public diplomacy. The key to true engagement and the successful wielding of influence – the essence of public diplomacy – is to be found in the relational strategies described in this book. Those who manage and study nations' foreign policy should pay close attention to these analyses of the new realities of connectivity."

—Philip Seib, *University of Southern California*

"Ambitious, thought provoking, and highly readable, this is the best available account of the relational approach to public diplomacy. These probing and insightful essays by accomplished scholars will prompt reflection, agreement, and counter-argument – precisely what is needed in the study and practice of 21st century diplomacy."

—Bruce Gregory, *George Washington University*

Relational, Networked, and Collaborative Approaches to Public Diplomacy

Over the past decade, scholars, practitioners, and leading diplomats have forcefully argued for the need to move beyond one-way, mass media–driven campaigns and develop more relational strategies. In the coming years, as the range of public diplomacy actors grows, the issues become more intertwined, and the use of social media proliferates, the focus on relations will intensify along with the demands for more sophisticated strategies. These changes in the international arena call for a connective mindshift: a shift from information control and dominance to skilled relationship management.

Leading international scholars and practitioners embark on a forward-looking exploration of creative conceptual frameworks, training methods, and case studies that advance relational, networking, and collaborative strategies in public diplomacy. Light on academic jargon and rich in analysis, this volume argues that while relationships have always been pivotal to the practice of public diplomacy, the relational dynamics are changing. Rather than focus on specific definitions, the contributors focus on the dynamic interplay of influence in the public diplomacy environment.

This book is an essential resource for students and practitioners interested in how to build relationships and transform them into more elaborate network structures through public communication.

R. S. Zaharna is an Associate Professor in the School of Communication and an affiliate Associate Professor in the School of International Service at American University. Dr. Zaharna has been one of the leading scholars in public diplomacy and has testified on several occasions before the U.S. Congress. She specializes in strategic communication and culture; her works include *Battles to Bridges: U.S. Strategic Communication and Public Diplomacy after 9/11* (2010) and *The Cultural Awakening of Public Diplomacy* (2012).

Amelia Arsenault is Assistant Professor of Communication at Georgia State University and is the Media and Democracy Research fellow at the Center for Global Communication Studies at the Annenberg School for Communication, University of Pennsylvania. She specializes in collaboration and digital media strategies in public diplomacy. Her previous scholarly work on networks and public diplomacy has appeared in edited volumes and journals such as the *ANNALS of the American Academy of Political* and *Social Science and Information, Communication, and Society*.

Ali Fisher is the Associate Director of Digital Media Research at Intermedia, where he moved from Mappa Mundi Consulting in 2011. He specializes in providing insight to enhance public diplomacy strategy and evaluation through network analysis. He has previously worked as a policy analyst for the Center for American progress. He received his Ph.D. at the University of Birmingham, and has worked as a lecturer in International Relations at Exeter University. His publications include *Trails of Engagement* (2010), and *Collaborative Public Diplomacy* (2012).

Routledge Studies in Global Information, Politics and Society

Edited by Kenneth Rogerson, Duke University and Laura Roselle, Elon University

International communication encompasses everything from one-to-one cross-cultural interactions to the global reach of the internet. *Routledge Studies in Global Information, Politics and Society* celebrates—and embraces—this depth and breadth. To completely understand communication, it must be studied in concert with many factors, since, most often, it is the foundational principle on which other subjects rest. This series provides a publishing space for scholarship in the expansive, yet intersecting, categories of communication and information processes and other disciplines.

Relational, Networked, and Collaborative Approaches to Public Diplomacy

The Connective Mindshift

Edited by R. S. Zaharna
Amelia Arsenault
Ali Fisher

Routledge
Taylor & Francis Group

NEW YORK AND LONDON

First published 2013
by Routledge
711 Third Avenue, New York, NY 10017

Simultaneously published in the UK
by Routledge
2 Park Square, Milton Park, Abingdon, Oxon OX14 4RN

*Routledge is an imprint of the Taylor & Francis Group,
an informa business*

Library of Congress Cataloging-in-Publication Data
   Relational, networked, and collaborative approaches to public diplomacy :
the connective mindshift / edited by R.S. Zaharna, Amelia Arsenault,
Ali Fisher.
      pages cm. — (Routledge studies in global information, politics
and society ; 1)
   1. Diplomacy.   2. Foreign relations administration.   3. Social networking.
I. Zaharna, R. S., 1956–   II. Arsenault, Amelia.   III. Fisher, Ali.
   JZ1305.R455 2013
   327.2—dc23
   2012044009

ISBN: 978-0-415-63607-0 (hbk)
ISBN: 978-0-415-82966-3 (pbk)

Typeset in Sabon
by Apex CoVantage, LLC

Printed and bound in the United States of America by Publishers Graphics,
LLC on sustainably sourced paper.

Contents

PART II
Conflict & Culture: Connectivity in Practice

Part III
Networks & Collaboration: The Connective Mindshift

Series Foreword

We are extremely pleased to launch the series Routledge Studies in Global Information, Politics and Society with the volume *Relational, Networked, and Collaborative Approaches to Public Diplomacy: The Connective Mindshift*, edited by R.S. Zaharna, Amelia Arsenault and Ali Fisher. The work brings together a broad-based and internationally diverse group of scholars who explore, analyze, discuss, and engage on issues at the nexus between politics and communication in the twenty-first century.

The focus of the work is Public Diplomacy—both in terms of interpersonal communication and in the digital realm. Addressing relational, network, and collaborative approaches to Public Diplomacy, the various authors highlight the importance of understanding context, power dynamics, and communication processes. Both scholars and practitioners contribute to the volume, adding a breadth and depth of experience to the work. In addition, the work makes suggestions for how public diplomacy may be more effectively pursued in the global realm. We believe that the work will interest a variety of readers—students and scholars interested in diplomacy and international relations in the twenty-first century, and practitioners reflecting on rapid changes in the communication environment.

As the authors set out: "This volume seeks to stimulate thinking about the mechanisms, benefits, and potential issues raised by a relational approach to public diplomacy and chart a new way forward."

—Kenneth Rogerson and Laura Roselle, Series Editors

Tables and Figures

Acknowledgments

Editing a collective volume certainly involves a connective mindshift. It is only made possible through the generous help, contributions, and support of numerous collaborators.

We would like to thank the contributors for their generous insights, work on drafts of the chapters, and patience with the process. Without your collaboration, this book would not be possible.

We wish to acknowledge current and former students for their prompt and careful attention to detail with research, preparing the manuscript, and other tasks. Thank you, Delaney Chambers, Adel El-Adway, Xiao He, Lucy Odigie, and Efe Sevin at American University; David Gardner at Georgia State University; Yu Zheng at the University of Southern California, Center on Public Diplomacy; and Hong Yu at Jinling College, Nanjing University.

We would also like to recognize our editor at Routledge, Natalja Mortensen, for her enthusiasm and encouragement on our project, Darcy Bullock for her thoroughness in guiding us through the process and Denise File of Apex CoVantage for her patience and attention to detail during production.

Finally, this book would not be possible without the support of our friends and family. Amelia Arsenault would like to thank Shawn Powers, her parents, Raymond and Kathy Arsenault, and her sister Anne. Ali Fisher would like to thank his wife, Erika Cerri. R. S. Zaharna would like to thank Kamal, Dad, Nadya, Dorene, and LeRoy.

Introduction
The Connective Mindshift

R. S. Zaharna, Ali Fisher, and Amelia Arsenault

A twenty-first-century approach to public diplomacy (PD) recognizes the complex architecture of the multi-hub, multi-directional networks that exist between communities around the world. We live in an interconnected world where many of the complex challenges that societies now face straddle borders and continents. Equally, the communities that make up these societies communicate through a wide range of networks. These networks pivot around multiple hubs, and influence flows in multiple directions. As a result of this complexity, public diplomacy will increasingly adopt an approach based on genuine cooperation and collaboration with these interconnected communities. Relational strategies will not be a public diplomacy add-on but a core imperative. We call this shift in public diplomacy the *connective mindshift*.

The connective mindshift goes beyond simply accepting mutuality and heterogeneity as a necessary evil of public diplomacy in a globalized world. The level of interconnectivity and complexity creates forbidding challenges for information dominance, assertions of identity, and soft power. Yet it is from this complexity that the connective mindshift draws strength.

The connective mindshift recognizes the power of connections and identifies the nature of these relationships as a key unit of analysis for public diplomacy. Yet relationships are not of equal value. They can be positive, facilitative, and empowering, as well as restrictive, coercive, exploitative, and abusive. Connections can enable but also constrain actions within this "network society."[1] The connective mindshift seizes on the dynamic interplay of influence in the contemporary public sphere. Public diplomacy is an attempt to change the odds of specific outcomes occurring.

The success of a public diplomacy strategy based on the connective mindshift depends on the ability of practitioners to successfully forge positive and productive connections to individuals and groups embedded within a network of communication networks. Vast, commonly transnational networks organized around religious, social, political, or other common interests are now a primary means through which many individuals exchange information and develop shared meanings and interpretations of events. For many individuals, official government sources are less credible than are autonomous social networks. The decentralized nature of contemporary communications privileges networks—not diplomats. Instead of seeking power over others to force change, the connective mindshift realizes that empowering and engaging with others is a more efficient path toward sustained change.

The connective mindshift responds to the changing political landscape and interworkings of power. A further challenge for public diplomacy is that its resurgence during the twenty-first century coincides with increasingly de-territorialized geographies of power, the emphasis on nonstate actors, and, by extension, groups that are not defined by their geographic location. Jan Melissen "takes the view that public diplomacy flourishes in a 'polylateral' world of multiple actors in which the state remains highly relevant in increasingly diverse international networks." [2] These networks of influence, however, challenge strategies based on national reputation, as their connections and activity flow comfortably across borders. While both soft power and competitive identity continue to play a role, they have specific limitations when applied to complex scenarios with common problems that require cooperative approaches and international collaboration involving nonstate or non-geographically located actors. [3]

At present, those prepared to work in genuine partnership or skilled in relational and networking dynamics are almost as rare as the scholarship that identifies methodologies or means through which collaborative forms of public diplomacy might function. This volume seeks to stimulate thinking about the mechanisms, benefits, and potential issues raised by a relational approach to public diplomacy and to chart a new way forward. This introductory chapter surveys the practice and perspectives of relational approaches in public diplomacy's past, present, and future.

RELATIONSHIPS IN THE SHADOWS

In some ways, the connective mindshift marks a return to earlier diplomatic practices that paid greater attention to the behaviors necessary to develop relationships. Prior to the advent of radio, television, and other mass media capable of reaching mass audiences, nations relied upon interpersonal channels as the primary means for communication. As many diplomats are quick to point out, building and managing relationships is fundamental to all forms of diplomacy, not just public diplomacy. Paul Sharp highlighted the representational function that diplomats played in managing relations between entities. [4] Negotiations, the core of traditional diplomacy, rest on relational elements such as the ability to listen, identify others' interests and concerns, search for mutual interests, and develop confidence-building measures to help foster trust and strengthen relations.

Long before the rise of classical diplomacy in Europe, flourishing trade and diplomatic networks linked kingdoms across Asia, Africa, and Mesoamerica. [5] Sending and accepting gifts, still popular in diplomacy, are among the oldest documented practices used to cultivate diplomatic relations.[6] Accepting gifts entails a degree of relational recognition. Exchanging gifts fulfills relational expectations of reciprocity and mutuality. Writings on the famed Chinese admiral Zheng He in the early 1400s are filled with tales of gifts exchanged during his voyages. Among the most notable was the emperor's giraffe, a gift delivered personally by ambassadors from the east African port city of Malindi.

If relations have always been an enduring feature of both traditional and public diplomacy, why does their resurgence seem new? This question sheds light on the foundation of public diplomacy as a field of study and provides direction for future research.

Today, public diplomacy is global in both practice and scholarship. However, the term "public diplomacy" and the field are strongly associated with the U.S. twentieth-century historical context.[7] If one considers contemporary public diplomacy practices, not only are several features unique to the U.S. experience, but these features undermine a relational orientation.

In the U.S. historical experience, public diplomacy evolved during the ebb and flow of war. Dating back to the American Revolution, U.S. public diplomacy has followed a recognizable pattern. It initiates public diplomacy activities with the start of war, intensifies them during hostilities, and then abruptly ends them at the close of war.[8] Thus formulated against the backdrop of war, American public diplomacy assumed an adversarial orientation. It represented one more tool or weapon with which to defeat the enemy. Strategies focused on isolating the enemy and controlling the communication terrain; tactics included deliberate deception and distortion of information, as well as manipulating public emotion.

Information, rather than relationships, provided the core focus for U.S. public diplomacy efforts. The names of various agencies charged with public diplomacy reflect the information orientation. There was the Committee on Public *Information* (World War I), the Office of the Coordinator of *Information*, followed by the Foreign *Information* Service (World War II), and the U.S. *Information* Agency (USIA). Until recently, U.S. government reports, congressional testimony, and other documents on public diplomacy activities were referred to as "overseas *information* programs." Information transmission was central to the definition of U.S. public diplomacy, "to inform, influence and understand."[9] Relationship building remained a caveat.

Public diplomacy's twentieth-century evolution also coincided with the emergence of the mass media and the refinement of propaganda techniques— two interrelated trends that further downplayed a relational emphasis. During World War I, major powers invested heavily in sophisticated public relations techniques targeting the domestic populations of both their allies and opponents."[10] During the interwar period, as the breadth and depth of propaganda activities, including those practiced by American allies on U.S.

soil, came to light, academics and governments began to pay greater attention to the study and practice of propaganda.[11] Following World War II and encounters with Nazi propaganda, U.S. research on persuasion, attitude change, and public opinion intensified. U.S. government-sponsored research laid the foundation for communication scholarship.[12]

Propaganda, as a form of persuasive communication, is strongly instrumental and goal oriented. Information may be deliberately withheld or manipulated to achieve a persuasive goal.[13] Elements such as trust, credibility, and mutuality—cornerstones for developing relations—were similarly manipulated to serve the goals of the communicator, what Harold Lasswell termed "friendship propaganda."[14] While public diplomacy has tried to distance itself from propaganda, it has retained an instrumental or goal-orientation focus.

The emergence of the mass media, first radio in the 1920s, then television in the late 1940s, solidified the focus on one-way influence. In many ways, the impersonal aspects of mass communication are antithetical to the relationship-building features of interpersonal communication: individually tailored messages, instantaneous feedback, and constant readjustment to the listener. In contrast, the mass media typically target the widest possible audience, feedback is delayed, and the audience is assumed to be passive.

The Cold War further entrenched the adversarial, unidirectional, instrumental, and impersonal orientation of early twentieth-century public diplomacy. Public diplomacy was a weapon in the U.S. arsenal; the strategic objective was, as Cull observed, to attain information dominance over the Soviet Union.[15] While relational initiatives such as the Fulbright Program, jazz tours, and other cultural events were spotlighted as particularly effective during the Cold War, their effectiveness was measured primarily based on their contributions to defeating communism and winning the Cold War.

Given the historical origins of public diplomacy, it is perhaps not surprising that when the United States resumed its interest in public diplomacy after the September 11, 2001, attacks, it assumed a familiar orientation. Public diplomacy was immediately cast as a weapon in the "battle for hearts and minds," a soft-power complement to the hard-power military offensives in Afghanistan and Iraq. The goal of influencing the target audience became a national security issue. As Lee Hamilton, co-chair of the influential 9/11 Commission, described it, public diplomacy was "an essential element of how we stop people from coming here to kill us."[16] President Bush led the "us versus them" information charge, saying: "We need to do a better job of making our case." Driven by the belief that anti-Americanism stemmed from an information shortage, initial high-profile initiatives were mass media ventures focused on refining the message rather than addressing underlying relations. U.S. public diplomacy relied on arm's-length, impersonal communication tools that kept the audience at a distance.

REGAINING THE RELATIONAL ORIENTATION

Public diplomacy's roots in American diplomacy circles, combined with its high-profile resurgence after 9/11, made U.S. public diplomacy a prominent model. However, that model, particularly its one-way information and mass media–driven approach, has come under increasing scrutiny. Robin Brown at the University of Leeds has advocated that public diplomacy needs to become more reflexive about the way its U.S. roots have shaped the field's concerns and focus.[17]

Recently, established middle powers such as the United Kingdom, Canada, and Norway have been particularly vocal in their calls for increased engagement and collaboration. Rising powers such as India and China, who are introducing their own models of public diplomacy, have similarly stressed relationship building as a pivotal way forward. Even within U.S. public diplomacy, relational dimensions are being explored more vigorously, as indicated by new programs seeking to leverage civilian power and collaborative public diplomacy.[18]

The chorus of scholars, politicians, diplomats, and laypeople arguing for a greater focus on relationship-building strategies, including dialogue, networks, and collaboration, has helped to bolster shifts in public diplomacy practice. Mark Leonard, executive director of the European Council on Foreign Relations, was one of the early vocal and influential advocates who spotlighted the importance of relationships in public diplomacy. Leonard argued that public diplomacy began with understanding other countries' needs, cultures, and peoples and then identifying areas of common cause.[19]

Scholars as well as practitioners drew attention to the long-term, relationship-building appeal of cultural programs such as France's Alliance Française or the German Goethe Institut.[20] Academic and longtime USIA service officer Richard Arndt, for example, pointed to culture as the "The First Resort of Kings," and hence the title of his book.[21] Cultural diplomacy has recently experienced a revival. Several countries have initiated new cultural programs (for example, China's Confucius Institutes) or reinvigorated their cultural programs (for example, the Indian Council for Cultural Relations).

Appeals for more dialogue and listening reflected another early prelude to the relational orientation. The Council on Foreign Relations (CFR) stressed that enhanced listening skills represented the best way forward to reduce perceptions of American arrogance.[22] In presenting public diplomacy options for influence, Fisher and Bröckerhoff emphasized that "listening to another country can be a public diplomacy act in itself."[23] Cull similarly singled out listening as the basic foundation for public diplomacy in his taxonomy of public diplomacy activities.[24] Former British diplomat Shaun Riordan highlighted the need for dialogue on the dramatic changes in the international arena.[25] Harold Saunders, a veteran U.S. diplomat of Arab-Israeli peace negotiations, cautioned that "human beings in relationship—acting in concert with one another—has too long been neglected in the study of politics."[26]

Concurrently, the emergence of the term "engagement" rapidly gained currency in Europe and the United States.[27] Engagement intuitively suggests active audience participation, as opposed to passive reception, as a means to building relationships. The British Foreign Commonwealth Office entitled its major 2008 report on public diplomacy *Engagement*,[28] which "must be the hallmark of contemporary public diplomacy."[29] A year into the Obama administration, Kristin Lord and Marc Lynch called engagement "a pillar and guiding principle of the U.S. foreign policy."[30]

Calls for a greater focus on relationships grew, as did the justification for doing so. In her book *The Future of U.S. Public Diplomacy*, Kathy Fitzpatrick, an early advocate of a relational approach in public diplomacy, put relationship management at the conceptual core of public diplomacy: "Public diplomacy's fundamental purpose is to help a nation establish and maintain mutually beneficial relationships with strategic publics that can affect national interests."[31]

In 2010, Anne-Marie Slaughter tied the need for a relational approach to the changing nature of global power, which she said would be increasingly defined by connections.[32] Peter van Ham spoke more broadly to the global audience about the changing power dynamic in his book *Social Power in International Relations*. On the surface, social power may appear similar to the "soft power" advocated by Joseph Nye. The distinction between the two may well lie in the relational dynamic. Whereas Nye rooted soft power in the individual attributes, or "soft power resources," namely the country's culture, political ideas, and policies,[33] van Ham's notion of social power is rooted in the social dynamic, which makes relationships central. Indeed, as van Ham points out, social power "derives from the understanding that power is fluid and nonlinear and that it moves through relationships and communication."[34]

While the application of network theory to public diplomacy is still in its nascent stage, more and more scholars are beginning to address the relevance of networks for public diplomacy. John Arquilla and David Ronfeldt of the RAND Corporation think tank first suggested the possibility of network approach as a part of a broader "revolution in diplomacy."[35] In 2001, Carnegie scholar Jamie Metzl pointed out that new technologies were fostering an environment that favored what he called "network diplomacy."[36] The Aspen Institute followed suit in 2003 with the idea of "netpolitiks," a network-based view of politics as an updated alternative to realpolitik.[37] R. S. Zaharna described networks as "the new model of global persuasion"[38] and illustrated the "soft power differential" of how network communication trumps mass communication in creating, as opposed to simply wielding, soft power.[39] In early 2010, Gerard Lemos and Ali Fisher proclaimed that we are "entering the network phase of public diplomacy," in which a community is able to draw on the collective ability of the network rather than build connections to tell others what they should do.[40]

The recent mantras of relationship building, networking, alliances, partnership, and engagement are all part of the vocabulary of collaboration. The opening of this chapter highlighted the complexity and global scope of contemporary problems such as global warming, terrorism, and human trafficking are prompting the movement toward collaboration. As Lucian Hudson detailed in his study on collaboration for the British Foreign and Commonwealth Office, governments increasingly have had to join hands with corporate and nongovernmental organizations to tackle complex "wicked" problems.[41] "Tame" problems can be solved in a linear, individual manner; one proceeds to study the problem, gather information, and then develop and implement solutions. "Wicked" problems are so intertwined that trying to solve one aspect of a problem often leads to the creation of new ones.[42]

In a complex environment, public diplomacy cannot be satisfied by how "we" appear to "others," whether we have the reputation we deserve, or thinking listening is about understanding how "they" hear "us."[43] Effective political and communication activity must be strategically aligned to the political and communication dynamics of the international arena. The communication dynamics of the contemporary international arena thrive on complex and multidirectional networks. This operational landscape requires cooperative approaches and international collaboration involving nonstate or non-geographically located actors.[44]

A collaborative approach builds on the third tier of public diplomacy envisaged by Geoffrey Cowan and Amelia Arsenault.[45] They described collaboration as:

> initiatives in which participants from different nations participate in a project together. . . . Collaborative projects almost without exception include dialogue between participants and stakeholders, but they also include concrete and typically easily identifiable goals and outcomes that provide a useful basis and structure upon which to form more lasting relationships.[46]

Although overlooked, they suggest that collaboration "can sometimes be *the* most important form of public diplomacy" (emphasis theirs).[47] Indeed, collaboration may well become the public diplomacy equivalent of negotiation in traditional diplomacy. Just as traditional diplomats finesse their negotiating skills on behalf of their respective nations, public diplomats will need to be well skilled in collaboration to tackle and address problems for the collective, public good.

Collaboration focuses on common challenges and contributing toward outcomes that are better for the larger community than is any one entity alone. As Keith Grint argues, the role of the "leader" is to ask the right *questions*, rather than provide the right *answer*, because the answers may not be self-evident and will require a collaborative process to make any kind of progress.[48] In environments such as the ones often faced by public diplomats, argues Ali Fisher, asserting answers or focusing on the exceptionalism of a particular country is likely to be counter-productive. The alternative is to focus on interaction intended to stimulate a collaborative process.[49] This process that starts with asking questions, and listening to a multiplicity of answers, is at the heart of a collaborative public diplomacy.

BOOK OVERVIEW

Since we began work on this book, the interest in networks and collaboration in public diplomacy has visibly grown. We expected as much, given both the evolving trends in the international arena and the adoption of social networking tools. We also expect the networking and collaboration will become key research topics in public diplomacy, paralleling the volumes on negotiations in traditional diplomacy.

Our goal for this collective volume was to explore theoretical and practical considerations in developing relational, network, and collaborative approaches in public diplomacy. We began with the premise that a relational approach is now an imperative for contemporary public diplomacy. Our question was how—how could a relational approach be implemented? Despite the growing interest, at present there appears to be little understanding of the underlying dynamics of relationship building and a shortage of practical knowledge about how to transform relationships into more elaborate and effective network structures through communication, engagement, and collaboration. It seems as if public diplomacy knows where it should go but needs more direction and a firmer footing for how to get there.

To help us tackle the question of how, we turned to a diverse range of scholars and practitioners who could lend their practical and theoretical insights on the intersection of relations and public diplomacy. Some contributors, primarily academics, offer the view from the 35,000-foot perspective and discuss insights from their research to outline conceptual frameworks. Other contributors, primarily practitioners, share their valuable on-the-ground experience of what works in the field.

The book proceeds in three parts. Part I, Visions of Connectivity, surveys the various contextual and conceptual complexities inherent in relational public diplomacy. Each chapter highlights a pivotal issue exposed by the relational perspective. Peter van Ham of the Clingendael Institute in the Netherlands leads off with a discussion of social power and its impact for shaping public diplomacy in "Social Power in Public Diplomacy." Whereas power has long been a prime focus in international relations, van Ham cautions that traditional views of power are no longer applicable in the contemporary political arena; power is increasingly fluid and nonlinear, and driven by relationships and communication rather than by traditional hard-power articulations.

Kathy Fitzpatrick of Qinnipiac University addresses the issue of ethics in her piece that moves from discussions of soft power to social conscience. Historically, credibility and dominance have been pivotal concerns in public diplomacy media and messaging strategies. Ethics have now moved to center stage. In relation-based public diplomacy, we are no longer dealing primarily with information but rather with behavior constituted by collaboration, mutuality, and dialogue. She argues that in order to be effective, relational public diplomacy must pay close attention to questions of power and establish clear ethical principles and values for global public diplomacy professionals.

In "The Politics of Relational Public Diplomacy," Robin Brown of the University of Leeds challenges the assumption of context and agency in public diplomacy. Current public diplomacy has tended to privileged the assumption of individual agency; that individual actors can use public diplomacy to shape relations. Brown raises a cautionary flag, arguing the reverse: the relations between nations are critical determinants of what type of public diplomacy that nations can use. Context is critical. He presents a typology of how political relationships constrain or enable different public diplomacy tools.

In "Taking Diplomacy Public," former Canadian diplomat Daryl Copeland addresses the element of change and warns that "contemporary Western diplomacy is facing a perfect storm." The gravest security threats—pandemic disease, food insecurity, resource scarcity, and climate change—are rooted in science and driven by technology and can only be solved through multinational collaboration and dialogue. Only by adopting a more agile and relational approach will diplomats and foreign ministries retain their relevance and efficacy.

Ambassador Kishan S. Rana, in "Diaspora Diplomacy and Public Diplomacy," focuses on the implications of globalization for how we approach the critical building blocks of the relational perspective, namely, the audience or public. Traditional views of public diplomacy assumed that the target audience was a foreign public. Rana's piece dispels that assumption through an expansive survey of how diaspora publics can intervene to assist their home as well as host country.

Yiwei Wang of Renmin University in China highlights the critical role of culture in "Relational Dimensions of a Chinese Model of Public Diplomacy." While public diplomacy is a global phenomenon, we cannot assume that there is or should be one theory or method. As Wang illustrates, different practices and theoretical perspectives reflect the "colorful national hues" of public diplomacy. Wang's exploration of the Chinese perspective of soft power, political relations, and communication practices exposes the many relational aspects of a Chinese model of public diplomacy.

In Part II, Conflict and Culture: Connectivity in Practice, we move from conceptual and theoretical issues to the on-the-ground challenges of deploying a relational approach to public diplomacy. Maureen Taylor and Michael L. Kent of the University of Oklahoma lead with original research on U.S. and European public diplomacy efforts in postwar Croatia to create a "network of organizations" based on shared values. The scholars highlight social capital, an important by-product of relational public diplomacy that has been overlooked in scholarship, which may help explain the long-term benefits and sustainability of relational initiatives.

In "New Frontier in Relational Public Diplomacy," Tadashi Ogawa draws upon his decades-long experience working with the Japan Foundation to explore how cultural initiatives can be used in peace building. Conditions wrought by the trauma of conflict often leave people isolated and angry. Ogawa shares a four-stage model of conflict, highlighting which types of cultural initiatives are appropriate at each stage. He highlights the dual role of culture in conflict situation; it can provide a prime source of division and destruction and, conversely, can play a decisive role in rebuilding and healing relationships.

"The Relational Paradigm and Sustained Dialogue," by Ambassador Harold H. Saunders, provides another sobering look at the challenges surrounding efforts to transform and ameliorate adversarial relationships. Public diplomacy practitioners and scholarship often assumes a benign or even positive view of relationships. Ambassador Saunders, who served as an advisor to five U.S. presidents, draws upon his diplomatic experience with the U.S.-Soviet relationship and Middle East conflict to outline two frameworks for transforming dialogue, the "relationship paradigm" and "sustained dialogue."

We move from the interpersonal realm of relationships to the digital realm in "Delivering Digital Public Diplomacy," by Charles Causey of the University of Washington and Philip N. Howard, who is currently a fellow at Princeton University. Public diplomacy scholars and practitioners increasingly embrace social media as a relational panacea. Through an examination of the diplomatic complexities surrounding the release of U.S. diplomatic cables to WikiLeaks in 2010 and the diplomatic deliberations over NATO involvement in Libya in 2011, Causey and Howard reveal the capacities and constraints that digital and social media have for the practice of contemporary public diplomacy.

Staying with the challenges of the social media, in "The 'Virtual Last Three Feet'," Hyunjin Seo of the University of Kansas examines the successes and failures of Café USA, an initiative of the U.S. embassy in Seoul, Korea. Seo's findings stress that social media, when utilized effectively, maximize the relational capacities of network-based public diplomacy. Culture, however, plays a decisive role; publics vary regarding how they understand relationships, and this variability has significant implications for public diplomacy relationship-building efforts.

In Part III, Networks and Collaborations: The Connective Mindshift, we recollect the various pieces of the relational, networking, and collaboration approach and flesh out the vision for the future of public diplomacy.

R. S. Zaharna, in "Network Purpose, Network Design," argues the need to view networks in public diplomacy as a dynamic organism that can grow and thrive—or wither and die. What makes a network initiative effective, she says, depends on the alignment between the public diplomacy purpose and the initiative's design. Because networks vary greatly, she says alignment between purpose and design is critical. To illustrate, she draws on examples from two prominent network-based collaborative initiatives: the International Campaign to Ban Landmines and China's Confucius Institutes. She distinguishes between networks as a structure and collaboration as a process and outlines an analytical framework for identifying key dimensions of effective network and collaborative initiatives in public diplomacy.

Amelia Arsenault, in "Networks of Freedom, Networks of Control," takes a next step by looking at the network initiatives and network public diplomacy approach within the network of networks, the internet. She cautions that attempts to exert relational power through connective technologies are inextricably linked to state attempts to exert power over technological resources, and the ability or inability to enlist the collaboration of governments, internet users, and the many businesses that produce the infrastructure through which electronically networked public diplomacy takes place. The rise of connective technologies has put a spotlight on Public Diplomacy 2.0, which, in turn, has focused attention on the internet as a the conduit that makes PD 2.0 possible. She focuses on the tension between the two. To mediate this tension, she proposes collaboration.

Ali Fisher, in "Standing on the Shoulders of Giants," moves the discussion of collaboration forward by taking an interdisciplinary approach to identifying factors that can facilitate sustainable collaborative behaviors. He first lays out core concepts of how open-source public diplomacy operates within the complex environment of the international arena and then proposes collaborative public diplomacy as the optimal approach in such an environment. He discusses what he views as four building blocks upon which to develop a collaborative theory of public diplomacy: the flow of information through a community, pathways; the power of coordination and aggregation, focal points; role of network position in innovation; and, finally, actions likely to encourage collaborative behavior.

The book is designed to appeal to researchers, educators, and practitioners. For researchers, the book presents a survey of the literature and cutting-edge research from leading scholars in the field of public diplomacy. For practitioners, the book provides practical applications, concrete examples, and case studies. For educators, the book provides a theoretical and conceptual foundation for discussing relational, networking, and collaborative approaches in public diplomacy.

Our vision for the book is that it be accessible, forward looking, and imaginative. By accessible, we mean that we want individual chapters to be light on academic jargon and rich in analysis, which scholars and educators as well as policymakers and practitioners find equally understandable and applicable. By forward looking, we envisage the volume as moving beyond calls for more two-way dialogues to focusing on how to actually create, explain, or analyze those dialogues. Finally, we want to challenge ourselves and our readers to push the boundaries of how we think about relations, networks, and collaboration and move into new, uncharted terrain. We believe that imaginative thinking is critical to meeting the current and unforeseen future challenges for the connective mindshift in public diplomacy.

NOTES

1. Manuel Castells, *The Rise of the Network Society* (New York: Blackwell, 1996).
2. Jan Melissen, "Beyond the New Public Diplomacy," *Clingendael Paper* 3 (October 2011).
3. Non-geographically located actors include the "digital insider"—discussed in Fisher, "Bullets with Butterfly Wings; Tweets, Protest Networks and the Iranian Election," in *Media, Power, and Politics in the Digital Age; The 2009 Presidential Election Uprising in Iran*, ed. Yahya R. Kamalipour (New York: Rowman & Littlefield, November 2010).
4. Paul Sharp, *Diplomatic Theory of International Relations* (Cambridge: Cambridge University Press, 2009).
5. Yale H. Ferguson and Richard W. Mansbach, "The Past as Prelude to the Future? Identities and Loyalties in Global Politics," in *The Return of Culture and Identity in IR Theory*, ed. Yosef Lapid and Freidrich Kratochwil (Boulder, CO: Lynne Rienner, 1996), 21–44.
6. Christer Jönsson and Martin Hall, *Essence of Diplomacy* (Basingstoke: Palgrave Macmillan, 2005), 86.
7. Nicholas J. Cull, " 'Public Diplomacy' before Gullion: The Evolution of a Phrase" (Los Angeles: USC, Center for Public Diplomacy, n.d.).
8. John Brown, "Historical Patterns of U.S. Government Overseas Propaganda, 1917–2007," http://ics.leeds.ac.uk/papers/vp01.cfm?outfit=pmt&folder=715& paper=2903
9. Planning Group for Integration of USIA into the Dept. of State, June 20, 1997. According to the U.S. State Department, "Public diplomacy seeks to promote the national interest of the United States through *understanding, informing, and influencing* foreign audiences."
10. Edwin L. James, "Try to Sow Discord in Allied Armies; Insidious Propaganda Used by Germans to Divide French and Americans," *New York Times*, January 20, 1919.
11. The first books on propaganda appeared within the first decade after the war. Several of those who participated in the U.S. wartime information activities became instrumental in developing the communication professions. Edward Bernays, who worked with the Creel Commission during World War I, authored *Crystallizing Public Opinion* (1923) and *Propaganda* (1925) and became known as the "father of public relations." The Advertising Council

of America, which helped rally the U.S. domestic public during the war, was established after World War II.

12. Christopher Simpson, *Science of Coercion: Communication Research and Psychological Warfare, 1945–1960* (New York: Oxford University Press, 1996).

13. Harold D. Lasswell, "The Theory of Political Propaganda," *American Political Science Review* 21 (August 1927): 627–631.

14. Harold D. Lasswell, "Propaganda," in *Encyclopedia of the Social Sciences* (New York: Macmillan, 1934).

15. Nicholas J. Cull, *The Cold War and the United States Information Agency: American Propaganda and Public Diplomacy, 1945–1989* (New York: Cambridge University Press, 2008).

16. Lee H. Hamilton, "U.S. Must Get Its Story Across to Arab World," *IndyStar. com* (March 14, 2005).

17. Robin Brown, "Public Diplomacy and Social Networks," paper prepared for the International Studies Association, Montreal, March 2011.

18. Hillary Rodham Clinton, "Leading through Civilian Power," *Foreign Affairs* 89 (2010): 13–24.

19. Mark Leonard, "Diplomacy by Other Means," *Foreign Policy* (September/October 2002): 50.

20. Martin Rose and Nick Wadham-Smith, *Mutuality, Trust and Cultural Relation* (London: Counterpoint, British Council, 2004), 15; Cynthia P. Schneider, "Culture Communicates: US Diplomacy That Works," in *The New Public Diplomacy*, ed. Jan Melissen (London: Palgrave Macmillan, 2005), 158.

21. Richard T. Arndt, *The First Resort of Kings: American Cultural Diplomacy in the Twentieth Century* (Dulles, VA: Potomac Books, 2005), xviii.

22. Council on Foreign Relations Independent Task Force on Public Diplomacy, *Public Diplomacy: A Strategy for Reform*, Peter Peterson, chair (New York: Council on Foreign Relations, 2002).

23. Ali Fisher and Aurélie Bröckerhoff, *Options for Influence: Global Campaigns of Persuasion in the New Worlds of Public Diplomacy* (London: Counterpoint, British Council, 2008), 23.

24. Nicholas J. Cull, "Public Diplomacy: Taxonomies and Histories," *ANNALS of the American Academy of Political and Social Science* 616 (March 2008): 31–54.

25. Shaun Riordan, *The New Diplomacy* (New York: Polity, 2002).

26. Harold H. Saunders, *Politics Is about Relationship: A Blueprint for the Citizens' Century* (London: Palgrave Macmillan, 2005), 27.

27. It is perhaps important to note that the calls for a more relational focus are coming primarily from Western sources, particularly U.S. and UK scholars and practitioners. Other scholars have suggested that many countries have a predominantly relational orientation in their public diplomacy. See, for example, Wang in this volume.

28. Jim Murphy, "Engagement," in *Engagement* (London: Foreign and Commonwealth Office, June 2008).

29. Ibid.

30. Kristin M. Lord and Marc Lynch, *America's Extended Hand: Assessing the Obama Administration's Global Engagement Strategy* (Washington, DC: Center for a New American Security, June 2010).

31. Kathy R. Fitzpatrick, *The Future of U.S. Public Diplomacy: An Uncertain Fate* (Boston: Brill, 2010), 105.

32. Anne-Marie Slaughter, "America's Edge," *Foreign Affairs* (January/February 2009): 112.

33. Joseph S. Nye, Jr., *Soft Power: The Means to Success in World Politics* (New York: Public Affairs, 2004), 8.
34. Peter van Ham, *Social Power* (New York: Routledge, 2011), 3.
35. John Arquilla and David Ronfeldt, *The Emergence of Noopolitik: Toward an American Information Strategy* (Santa Monica, CA: RAND Corporation, 1999).
36. Jamie Metzl, "Network Diplomacy," *Georgetown Journal of International Affairs* 2 (2001): 77–87.
37. David Bollier, *The Rise of Netpolitik: How the Internet Is Changing International Politics and Diplomacy* (Washington, DC: The Aspen Institute, 2003).
38. R. S. Zaharna, "The Network Paradigm of Strategic Public Diplomacy," *Foreign Policy in Focus* 10 (2005): 1–4.
39. R. S. Zaharna, "The Soft Power Differential: Network Communication and Mass Communication in Public Diplomacy," *The Hague Journal of Diplomacy* 2, no. 3 (October 2007): 213–228.
40. Gerard Lemos and Ali Fisher, "Entering the Network Phase in Public Diplomacy | USC Center on Public Diplomacy | Newswire—CPD Blog," March 26, 2010, http://uscpublicdiplomacy.org/index.php/newswire/ cpdblog_detail/entering_the_network_phase_in_public_diplomacy/.
41. L. Hudson, *The Enabling State: Collaborating for Success* (London: Foreign and Commonwealth Office, 2009), http://www.mbsportal.bl.uk/taster/ subjareas/ . . . /fco/102378enabling09.pdf
42. Jeff Conklin, "Wick Problems and Social Complexity," in J. Conklin, *Dialogue Mapping: Building Shared Understanding of Wicked Problems* (Wiley, October 2005); http://cognexus.org/wpf/wickedproblems.pdf.
43. Nye, *Soft Power*, 111.
44. See note 3.
45. Geoffrey Cowan and Amelia Arsenault, "Moving from Monologue to Dialogue to Collaboration: The Three Layers of Public Diplomacy," *ANNALS of the American Academy of Political and Social Science* 616 (March 2008): 10–30.
46. Ibid., 21.
47. Ibid., 22.
48. Keith Grint, "Problems, Problems, Problems: The Social Construction of Leadership," *Human Relations* 58 (2005): 1467–1494.
49. Ali Fisher, *Collaborative Public Diplomacy* (New York: Palgrave, 2012).

Part I

Visions of Connectivity

1 Social Power in Public Diplomacy

Peter van Ham

INTRODUCTION

Who has power in international politics? This central question has become increasingly hard to answer, due to the growing complexity of national and global policy processes. Often this results in fast and furious statements on the demise of the nation-state, the growing power of nongovernmental organizations (NGOs), or even the impact of celebrities in shaping agendas and influencing decisions. Since we don't know who or what is driving change, media headlines about Twitter- and Facebook-revolutions in Moldova, Tunisia, and Egypt have caught the public imagination.[1] Public diplomacy is also considered a new approach to study the impact of (foreign) publics to influence decisions, often by using modern technology and social media. Especially China's forays into public diplomacy have indicated that image building and networking are now integral aspects of the foreign policies of all states, regardless of their size and their capabilities. Today, utilizing the opportunities offered by public diplomacy is considered a marker of sophistication and cleverness. Why threaten with sanctions and warships if the pressure of the "international community" can be equally effective? Why not use social media to get a message across and influence the policy agendas of influential actors? Everyone—from Al Qaeda to the CIA, from Greenpeace to Shell—uses this media-saturated playing field of international politics to spread their messages and guard their interests.

But how is power actually *wielded*, in such a messy terrain of influence, manipulation, pressure, and persuasion? How do we actually *know* who is pulling which strings, with what results? Obviously, the classical question of who gets what, when, why, and how remains crucial to understanding contemporary politics, if only because the answers are crucial to maintaining accountable and transparent—and hence: democratic—government and governance. So how should we study power? Is it based on, or embedded in, resources or in relationships? Should we examine structures or focus on agency? Is power a potentiality or an actuality? Which actors are the most salient, deserving our attention?

This chapter conceptualizes the notion of social power and examines its relevance for understanding public diplomacy. It argues that the concept of social power contributes to our understanding of the academic study of power in today's complex international environment. The case study of public diplomacy is especially instructive, since it involves the full scope of policy actors, ranging from states (big and small), to non-state actors (from established NGOs to the eclectic Occupy Movement), to individuals (from Hollywood stars to concerned citizens). It concludes that the complexity of politics and the speed of societal and technological change should not fool us: Despite all these revisions and revolutions, we should still be concerned with power and consider it the key variable in an ever-more-muddled political formula.

SOCIAL POWER—DEFINING THE CONCEPT

The notion of social power is hardly new, and has obviously been used more widely and often in sociology than in the study of international relations.[2] The "social" in social power derives from the understanding that power is fluid and non-linear, and that it moves through relationships and communication. For example, merely looking at resources and objective capabilities is hardly useful without examining how they are used and perceived by relevant other actors. Realists generally examine power in terms of coercion, as something that is possessed and accumulated, measurable, visible, and working on the surface. The study of social power, however, takes a markedly different approach, looking for power beneath the surface, as permeating all social relationships, institutions, discourses, and media.[3] The notion of social power aims to offer a necessary alternative conceptualization of power, since it acknowledges that the exercise of power always takes place in a specific social situation and is, therefore, inherently contextual. Just as a gun secretly hidden in a closet without anyone knowing about it does not result in a credible threat of force, social power is contingent upon interaction, communication, relationships, and institutions. Or, as Yale H. Ferguson argues, "[p]ower is not like money in the bank, [but] rather a relative matter. The effective exercise of potential power is dependent on the actors being targeted, the issue involved, and prevailing circumstances."[4]

Power, therefore, comprises a dual ontology: one based on social interaction, and one as an essential condition and resource. This is obviously confusing. Social power's ontology, however, is much clearer, since (as the concept itself indicates) it is predicated on the notion that this face of power derives from communication, social knowledge, and economic and political interaction. This implies that social power only works in relationships and is ultimately dependent on the perception of others. For social power to become part of a strategic doctrine, policymakers must think carefully about how to *use* power. Policymakers realize that they can never take social

Politics?

power for granted, although they generally remain confused about how to use it. Moreover, since continuing relations give rise to social learning, social power is, inevitably, a long-term process, and should be studied as such.

Social power can be defined as the ability to set standards and create norms and values that are deemed legitimate and desirable, without resorting to coercion or payment.[5] Soft power's core components are attraction and persuasion; social power clearly goes beyond that. Joseph Nye's notion remains agent centered, assuming that soft power remains largely based on resources, which can be used, applied, and wielded.[6] Social power, on the other hand, also involves discursive power, drawing attention to the impact of framing, norm advocacy, agenda setting, and the impact of media and communication, as well as practices such as place branding and public diplomacy. Like soft power, social power eschews the use of coercion and force, giving it a certain ethical appeal and making it morally superior to hard power. By reneging coercion, social power finds its basis on grounds other than territory, economic resources, and/or the capacity and willingness to threaten with violence.

Still, this leaves unanswered the question as to why certain standards, norms, and values become privileged, accepted, and institutionalized, whereas others become (or remain) marginalized. As Daniel Philpott argues in his *Revolutions in Sovereignty* (2001), what is "normal" in international society is not fixed but dynamic, and changes with the geopolitical tide and fashion. In this context, norm advocacy obviously is of key concern. Martha Finnemore and Kathryn Sikkink define norm advocates (or norm entrepreneurs) as actors with "strong notions about appropriate or desirable behavior in their community."[7] The literature on norm advocacy has cast its net widely, including studies on non-state actors such as transnational advocacy networks, individuals, and NGOs, as well as, of course, states and international organizations (IOs). The emerging arena of transnational governance offers ample space to transnational actors to act as "honest brokers" or "meaning architects," oftentimes forming "discourse coalitions" among themselves to either shape or challenge the rules of the game of (global) politics.[8] Since NGOs play such an important role in agenda setting, opinion building, and drafting of plans and policy proposals, they compel us to reconsider the understanding of power as a predominantly coercive process.

For the study of social power, framing is a key concept. The discussion on framing takes place in a crowded conceptual field with overlapping terminology used by cognitive scientists, psychologists, and political scientists, who use notions such as frame, image, script, and paradigm to refer to approximately similar processes of creating (social) meaning. Frames offer mental structures shaping the way we see the world, and therefore limit the range of interpretive possibilities; they tell us what is important, and what the range of options and solutions is for which problems.[9] Framing helps to place issues and problems within a broader social and historical context. All norm entrepreneurs using social power engage in frame competition, trying to persuade relevant audiences and actors to see things their way. Finnemore and Sikkink argue that framing is necessary because "the linkages between existing norms and emergent norms are not often obvious and must be actively constructed by proponents of new norms." Norm entrepreneurs must actively create new standards by "using language that names, interprets, and dramatizes them."[10] The concept of "grafting" is obviously closely related to framing, and can be defined as "incremental norm transplantation," usually by associating the new norm with a pre-existing norm in the same issue area.[11]

It is clear that social power can be as contested as hard power, since advocating and uploading new standards, norms, and values is a competitive, and at times even combative, process, positing new notions of desirable and normal behavior vis-à-vis settled ways of doing things. Social power only very rarely takes place in a normative void, but has to compete in a normative, political space. Social power can be used conservatively, by maintaining existing standards and norms, or revolutionarily, by uploading new ones. Often, paradigms shift due to shocking, or symbolic, events that "recast or challenge prevailing definitions of the situation, thus changing perceptions of costs and benefits of policies and programs and the perception of injustice of the status quo."[12] Pepper D. Culpepper suggests that common knowledge *creation* occurs only after periods of institutional crisis, once most actors call into question old norms, values, and institutions.[13] Crisis undermines the taken-for-grantedness of these old rules and habits, destabilizing the cognitive basis of existing institutions. But, as Culpepper also points out, "[o]bserving how ideas become shared is much like watching grass grow: nothing seems to be happening in the short term, but after one day a former patch of mud is suddenly green."[14]

Paradigm-shifting events—ranging from the fall of the Berlin Wall, to 9/11, to the current global financial and economic crisis—obviously constitute a crisis in common knowledge, offering opportunities to create new norms, and ultimately new socially agreed "facts." Major norm changes are always disruptive.[15] Most often, however, social power is used to introduce new standards and norms that fit rather coherently within the status quo, since new norms that "fit" are generally considered less threatening and, therefore, more legitimate.[16] Like all aspects of social power, framing is highly contextual, which implies that the "frame resonance" varies between different target audiences, as American public diplomacy has found out. The Bush administration's rhetorical framing of the Iraq invasion as an effort to "spread freedom and democracy" has lost out to competing conceptual frames highlighting an on-going "civil war," or even the return of a Vietnam-like quagmire.[17] Robert M. Entman suggests that in the absence of an overwhelming Cold War frame of reference to analyze international politics, the competition over "news frames" has increased. Since foreign policy frames are more likely to be accepted when they "fit"—i.e., are culturally congruent to existing values, norms, and interpretations—the Bush administration has depicted 9/11 as a terrorist plot of extremists "hating our freedoms."

Asking why and how frames change offers insight in the workings of social power. Two different methodologies can be identified: the actor representation approach (with a focus on the changing *distribution* of actors who participate in policy debates) and a frame adoption approach (with a focus of the *different frames* that actors attach to a policy issue).[18] Often, these two approaches can, and should, be linked, since when new political actors get their voices heard, new frames are generally introduced. Connecting policy frames to their sponsors indicates who has social power within a certain discursive field.[19] Which prompts the question, how can policies and frames become common practice without force and other forms of coercion?

Amitav Acharya suggests that the success of norm diffusion strategies depends primarily "on the extent to which they provide opportunities for localization," which involves "a complex process and outcome by which norm-takers build congruence between transnational norms . . . and local beliefs and practices."[20] Acharya, therefore, suggests that norm-takers have considerable agency through a process of dynamic congruence building, implying that the "fit" between international and domestic norms is of key importance. Both Jeffrey W. Legro and Jeffrey T. Checkel point to the importance of a compatible "organizational culture" and "cultural match" between international and domestic norms, which explains why some norms are accepted swiftly and others remain contested.[21] Acharya's emphasis on the role of norm-takers is especially appropriate, since norm entrepreneurs are highly dependent on local elites to "download" foreign norms. As Acharya argues, the prospect for localization depends on "its positive impact on the legitimacy and authority of key norm-takers, the strength of prior local norms, the credibility and prestige of local agents, indigenous cultural traits and traditions, and the scope for grafting and pruning presented by foreign norms."[22]

As we will see in the next section on public diplomacy, norm entrepreneurs may now also enter into relationships with foreign publics, approaching them as both consumers and citizens. Both elites and the general public may be instrumental in adopting new norms and rules, by recognizing their merit and legitimacy.

PUBLIC DIPLOMACY—SETTING AGENDAS AND SHAPING NORMS

Today's public diplomacy fits well in a world where networks and fluid relationships among multiple actors with fuzzy roles abound. Where classical diplomacy centers on high-level talks and conferences, public diplomacy is about direct interaction, for example through blogs and music festivals. It is argued that this shift is due to the fact that in a globalized, networked international environment, ordinary people have become increasingly important. In politics, state sovereignty is challenged by "people power," generated by the global triumph of democracy.[23] In economics, wealth is created more by weightless assets such as knowledge and skills (which belong to individuals) than by physical assets and resources (which belong to states). Even in the area of security, human security and identity questions are crowding out classical inter-state rivalry as the key concern and dominant paradigm.[24] As Mark Leonard and Vidhya Alakeson argue in their study *Going Public* (2000), "with an unprecedented spread of democracy, our ability to win over other governments will depend in part on how we are perceived by the populations they serve."[25]

Public diplomacy depends on, and is rooted in, communication. The social power derived from this strategy hinges on other actors knowing one's positive and alluring policies and qualities. It is key to spread the social knowledge about one's attractiveness—or, in case of new public diplomacy, the importance of certain policy issues;[26] otherwise, little social power can be derived and used. This explains why the importance of social power has increased with the onset of a new media era, since in a world where information technology is cheap, widespread, and evasive, communication has become simpler. The mechanisms used to communicate with foreign audiences, often across the world, have moved to new, real-time, and global technologies, especially the internet. Radio, TV, and printed media are still important, but satellites, YouTube, and Twitter are now considered more effective, and certainly quicker and more economical. As a result, these new technologies blur the once rigid lines between domestic and international news spheres. What is said in Berlin for a specific German audience is heard in Beijing, Baghdad, and beyond.

But today's public diplomacy is not focused only on bringing out a targeted message; it also strives to build relationships with others. It is, therefore, less about authority, telling others what to do, than about showing others what we consider to be desirable, in the hope (and expectation) that it will be emulated. This relationship does not need to be between a government and a foreign audience, but could well be between two audiences, foreign to each other, whose communication and interaction a specific government wishes to facilitate. For example, in 2008, British diplomats started a public diplomacy campaign to appeal to public opinion in twenty countries across the globe to get support for a plan to deal with climate change. Interestingly, British public diplomacy included engagement with American public opinion as well as key public officials in American states that have agreed to cut carbon emissions, regardless of Washington's refusal to commit itself to binding targets at a national level. By successfully engaging American and European publics, public diplomacy is considered a useful way to shape a cooperative transatlantic foreign policy agenda.[27] Unlike propaganda, public diplomacy is, therefore, less about "getting the message out" than about creating a wider, perhaps even global community, which is susceptible to a way of thinking that is considered desirable. As a consequence, it is less about telling than about listening; it is less about spreading information than about facilitating and networking.[28]

The problem with public diplomacy as a social power phenomenon is that we still lack detailed knowledge and a thorough understanding of how it works. How do certain fringe ideas become received wisdoms? What is the most effective way to change minds and win over hearts? What are the triggers that encourage the general public and elites to reframe the issues and think (as well as feel) differently? Knowledge is still very patchy on both the psychological and sociological aspects of these questions. What we do know, however, is that influencing the way people think, what they consider normal and desirable, is a key goal of any foreign policy, and touches on the very roots of our debate on social power. In the emerging literature on new public diplomacy,[29] two features stand out, illustrating how social power is both generated and used in contemporary international politics.

First, new public diplomacy aims to create partnerships and platforms, which embodies the shift from the standard practice of advocacy to a so-called ideas-based public diplomacy strategy. Advocacy has been central to diplomatic practice, using communication tools to actively promote a particular policy or cause. The style of an ideas-based public diplomacy is not to use the megaphone and make claims, but to shape an idea or argument that will eventually be taken up and reproduced by others, and hence take on a life of its own. It effectively applies social power and shapes (new) norms and values, but using different tactics. This is why the new public diplomacy may well try to boost the credibility of an idea by dissociating itself from it. For example, given America's limited credibility in the Muslim world, Washington often uses other, more neutral channels to spread its ideas and arguments. It also implies that an ideas-based public diplomacy may adopt an even broader approach by promoting an international environment that makes the spread of ideas possible in the first place. Here examples can be found in the United Kingdom, where the British Council worked together with the consultancy agency River Path Associates. River Path set up several blogs (e.g., during the World Summit on Sustainable Development in Johannesburg in 2002, and around the debate on the new president of the World Bank in 2005), which were actively used and provided a valuable opportunity for international dialogue on matters high on London's foreign policy agenda. Similarly, the EU sponsored the launch of a joint Israeli-Palestinian web-based dialogue project (called *bitterlemons.org*, set up in 2006), which soon reached more than 100,000 active participants in the region.[30] The new public diplomacy, therefore, goes beyond spreading ideas, but aims to facilitate and generate an international public platform that did not exist before.

indiv. vs 'manuals'. opinion + leaders are not only adopters, manufacturers are

There are good reasons why states have given leeway to NGOs in the public diplomacy process. States should perhaps acknowledge that NGOs may be better equipped, both mentally and in organizational set-up, to make optimal use of the new dynamic and rules of the social power game. States may still be good in mass media–driven, one-way communication, supported by cultural and educational exchanges. But over the last decade, NGOs have clearly demonstrated their power to set the international political agenda by framing debates on dealing with global poverty and global warming, as well as by campaigning to ban landmines. The success of the International Campaign to Ban Landmines (ICBL) illustrates how an informal network communication approach has made excellent use of social power's potential to shape policy outcomes. The story of the so-called Ottawa process[31] is well-known: Six prominent NGOs formed the ICBL in the early 1990s and had attracted more than 1,000 NGOs from more than 60 countries by 1996. The ICBL was a typical loose network, without a clear hierarchical structure, but making the most of its social power through network synergy. Relationships, coalitions, and trust were built up over the years, while its many members all over the world communicated via the internet to coordinate events, distribute petitions, raise money, and, perhaps most important, educate the public media. This loose network of NGOs used their collective social power by gradually changing the attitude of key players toward banning anti-personnel landmines, effectively altering the standards and norm for responsible behavior in international politics. This did not occur through the classical negotiating pattern of conventional arms treaties where states would often take a decade to bargain behind closed doors, but in the astonishingly short period of less than two years, using an open, public debate where everyone could join in.

A *second* element of the new public diplomacy involves the practices of cultural, exchange, and broadcasting diplomacy, which make optimal use of the opportunities offered by today's new media. The days when an exhibition or opera company could transgress the international cultural boundary and win hearts and minds are long gone. With increased technological connectivity, the porosity of borders, and the reality of mass migration, cultural exchange has acquired a truly new meaning. The United States and Europe host, oftentimes involuntarily, millions of migrants from all over the world, whose impressions of their new "home" country turn them into unpretentious, yet important opinion formers. Diasporic populations have always communicated with their kin at home through the mail. But with the increase of new and cheap mass communication, these millions of (legal or illegal) ex-patriots play an important role in how host countries, especially Western ones, are perceived around the world. Increasingly, the role of immigrants as a mechanism of international cultural communication is taken into account as an integral part of the new public diplomacy. In a way, it reflects the democratization of diplomacy, which implies that ordinary people become the main focus of diplomacy, rather than traditional elites.

These new developments suggest that the very nature of public diplomacy is changing rapidly. Traditional diplomatic actors (such as states and IOs) have lost their monopoly and have to run very fast just to stay in the same place. Since gatekeepers, be they diplomats or other government officials, no longer control the flow of information on any issue of public relevance, citizens around the globe can react in any way they want using global media at a negligible cost. It also means that diplomacy now increasingly takes shape in global public policy networks, which bring together actors from government, private business, and civil society, all aimed at finding common solutions to policy problems. Proponents of these new networks expect both more effectiveness and democratic legitimacy from governance that goes "beyond the nation-state."[32]

CONCLUDING REMARKS—HOW TO RAISE THE LEARNING CURVE

One of the daunting problems with studying power in international politics is that, no matter how many case studies we generate, the learning curve remains rather flat. What may work for countries A and B at moment T may be utterly inapplicable to countries C and D in moment $T+5$. Not only is this frustrating, but it also undermines the credibility of social scientists studying the role and relevance of public diplomacy and related processes, not to speak of the reluctance of relevant actors to fund further research on these matters. Given today's over-activity in the area of public diplomacy, plenty of actors seem to plunge into the fray and hope for the best, keen as they are not to be left behind in the pursuit of dusty "Diplomacy 1.0" activities. But one should seriously question whether this triumph of hope over knowledge is sustainable.

The underlying problem is that both academics and policymakers want to solve the so-called wielding problem: how can we connect the dots between power tools, instruments, and resources, and concrete policy outcomes? One could argue that social power has a Newtonian quality to it, since its effect may be visible, whereas the source of power normally is not. Since social power is most often set in institutions and relationships, it is difficult to actually wield it. Institutions and relationships are socially embedded, molded as they are by traditions, culture, and media, as well as by fads and fashions. Since social power centers around being able to determine what is normal, desirable, and the law-of-the-land, legitimacy and credibility are important, if not essential, requirements to successfully upload one's norms and values. In contemporary international politics, legitimacy and credibility have become powerful resources and tools to justify and gather support for foreign policy actions. The ability and capability to legitimate foreign policy *in the eyes of others* is the staple of social power, and the objective of most public diplomacy activities. Legitimacy assumes tacit or explicit agreement on the rules-of-the-game, based on, or rooted in, a shared set of norms. Credibility is based on trust that policies will be conducted effectively. The ability to acquire and sustain both legitimacy and credibility requires social capital, which can be defined as the set of norms and values that is shared among members of a group, permitting cooperation among them.

How, and even whether, social capital can be accumulated in international politics remains somewhat elusive. States and international organizations obviously still have credibility and legitimacy, to a widely varying degree. They increasingly compete with emerging transgovernmental policy networks, which have become important conduits for social power. These transgovernmental arrangements (or global public policy networks—GPPNs) are loose alliances between governments, IOs, firms, NGOs, professional organizations, and cultural and religious groups, joining together to achieve common goals. They embody the new fluid (or liquid) nature of today's governance and public diplomacy environment, which privileges arrangements lacking institutional fixity, but rewards flexibility. This also explains the proliferation of Friends groupings, Troikas, Quartets, and Quints, which are merely the tip of the iceberg of a major recalibration of the institutional foundation of global governance. The important novelty of these networks is that they are not driven by formal institutions and bureaucracies, and are not managed in a modern, top-down hierarchical style. Instead, GPPNs are "owned" by relevant slices of society, comprising as many stakeholders as is deemed necessary to be effective, efficient, and legitimate.

Especially transnational advocacy coalitions, whose power derives from managing information and mobilizing public support, have shown themselves remarkably adept to influence both formal government channels and GPPNs. Norms established within the UN-sponsored Global Compact and Corporate Social Responsibility (CRS) agreements, for example, are encouraging firms to act as good, responsible corporate citizens. Especially firms selling directly to consumers realize that their credibility and likeability are essential elements of their brand. This implies that NGOs and the wider public of consumers may steer business actors to comply with a wide range of social and environmental goals. Together with the phenomenon of private authority—based on gentlemen's agreements, codes of conduct, ethical guidelines, and partnerships—today's policymaking environment has become a crowded field of actors, all with diverging claims to legitimacy and credibility. The state has become only one of these competing actors, who all try to define the situation and aim to set rules and standards.

Social power can be used to tilt the playing field, by setting the structural conditions to achieve foreign policy goals and limit the costs to do so. Public diplomacy, especially, has emerged as a strategy used by new players—ranging from emerging Great Powers like China to IOs such as NATO—in order to enhance and capitalize on their social capital—not always successfully, to be sure, since many of these rather inexperienced actors are feeling their way forward, trying to learn the largely unwritten mores and mechanisms of global governance's rulebook. One of the bigger challenges for *all* actors involved in public diplomacy has been to shed the mindset of power politics, based on control and hierarchy. Instead, the new paradigm of social power must be embraced, which does not use the megaphone to make claims but aims to shape an idea or argument in the hope that it will eventually be taken up and reproduced by others, and hence take on a life of its own. Without an appreciation of the nature and workings of social power, contemporary international politics can no longer be understood.

NOTES

1. Evgeny Morozov, *The Net Delusion: The Dark Side of Internet Freedom* (New York: Public Affairs, 2011).
2. Michael Mann, *The Sources of Social Power: A History of Power from the Beginning to A.D. 1760* (Cambridge: Cambridge University Press, 1986); and Daniel Philpott, *Revolutions in Sovereignty: How Ideas Shaped Modern International Relations* (Princeton, NJ: Princeton University Press, 2001).
3. Jennifer Sterling-Folker and Rosemary E. Shinko, "Discourses of Power: Traversing the Realist-Postmodern Divide," *Millennium* 33 (June 2005): 637–64.
4. Yale H. Ferguson, "Approaches to Defining 'Empire' and Characterizing United States Influence in the Contemporary World," *International Studies Perspectives* 9 (August 2008): 279.
5. Peter van Ham, *Social Power in International Politics* (New York: Routledge, 2010).
6. Joseph S. Nye, Jr., *Soft Power: The Means to Success in World Politics* (New York: Public Affairs, 2004).
7. Martha Finnemore and Kathryn Sikkink, "International Norm Dynamics and Political Change," *International Organization* 52 (Autumn 1998): 897.
8. Thomas Hale and David Held, eds., *Handbook of Transnational Governance. Institutions and Innovations* (Cambridge: Polity, 2011); and Klaus Dingwerth, *The New Transnationalism: Transnational Governance and Democratic Legitimacy* (New York: Palgrave Macmillan, 2007).
9. George Lakoff, *Don't Think of an Elephant: Know Your Values and Frame the Debate* (White River Jct., VT: Chelsea Green, 2004); and Robert D. Benford and David A. Snow, "Framing Processes and Social Movements: An Overview and Assessment, *Annual Review of Sociology* 26 (2000): 611–39.
10. Finnemore and Sikkink, "International Norm Dynamics and Political Change," 908.
11. Theo Farrell, "Transnational Norms and Military Development: Constructing Ireland's Professional Army," *European Journal of International Relations* 7 (March 2001): 63–102.
12. Mayer N. Zald, "Culture, Ideology, and Strategic Framing," in *Comparative Perspectives on Social Movements: Political Opportunities, Mobilizing Structures, and Cultural Framings*, ed. Doug McAdam, John D. McCarthy, and Mayer N. Zald (New York: Cambridge University Press, 1996), 268.
13. Pepper D. Culpepper, "The Politics of Common Knowledge: Ideas and Institutional Change in Wage Bargaining," *International Organization* 62 (2008): 5.
14. Culpepper, "The Politics of Common Knowledge," 9.

15. Margaret E. Keck and Kathryn Sikkink, *Activists beyond Borders: Advocacy Networks in International Politics* (Ithaca, NY: Cornell University Press, 1998), 35.
16. Ann Florini, "The Evolution of International Norms," *International Studies Quarterly* 40:3 (September 1996): 363–89; Edna Ullmann-Margalit, *The Emergence of Norms* (Oxford: Clarendon Press, 1977).
17. Robert M. Entman, *Projections of Power: Framing News, Public Opinion, and U.S. Foreign Policy* (Chicago: University of Chicago Press, 2004).
18. Brian Steensland, "Why Do Policy Frames Change? Actor-Idea Coevolution in Debates over Welfare Reform," *Social Forces* 86:3 (March 2008): 1028.
19. Myra Marx Ferree, William A. Gamson, Jürgen Gerhards, and Dieter Ruchs, *Shaping Abortion Discourse: Democracy and the Public Sphere in Germany and the United States* (Cambridge: Cambridge University Press, 2002).
20. Amitav Acharya, "How Ideas Spread: Whose Norms Matter? Norm Localization and Institutional Change in Asian Regionalism," *International Organization* 58 (2004): 241.
21. Jeffrey W. Legro, "Which Norms Matter? Revisiting the 'Failure' of Internationalism," *International Organization* 51 (1997): 31–63; Jeffrey T. Checkel, "Why Comply? Social Learning and European Identity Change," *International Organization* 55 (2001): 553–88.
22. Acharya, "How Ideas Spread," 247–48.
23. Michael True, *People Power: Fifty Peacemakers and Their Communities* (Jaipur: Rawat, 2007).
24. See, for example, the special issue on human security of *Security Dialogue* 35 (2004).
25. Mark Leonard and Vidhya Alakeson, *Going Public: Diplomacy for the Information Society* (London: The Foreign Policy Center, 2000), 3.
26. Kathy Fitzpatrick, "Advancing the New Public Diplomacy: A Public Relations Perspective," *The Hague Journal of Diplomacy* 2 (2007): 187–211.
27. Kristin M. Lord, "Public Diplomacy and the New Transatlantic Agenda," *Brookings US-Europe Analysis Series* (August 15, 2008), http://www.brookings.edu/research/papers/2008/08/15-public-diplomacy-lord
28. Nicholas J. Cull, "Public Diplomacy: Lessons from the Past" (April 2007), unpublished report.
29. Jan Melissen, *The New Public Diplomacy: Soft Power in International Relations* (New York: Palgrave Macmillan, 2005).
30. Yossi Alpher, "Bitterlemons.org and the Lebanon War," *Foreign Service Journal* 83 (December 2006): 27–32.
31. Nicola Short, "A Review of the Ottawa Process to Ban Landmines," *ISIS Briefing Paper Number 15* (November 1997).
32. Wolfgang H. Reinecke, *Global Public Policy: Governing without Government?* (Washington, DC: Brookings Institution Press, 1998).

2 Public Diplomacy and Ethics
From Soft Power to Social Conscience

Kathy R. Fitzpatrick

INTRODUCTION

In the popular 1958 novel *The Ugly American*, authors William J. Lederer and Eugene Burdick offered a blistering indictment of American foreign policy.[1] The book was set in the fictional country of Sarkhan in Southeast Asia, where the United States was locked in a fierce battle with Russia against communism. In this struggle, Lederer and Burdick contended, the United States lacked both the capabilities and values needed to win the support of local citizens.

Drawing on their personal experiences overseas, the authors portrayed American diplomats as arrogant, rude, and insensitive to the needs and opinions of the Sarkhanese people. Not only did U.S. officials not speak the language of their host country, but they had no more than an academic understanding of the area's customs, beliefs, religion, humor, and values. U.S. officials seldom interacted with local citizens, staying close to U.S. compounds near the embassies. The locals had a term they used to describe the lack of interest demonstrated by the Americans in community affairs— "S.I.G.G.," or "Social Incest in the Golden Ghetto." How, Lederer and Burdick asked, could the United States expect to win the support of people abroad if they didn't understand or talk to them?

The authors derided the lack of respect demonstrated by the United States for the Sarkhanese people with anecdotes illustrating how U.S. officials simply decided what was best for the local communities—typically roads or dams or other big-ticket infrastructure items—without bothering to ask community members what *they* thought was needed. Most important was making sure local citizens knew that foreign aid was provided by the United States of America. Presumably, this knowledge alone would win their favor.

On the flip side, Lederer and Burdick showed the effectiveness of American envoys genuinely interested in helping the Sarkhanese by working with communities on matters of interest and concern to them. For example, one collaborative effort led by an American engineer resulted in the development of a much-needed water pump made from locally available bicycle parts. In the book's factual epilogue, Lederer and Burdick argued that if the United States is to succeed in establishing good relations with people abroad, then more is required than self-serving initiatives focused solely on advancing American interests with little regard for the interests of foreign publics. In other words:

> The little things we do must be moral acts and they must be done in the real interest of the peoples whose friendship we need—not just in the interest of propaganda.[2]

Sound familiar? The same criticisms of U.S. public diplomacy abound today. Perhaps that's why *The Ugly American* continues to be republished and is still required reading in many university classrooms. While much has changed in global society as a result of globalization and new technology, the human dimension of international relations has not changed. In fact, the need for a relational approach to public diplomacy has never been greater. A highly connected, increasingly interdependent world requires nations and peoples to work together for the advancement of global peace and prosperity. For public diplomacy, this means "moving from monologue to dialogue to collaboration."[3]

At the same time, in order to be effective over the long term, contemporary public diplomacy requires more than a bigger strategic toolbox that includes a broader array of listening and two-way communication and engagement devices—all of which are very important and all of which can be used for asymmetric purposes. It also requires a new worldview, or set of assumptions, that rejects traditional conceptions of public diplomacy as a means for promoting the self-interest of nations, as well as more contemporary views of public diplomacy as a means for accruing and wielding power. A truly relational public diplomacy requires a worldview that sees public diplomacy as a means for achieving *mutual* understanding and advancing *shared* interests among nations and peoples. Such a view recognizes both the centrality of ethics and values in a nation's relationships with foreign publics and the evolving role and function of public diplomacy in global society.

This chapter addresses the often-overlooked ethical dimensions of public diplomacy that are critical to a relational framework. It begins by examining the ethical foundations of public diplomacy through the lens of soft power, which has been widely adopted to explain public diplomacy's purpose and value. This analysis, which challenges the idea of public diplomacy as an instrument of power, reveals both the ethical shortcomings of a self-interested approach to global public engagement and the need for a more ethical alternative based on relationships. The chapter considers the expanding obligations of public diplomats in global society and suggests the time has come to articulate principles and values that could provide ethical guideposts for global public diplomacy professionals. It identifies six core relational values that reflect both lessons learned in the field and a commitment to ethical public diplomacy practices.

ETHICAL FOUNDATIONS

In *Soft Power: The Means to Success in World Politics*, Joseph S. Nye, Jr., introduced the idea of "soft power," which he defined as "the ability to get what you want through attraction rather than coercion or payments."[4] According to Nye, "soft power rests on the ability to shape the preferences of others."[5] The currency of soft power in international relations, Nye said, is different from that of hard power (i.e., military might and economic muscle); rather, it is "an attraction to shared values and the justness and duty of others to contribute to policies consistent with those shared values."[6] Soft power "co-opts people rather than coerces them," Nye explained.[7] Co-optive power rests on "the attractiveness of one's culture, political ideals, and policies, or on one's ability to manipulate other countries' political agendas."[8]

In an environment in which foreign public opinion has become increasingly important to a nation's ability to advance global interests, and the global flow of information is enhanced by new media, Nye said, a nation's key soft-power resource is public diplomacy, which plays a central role in shaping the global climate in which policy making takes place and in creating an attractive image of a country, its values, and its policies. There are three ways that public diplomacy works, according to Nye. First, it manages daily communication to explain the context of foreign policy decisions to foreign publics. Second, it develops strategic communication programs involving symbolic events and branding activities to advance specific government policies. And, third, it helps to build long-term supportive relationships between nations and people abroad. Combined, Nye said, these efforts "create an attractive image of a country and this can improve its prospects for obtaining its desired outcomes."[9] In other words, when practiced effectively, public diplomacy enhances a nation's ability to accrue and wield power in global society.

The concept of soft power has been widely adopted both in the United States and elsewhere to explain the function and value of public diplomacy. For example, in writing about American public diplomacy, Wilson P. Dizard observed that in this new era, " 'soft power' is the major factor influencing the role of US public diplomacy."[10] Carnes Lord similarly suggested that "public diplomacy, in order to be truly effective, must be about the active projection of soft power in order to reinforce American influence—or to generate it where otherwise absent."[11] The idea of public diplomacy as soft power also has been embraced by those involved in U.S. cultural diplomacy aimed at fostering mutual understanding between nations and peoples. According to Cynthia P. Schneider, "Cultural diplomacy is a prime example of 'soft power,' or the ability to persuade through culture, values and ideas."[12]

Reflecting a more global perspective, Josef Batora observed that public diplomacy "comprises all activities by state and nonstate actors that contribute to the maintenance and promotion of a country's soft power."[13] Brian Hocking similarly pointed out that "the limitations of hard, or military power and the advantages that can accrue from the use of 'attractive' power rooted in factors such as culture, ideals and values, which, it is argued, encourages others to want what you want, are *basic assumptions* among advocates of an enhanced role for public diplomacy" in global affairs (emphasis added).[14]

Such assumptions can be explained by a number of factors. First, and perhaps most important, is that public diplomacy is an elusive concept that lacks a clear and consistent definition that articulates its fundamental purpose. As a result, the idea of soft power has provided a unifying concept. Second is that public diplomacy has long been viewed as an instrument of "war"—due in part to the role of U.S. public diplomacy in helping to combat communism during the Cold War. Third is that public diplomacy is generally discussed in political contexts in which the dominant ideology—realism—is based on the goal of maximizing national power and the supremacy of state interests.

Additionally, public diplomacy has been equated with nation branding, which has direct links to soft power. Simon Anholt—who coined the phrase "nation branding" and later changed it to "competitive identity"—pointed out that a nation-branding view of the world as a competitive marketplace in which nations must compete for the affection of world citizens is in line with Nye's view of soft power. Much like soft power, which is "about making people want to do what you want them to do," Anholt said, competitive identity is "about making people want to pay attention to a country's achievements, and believe in its qualities."[15] According to Anholt, competitive identity "is the quintessential modern exemplar of soft power."[16]

Associations between public diplomacy and power, which contribute to the notion that public diplomacy is more about competing and "winning" in the global marketplace of ideas than about building and sustaining mutually beneficial relationships, have had significant consequences for the advancement of public diplomacy theory and practice. The biggest impact is that alternative conceptualizations have been slow to emerge. As a result, the seemingly inherent contradictions in a *power*-based model of public diplomacy guided by *relational* principles have received little attention. If public diplomacy is to advance as a relational enterprise, however, links between power and public diplomacy require more serious scrutiny.

For example, is the true purpose of public diplomacy to acquire and/or wield power in global society? If public diplomacy is viewed as an instrument of power, then how does relationship building fit within such a construct? If symmetrical, collaborative relationships with people abroad are desired—indeed required—(as relational conceptions of public diplomacy suggest) for successful public diplomacy, how does a power-based model of public diplomacy address power imbalances in such relationships? How are principles of mutuality and dialogue—which characterize contemporary public diplomacy—operationalized in a power-based model of public diplomacy? And, most important in a discussion of ethics, does a power-based model of public diplomacy motivated and directed by self-interest—even one based on dialogue and relationship building—reflect the ethical values and moral legitimacy required for public diplomacy to be effective in contemporary global society?

ETHICAL SHORTCOMINGS

In one of the few works to consider the meaning of power in public diplomacy, Ali Fisher identified a tension between "those that seek to exert 'power over' a target audience and those that intend to engage or empower a community,"[17] which, he says, "has greater potential to attract engagement from the foreign population as it relies not on honing attractive things for their consumption but in engaging through actions in which they are already interested."[18] Fisher contrasted the asymmetry of soft power with "genuine, symmetrical engagement," or the point at which two parties who "meet as participants are equally open to the influence of the other while seeking to exert influence."[19] According to Fisher, the assumptions of a soft-power approach to public diplomacy "characterize it as neither mutual nor based on a reciprocal relationship. It excludes the development of common goals through dialogue, nor provides support to empower others to realise their goals. It is neither compromise nor negotiation. It is a belief in one's own perspective over another. It is an asymmetric power relationship in favour of the actor over the foreign public."[20]

Such a description reveals the ethical shortcomings of soft power as a conceptual foundation for public diplomacy. Public diplomacy initiatives aimed at accruing or wielding power fail to recognize the importance of mutuality and dialogue in which *both* parties are conducive to change in attitudes and behavior and in which the achievement of *mutual* benefit is the designed outcome.[21] They also miss the point that moral legitimacy is not mandated by a nation or other international actor engaged in public diplomacy. Rather, it is bestowed by foreign publics on such actors. As such, the ethical expectations of the people with whom a nation engages must be accommodated if public diplomacy is to be effective. This means that instead of focusing solely on how a nation can make its voice stand out in a crowded global marketplace of ideas, public diplomats also must consider how they can help facilitate other voices in that marketplace.

This fact was most evident in the United States' post-9/11 public diplomacy efforts that—rightly or wrongly—appeared to foreign publics to be more geared toward molding their views to mirror those of the United States than in engaging in a true dialogue in which American views might be adjusted to accommodate the interests of foreign publics. A study by Patrick Plaisance found that public diplomacy initiatives undertaken in the early post-9/11 period likely created perceptions among people abroad that the American government was engaged in propaganda campaigns to convert them to U.S. ways of thinking.[22] For example, in evaluating the "Shared Values" initiative, which was designed to promote America as a tolerant nation and featured happy Muslims living happy lives in the United States, Plaisance identified three "serious ethical shortcomings."[23] First, the campaign engaged in selective truth-telling in presenting America as a tolerant nation. Second, it treated people abroad as means rather than ends in "pursuing a goal of changing the opinions that Muslims have of the United States because it benefits the United States to do so—rather than seeking genuine, more comprehensive mutual understanding."[24] Third, the apparent intent of the campaign was to effect the "evaluative narrowing" of receivers by oversimplifying the reality of life in America.[25]

These findings revealed the attitudes of an administration that viewed U.S. public diplomacy's charge as "making America's case," or developing "a long-term strategy to make sure that our ideals prevail."[26] According to one former undersecretary of state for public diplomacy and public affairs, U.S. public diplomacy needed to "create the conditions and the climate that allow people to give our ideas a fair hearing." She said, "We are confident, if they are able to think for themselves, if they're able to give that fair hearing, that people will choose the power of our ideals."[27]

A Pew Global Attitudes Project study, which examined global public opinion of the United States during that time period, revealed weaknesses in the Bush administration's efforts to sway global attitudes toward the United States, finding that "anti-Americanism is deeper and broader now than at any time in modern history."[28] According to the report, at the heart of the decline was "the perception that the United States acts internationally without taking into account the interests of other nations."[29] The study also showed that foreign publics simply don't trust America. On matters of international security particularly, "the rest of the world has become deeply suspicious of U.S. motives and openly skeptical of its word."[30] Duke University researchers who synthesized polling data on increasing anti-Americanism throughout the world similarly found "widespread erosion of America's image abroad" with U.S. policies "widely viewed with increasing skepticism, even among traditional allies."[31]

Although such findings cannot be attributed solely to bad public diplomacy, they do suggest a lack of moral awareness on the part of U.S. officials.

As Julia E. Sweig observed in *Friendly Fire: Losing Friends and Making Enemies in the Anti-American Century*, a perceived lack of concern for others' interests contributes to feelings of anti-Americanism and hostility toward the United States. Put another way, she said, a significant element of global antipathy toward America is "the near inability of the United States to see its power from the perspective of the powerless."[32]

The important lesson from these U.S. examples for public diplomats is that in a multicultural, highly connected, increasingly interdependent world, public diplomacy must *adapt* to changing conditions and societal expectations, rather than try to—or be perceived as trying to—manipulate the global environment or the people in it solely for the good of a nation. Public diplomacy is most effective when it helps reconcile a nation's goals with the expectations of its key foreign publics.[33] Such reconciliation requires careful balancing of the interests involved and recognition that foreign publics should have a voice in public diplomacy outcomes. This does not mean that national self-interest should be subordinated to other interests. As David Martinson observed, "The problem is not self-interest per se, but using organizational . . . self-interest to designate the baseline as to what will be considered ethical behavior."[34]

ETHICAL OBLIGATIONS

In a recent issue of *The Hague Journal of Diplomacy*, former British diplomat Brian Barder asked the intriguing question: "What are diplomats for?"[35] Barder considered what he called the "rival concepts" of the diplomat's functions—"competitively and exclusively promoting the national interest versus concentrating on internationalist, ethical obligations that should govern diplomatic behavior."[36] He contended that "[t]he golden rule for diplomats, as for others, must be to act in a way that brings the greatest good for the greatest number, *irrespective of the nationalities of those who are to benefit*, even if in real life a degree of priority is likely to be accorded to one's own fellow citizens" (emphasis in original).[37] At the same time, Barder recognized that whether "ministers who live or (metaphorically) die by the domestic vote will generally obey such an elevated internationalist rule is another matter. But there seems to be no basis—*pace* that old-fashioned Foreign Office tradition—for excusing diplomats from it" (emphasis in original).[38]

In calling for a more socially responsible diplomacy, Barder waded into some relatively unexplored territory in diplomatic studies, in which questions related to morality and ethics have received little consideration. For scholars and diplomats contemplating a more "public" diplomacy in the twenty-first century,[39] he also identified a central challenge for public diplomacy practitioners—that is, "balanc[ing] daily what they judge to be the ethical demands of the issues that they face against their pursuit of national interest and the promotion of their government's policies."[40] In this effort, he suggested, it should be recognized that pursuit of the national interest "is not a zero-sum game."[41]

The ethical standards that should guide public diplomacy practices, however, are unclear, as scholars and practitioners have just begun to explore the assumptions and requirements of a relational framework.[42] At the same time, the idea of a more socially conscious public diplomacy that has relevance and impact beyond its organizational function fits well within—perhaps defines—a relational paradigm. It reflects the complexity and diversity of the contemporary diplomatic environment and the need for a more collaborative approach to public diplomacy that "understands the international environment [as] a network of interconnected communities and interests."[43]

Additionally, the idea of the public diplomat as a social conscience embraces the policy advisory role of public diplomacy professionals who counsel and advise on the public implications of a nation's decisions and actions. It also recognizes that public diplomacy plays a critical role in bringing nations and peoples together for the good of not just the interacting nations and peoples but also broader global society. In participating in and helping to build and facilitate networks of international actors—and in managing the mutual interdependence of these actors—public diplomacy helps to maintain relationships necessary for the advancement of peace and prosperity for all the world's citizens.[44]

As advisors, public diplomats help their nations interpret and respond to the global environment of attitudes and opinions and bring the concerns of people abroad back to policy makers at home. As advocates, they represent the interests of their nations with foreign publics. In both these roles, it is the job of public diplomats to ensure that national goals and actions are congruent with public expectations. As members of the Public Diplomacy Council observed about U.S. public diplomacy, the nation's credibility in the world will turn not on how effectively the nation's interests are served, but rather on how effectively America serves the interests of people abroad, or "the extent that we are seen to be working to solve global problems that affect their lives . . . the extent that we recognize their hopes and ambitions . . . the extent that we satisfy their desire for equal recognition."[45]

As scholars and practitioners contemplate an expanded role for public diplomacy in global society, they must consider not only the analytical boundaries that define public diplomacy as a field and function; they also must consider the ethical principles and values that (should) guide public diplomacy in practice. Admittedly, continuing debate on what public diplomacy is and how it should be used—as illustrated by the earlier discussion on soft power—complicates the process of defining ethical standards. The diversity of cultures, beliefs, and values in which public diplomacy is conducted in various communities throughout the world creates additional difficulty. At the same time, the adoption of a relational framework for public diplomacy provides a foundation upon which countries can begin to build professional standards for practice.

ETHICAL STANDARDS

Career Diplomacy by Henry W. Kopp and Charles A. Gillespie, intended as a guide for work in the U.S. Foreign Service, describes the Foreign Service as "an institution, a profession, and a career."[46] According to Kopp and Gillespie, members of the Foreign Service "like to say that they are professionals" and they "see diplomacy as a profession—a set of skills to be mastered through apprenticeship and training, with restrictions on entry, advancement by merit, and codes of behavior."[47] However, these writers explained, "diplomacy is different from other professions" in that "amateurs are allowed to participate."[48] Diplomacy is also different from other professions in that most diplomats operate without a formal code of professional conduct. According to the president of the U.S. Foreign Service Association, "Our foreign affairs agencies seem to have notional values that we espouse from time to time, but these have not been set down in specific codes of ethical and professional conduct."[49]

In years past, when diplomacy specialists served apprenticeships with more seasoned practitioners, written standards that could be passed on to new recruits were considered unnecessary. As Kopp and Gillespie observed, "most governments recognize that diplomatic skills, though accessible in many ways, are most surely gained through diplomatic experience."[50] Additionally, the idea of developing a formal code of conduct did not sit well with some American diplomats. For example, in 1976, Kenneth Thompson cautioned that diplomacy cannot—should not—follow rigid codes or binding rules and precepts, but rather "moral maxims"—signposts and rough guidelines—that are "lived out in practice."[51]

While an apprenticeship system might have served the U.S. Foreign Service well during the Cold War, however, that is no longer the case. Severe cutbacks in the 1990s depleted the ranks of U.S. Foreign Service officers experienced in all areas, taking a very serious toll on the nation's diplomatic capabilities. As Thomas Hansen observed, nearly half of all U.S. Foreign Service officers (including public diplomats) today have less than ten years of experience.[52] As a result, there is a "critical shortage" of experienced professionals to mentor new officers.[53]

A lack of experienced public diplomacy professionals is not unique to the United States. Yet, as foreign ministries throughout the world continue to expand their public diplomacy operations, there has been little discussion among public diplomacy scholars and practitioners about the principles and values that should guide the behavior of public diplomats.[54] Part of the reason for the lack of professional standards is that the profile of the public diplomacy professional is still being formed. As Daryl Copeland observed, "[T]he essence of the public diplomat as a person and as a professional has attracted almost no notice."[55]

Rather than wait for others to notice their ascent in international relations, however, public diplomats should take the lead in defining the professional standards by which they will operate. In writing about ethics in public relations, Dean Kruckeberg explained the importance of establishing professional values: "Ethical values are important because they allow us to define ourselves as a professional community by defining our relationship with society. It is we—not society—who are the primary beneficiaries of our professional ethics, and we must guard jealously the manifest right and obligation to prescribe and then practice such ethical behavior—and to banish from our professional community those transgressors who choose not to conform"[56]

ETHICAL PRINCIPLES AND VALUES

The development of global professional standards would help to establish public diplomacy as a distinct profession whose members are bound by particular principles and values. It would establish expectations and provide guidance for new as well as experienced public diplomats to help ensure that their decisions are grounded in ethical precepts. Perhaps most important, it would force public diplomacy professionals to define public diplomacy's obligations to foreign publics and to broader global society. In this respect, they would be responding to Jan Melissen and Paul Sharp's call in the launch issue of *The Hague Journal of Diplomacy* for diplomats "to reflect more, and more explicitly, on what they do, why they do it, and why it is worth doing."[57] Those who fail to do so, they suggested, run the risk of others stepping in and imposing their views of what diplomacy should be and how it should be conducted.

In contemplating the development of a code of ethics for public diplomats, data from the *USIA Alumni Study* offer a starting point.[58] This study, in which more than 200 members of the USIA Alumni Association participated, surveyed the views of senior officers in the U.S. Information Agency (USIA)—for nearly half a century the largest public diplomacy operation in the world—on a range of matters related to public diplomacy, including ethics and values.[59] Although the global context in which public diplomacy is practiced has changed in significant ways since the end of the Cold War and the agency's dissolution in 1999—making it necessary to consider new ways of thinking about and doing public diplomacy—the survey revealed that fundamental tenets of ethical public diplomacy may not have changed all that much.

An overwhelming majority (89 percent) of the USIA alumni—who reported an average of twenty-five years of public diplomacy experience in all corners of the world—agreed that ethical issues are important considerations in the practice of public diplomacy.[60] When provided a list of values and asked to choose the five most important to public diplomacy professionals in working with people abroad, the former public diplomats rated the following values highest: credibility, respect, truthfulness, dialogue, and openness.[61] These values suggest that although a primary objective of U.S. public diplomacy during the Cold War was *telling* America's story to the world, public diplomats on the front lines recognized the importance of relationship building in their efforts to achieve the USIA mission "to bring about understanding for [the] nation's ideas and ideals, its institutions and its culture, as well as its national goals and current policies."[62]

Open-ended comments by the USIA alumni further emphasized the importance of ethical values in the professional practice of public diplomacy. For example, one of the officers explained, "Just putting out a message is only part of the process, and a small part at that. There needs to be more true dialogue, to build an atmosphere of understanding and trust."[63] According to another, "Credibility is hard-won and fragile."[64] Others said, "Honesty and openness are the best attributes of a successful public diplomacy effort," and "U.S. officials should tell the truth . . . warts and all."[65] The former public diplomats' comments also reflected a broader theme that was summarized by one: "Good public diplomacy requires sustained relationships of trust and goodwill."[66]

A recent study that identified the defining characteristics of the "new" public diplomacy revealed both the enduring nature of these values and evolving perspectives on how public diplomacy should be practiced.[67] According to this report, the new public diplomacy (1) anticipates a more collaborative approach to international relations; (2) contributes to mutual understanding among nations/international actors and foreign publics; (3) helps to build and sustain relationships between nations/international actors and foreign publics; (4) facilitates networks of relationships between nations/international actors and people in both the public and private sectors; (5) involves both foreign and domestic publics; (6) includes foreign publics in policy processes; (7) is based on principles of dialogue and mutuality; (8) emphasizes two-way communication and interactions; (9) favors people-to-people interactions over mass-messaging techniques; and (10) has a primarily proactive, long-term focus on relationship building.[68]

Viewed together, the findings of the *USIA Alumni Study* and the defining features of the new public diplomacy reveal striking similarities in the ethical principles and values considered important to public diplomacy's success, while also showing movement toward a more collaborative model of public diplomacy. These works suggest that six core relational values might form the basis of a code of ethics for contemporary public diplomacy professionals:

1. Credibility—reflecting the importance of authenticity and believability in words and actions;
2. Mutuality—reflecting principles of dialogue and reciprocity;
3. Collaboration—reflecting a commitment to engage and work with others toward shared goals;
4. Honesty—reflecting adherence to the highest standards of accuracy and truth;
5. Respect—reflecting openness to and acceptance of others' beliefs, ideals and values;
6. Trust—reflecting the importance of integrity and reliability.

These relational values reflect both the "lessons of experience"[69] in the field and the keen insights of contemporary public diplomacy practitioners and scholars. They provide guideposts for public diplomats to consider in carrying out their ethical obligations to those affected by their nations' decisions and actions. They provide a foundation for contemplating public diplomacy's broader role and impact in global society. Most important, these values demonstrate that public diplomats are committed to ethical practices.

Going forward, public diplomacy scholars and practitioners will be challenged to define and apply these values in vastly different contexts and cultures. They will be tasked with reconciling the ethical dimensions of public diplomacy with diverse perspectives on public diplomacy's function(s) in global society. They also will be asked to demonstrate links between ethics and effectiveness in the field. Future research will help to address such challenges and define the parameters of ethical public diplomacy practices in various regions of the world. Key questions for future studies include: Is a global code of ethics in public diplomacy possible (desirable)? What are the advantages/disadvantages of a global code? What issues related to professional responsibility and accountability should be addressed in a global code of ethics? What would be (should be) the philosophical foundation of such a code? Could (how could) a global code of ethics in public diplomacy be enforced? What are the consequences of engaging in unethical public diplomacy practices (as defined by the code)? What types of education and training would be required to ensure ethical public diplomacy practices on a global scale? How should ethical standards of practice be promoted and advanced?

CONCLUSION

If public diplomacy's fundamental purpose is to establish and sustain mutually beneficial relations between nations and peoples for the advancement of global peace and prosperity, then a relational framework is the clear alternative to soft power as a conceptual foundation. A relational model integrates a more global—and less nationalistic—perspective than do promotional or power-based models of public diplomacy. It incorporates dialogue in which foreign publics are viewed as participants in policy processes rather than as means to self-interested ends. And it is based on collaboration, meaning that it is not about competition or defeating others' ideas but about advancing shared goals. As such, a relational perspective reflects not only "best practices" in contemporary public diplomacy but also a move toward more ethical practices.

The next step in public diplomacy's development is the establishment of professional standards that advance the relational paradigm. Although a shift toward a more collaborative public diplomacy is underway in foreign ministries throughout the world, there is still a long way to go before public diplomacy fully integrates the principles and values of a relational framework. As *New York Times* writer Michael Meyer noted in contemplating the continuing relevance of *The Ugly American* in a post-9/11 world, "As the battle for hearts and minds has shifted to the Middle East, we still can't speak Sarkhanese."[70]

NOTES

1. William J. Lederer and Eugene Burdick, *The Ugly American* (New York: W.W. Norton, 1999).
2. Ibid.
3. Geoffrey Cowan and Amelia Arsenault, "Moving from Monologue to Dialogue to Collaboration," *ANNALS of the American Academy of Political and Social Science* 616 (2008): 10.
4. Joseph S. Nye, Jr., *Soft Power: The Means to Success in World Politics* (New York: Public Affairs, 2004), x.
5. Ibid., 5.
6. Ibid., 64.
7. Ibid., 5.
8. Joseph S. Nye, Jr., "The Velvet Hegemon: How Soft Power Can Help Defeat Terrorism," *Foreign Policy* (May 2003): 74.
9. Nye, *Soft Power: The Means to Success in World Politics*, 110.
10. Wilson P. Dizard Jr., *Inventing Public Diplomacy: The Story of the U.S. Information Agency* (Boulder, CO: Lynne Rienner, 2004), 227.
11. Carnes Lord, *Losing Hearts and Minds? Public Diplomacy and Strategic Influence in the Age of Terror* (Westport, CT: Praeger Security International, 2001), 20.
12. Cynthia P. Schneider, "Culture Communicates: US Diplomacy That Works," in *The New Public Diplomacy: Soft Power in International Relations*, ed. Jan Melissen (Houndmills: Palgrave Macmillan, 2005), 147.
13. Quoted in Eytan Gilboa, "Public Diplomacy: The Missing Component in Israel's Foreign Policy," *Israel Affairs* 12 (2006): 719.
14. Brian Hocking, "Rethinking the 'New' Public Diplomacy," in Melissen, *The New Public Diplomacy*, 33.
15. Simon Anholt, *Competitive Identity: The New Brand Management for Nations, Cities and Regions* (Houndmills: Palgrave Macmillan, 2007), 127.

16. Ibid.
17. Ali Fisher, "Looking at the Man in the Mirror: Understanding of Power and Influence in Public Diplomacy," in *Trials of Engagement: The Future of US Public Diplomacy*, ed. Ali Fisher and Scott Lucas (Leiden: Martinus Nijhoff, 2011), 271.
18. Ibid., 282.
19. Ibid., 272.
20. Ibid., 281.
21. Kathy R. Fitzpatrick, *U.S. Public Diplomacy in a Post-9/11 World: From Messaging to Mutuality* (Los Angeles: Figueroa Press, 2011).
22. Patrick Lee Plaisance, "The Propaganda War on Terrorism: An Analysis of the United States' 'Shared Values' Public Diplomacy Campaign after September 11, 2011," *Journal of Mass Media Ethics* 20 (2005): 250–68.
23. Ibid., 266.
24. Ibid., 263–64.
25. Ibid., 265.
26. Kathy R. Fitzpatrick, *The Future of U.S. Public Diplomacy: An Uncertain Fate* (Leiden: Martinus Nijhoff, 2010), 50.
27. Ibid.
28. Pew Research Center for the People and the Press, "Global Opinion: The Spread of Anti-Americanism," *Pew Global Attitudes Project* (2005): 106, http://pewglobal.org.
29. Ibid., 108.
30. Ibid., 106.
31. Ole R. Holsti and Natasha C. Roetter, "How Publics Abroad View the United States" (paper presented at the annual meeting of the American Political Science Association, Washington, DC, September 1–4, 2005).
32. Julia E. Sweig, *Friendly Fire: Losing Friends and Making Enemies in the Anti-American Century* (New York: Public Affairs, 2006), 34.
33. James E. Grunig, Larissa A. Grunig, and William P. Ehling, "What Is an Effective Organization?" in *Excellence in Public Relations and Communication Management: Contributions to Effective Organizations*, ed. James E. Grunig (Mahwah, NJ: Lawrence Erlbaum, 1991), 86.
34. David L. Martinson, "Enlightened Self-Interest Fails as an Ethical Baseline in Public Relations," *Journal of Mass Media Ethics* 9 (1994): 102.
35. Brian Barder, "Diplomacy, Ethics and the National Interest: What Are Diplomats For?" *The Hague Journal of Diplomacy* 5 (2010): 289.
36. Ibid.
37. Ibid., 296.
38. Ibid.
39. Shaun Riordan, "Dialogue-Based Public Diplomacy: A New Foreign Policy Paradigm?" in Melissen, *The New Public Diplomacy*, 5.
40. Barder, "Diplomacy, Ethics and the National Interest," 297.
41. Ibid., 294.
42. Fitzpatrick, *U.S. Public Diplomacy in a Post-9/11 World.*
43. Ali Fisher and Scott Lucas, "Conclusion," in Fisher and Lucas, *Trials of Engagement*, 300.
44. W. Timothy Coombs and Sherry J. Holladay, *It's Not Just PR: Public Relations in Society* (Malden, MA: Blackwell, 2007), 127.
45. Barry Fulton, Bruce Gregory, Donna Marie Oglesby, Walter R. Roberts, and Barry Zorthian, "Public Diplomacy: A Dissent: Transformation Not Restoration," in *America's Dialogue with the World*, ed. William P. Kiehl (Washington, DC: Public Diplomacy Council, 2006), 191.

46. Harry W. Kopp and Charles A. Gillespie, *Career Diplomacy: Life and Work in the U.S. Foreign Service* (Washington, DC: Georgetown University Press, 2008), 5.
47. Ibid., 51.
48. Ibid.
49. Susan R. Johnson, "Essential Ingredients for a Professional Foreign Service," *Foreign Service Journal* April (2012): 5.
50. Ibid., 7.
51. Kenneth Thompson, "Moral Maxims in Statecraft," *International Relations* 6 (1979): 693.
52. Thomas Hanson, "The Traditions and Travails of Career Diplomacy in the United States," *The Hague Journal of Diplomacy* 6 (2011): 447.
53. Ibid.
54. One exception is Richard Nelson and Foad Izadi, "Ethics and Social Issues in Public Diplomacy," in *Routledge Handbook of Public Diplomacy*, ed. Nancy Snow and Philip M. Taylor (New York: Routledge, 2009).
55. Daryl Copeland, "No Dangling Conversation: Portrait of the Public Diplomat," in *Engagement: Public Diplomacy in a Globalized World: A Collection of Essays and Case Studies* (London: UK Foreign & Commonwealth Office, 2008).
56. Dean Kruckeberg, "Ethical Values Define Public Relations Community," *PR Update* 2 (1993): 1–2.
57. Jan Melissen and Paul Sharp, "Editorial," *The Hague Journal of Diplomacy* 1 (2006): 1.
58. Fitzpatrick, *The Future of U.S. Public Diplomacy*, Appendix One.
59. Ibid.
60. Ibid., 213.
61. Ibid.
62. Hans N. Tuch, *Communicating with the World: U.S. Public Diplomacy Overseas* (New York: St. Martin's Press, 1990), 3.
63. Fitzpatrick, *The Future of U.S. Public Diplomacy*, 235.
64. Ibid., 237.
65. Ibid.
66. Ibid., 236.
67. Fitzpatrick, *U.S. Public Diplomacy in a Post-9/11 World*.
68. Ibid., 12–13.
69. Alan K. Henrikson, "Diplomacy's Possible Futures," *The Hague Journal of Diplomacy* 1 (2006): 4.
70. Michael Meyer, "Still 'Ugly' after All These Years," *New York Times Sunday Book Review* online, July 10, 2009.

3   The Politics of Relational Public Diplomacy

Robin Brown

INTRODUCTION

The emergence of the relational approach to public diplomacy has been driven by the belief that it offers a better way to approach the practice of public diplomacy. Particularly in the wake of 9/11, "relationalism," as it might be termed, has been seen as an approach that is both more effective and more ethical. The first claim of effectiveness is rooted in the view that "informational" or "messaging" approaches have proved ineffective in the task of improving relations between Western countries and foreign publics. Implicit in this view is that relational activities can play a role in improving the broader political context within international relations. The second claim of ethical character stems from the idea that a relational approach requires a commitment to mutuality, symmetry, dialogue, or trust building that differentiates the approach from the pursuit of information dominance or some other version of propaganda. In particular, this second claim stems from the origination of the relational approach in normative theories of communications and technology, for instance symmetrical theories of public relations, theories of dialogue, or the claims of the superiority of open-source methods.

This chapter argues that a relational theory of public diplomacy needs to move beyond its roots in normative theories of communications. While empirical considerations cannot be taken as decisive objections to normative theories, they do raise the question of what public diplomacy can be expected to achieve as a real-world activity. Public diplomacy is a practical activity undertaken by collective (often governmental or quasi-governmental) actors for particular purposes in specific contexts. These issues require a much more extensive treatment than can be given here, so this discussion focuses on the question of context of public diplomacy activities. In particular, the interaction between objectives and diplomatic context creates a "politics of public diplomacy." Practitioners and academic researchers rarely address this facet, but rather focus is on the public diplomacy act itself. Understanding this politics goes a considerable distance toward explaining the operations and prospects for public diplomacy. If the working assumption

is that public diplomacy has the capacity to transform diplomatic and political relationships, there is considerable evidence that, in many cases, it is
the reverse of this relationship that is decisive; the political and diplomatic
environment more strongly affects the public diplomacy environment than
the other way round.

This argument is developed in four stages. The first section looks at how
we should conceptualize the context for public diplomacy action. It argues
that the network perspective offers considerable resources for addressing
context in a consistent way. The second section discusses the tendency to
neglect the idea that the politics of public diplomacy is located in a mixture
of practical and conceptual sources. The third section explores the intersection between the motivations for public diplomacy activity and the political
context. This framework allows the identification of a set of cases, where,
if anything, public diplomacy is likely to worsen diplomatic relationships.
The concluding section identifies the implications of this analysis for the
development of public diplomacy research and practice.

CONCEPTUALIZING RELATIONAL
PUBLIC DIPLOMACY

Public diplomacy is understood here as the set of communication activities carried out by governmental or quasi-governmental organizations that
are intended to have an influence on external publics. The relational approach to public diplomacy grows out of communications theories. This
approach leads to a focus on the communicative act. But the effect of
any communicative act is shaped by the context in which it occurs; it
then follows that the fit between action and context is an important element of explaining the success or failure of that action. Theoretically, it
makes sense to achieve this contextualization of public diplomacy action
through an engagement with the vocabulary of relational sociology and
social network analysis.

Relational sociology starts from the insight that relationships are the
building blocks of all social formations and that a set of relationships can
be treated as a network.[1] Thus, there is a movement from a single relationship (or dyad) to a set of interdependent relationships. The formation and
maintenance of relationships depends on communication, but is not simply
communications; it may also involve the exchange of resources. Relationships are interdependent, and the pattern of relationships gives insights into
pressures for conformity versus the degree of autonomy that agents enjoy
within a network.[2]

Relationships can be conceptualized in terms of their content (what are
they about) and their strength, understood in terms of the relative priority for the members of the dyad.[3] This in turn gives rise to the question of
asymmetry in the relationship. A dyad may be more important for one side

than the other, which in turn creates an imbalance of power that can be exploited. The relative importance of particular relationships stems, in part, from the overall structure of the network.[4]

Relational public diplomacy occurs in a world of relationships. It follows that the impact of a public diplomacy initiative depends less on the quality of that initiative in itself than the relationships around the interlocutors. Two people may enjoy a successful dialogue, but the impact of that dialogue depends on their other relationships. Can the discussants persuade their counterparts to adopt their views or are the pressures on the discussants, whether social disapproval or bureaucratic inertia, too great? The typical rationale for relational public diplomacy activities is that they will have an impact beyond those directly engaged in the activity. For instance, the efforts of a public diplomat to forge relations with a nongovernmental organization (NGO) are likely to be predicated on the belief that the NGO has some broader impact. Alternatively, the selection of a recipient for a scholarship is based on the belief that the recipient will subsequently take on a significant role in his or her home country. Social networks are not the same as technological networks. Social networks are prone to separation and closure as much as to openness and diffusion.[5] Indeed, one of the attractions of the network approach is the ability to treat these phenomena as aspects of the same social structures. The key question becomes, under what circumstances will communication and influence flow across social networks?

Treating social formations as a set of networks provides two further insights into the place of public diplomacy within the broader set of international relationships. First, when does public diplomacy have the greatest impact? Relationships built or facilitated by public diplomacy programs are a subset of all governmental relations with that country, which, in turn, are a subset of all relationships between two countries. Public diplomacy is a tool used to support or modify the broader set of relationships. For instance, by developing a student exchange programs, a country seeks to influence the broader governmental relationships or to influence the society-to-society set of relationships in the present and in the future. This analysis suggests that, all things being equal, the impact of public diplomacy will be greater where there are fewer intergovernmental and intersocietal relationships, because public diplomacy will be a greater share of the total set of relationships. As the volume of interaction increases, it is likely that public diplomacy programs will constitute a smaller fraction of the whole; hence, the overall potential to influence the totality of relationships will decline.

One of the recurring motifs in thinking about public diplomacy is the gap between "policy" and "communication." In other words, policy decisions are made without regard for how they will look to foreign audiences. The implication of the policy/communication discussion is that a government made the right policy decision but a more skillful communication would have reduced the damaging consequences. Consequently, communications was asked to manage the consequences of unpopular policy decisions.

After his appointment as minister with responsibility for the overseas information services in the wake of the 1956 Suez Crisis, the British politician Charles Hill made a classic statement of this argument:

> The enterprise had failed; everybody was smarting under the sting of defeat and, naturally enough, the search for scapegoats was on. Those who disagreed with the Suez policy did not have to look very far for their target—Anthony Eden was their man and they abused him bitterly. But those that had supported or tolerated the venture, including Cabinet Ministers who shared the responsibility for it with Eden, did not take long to find another scapegoat—the information services.[6]

From a relational point of view, "policy" can be understood as one set of decisions about relationships. In this case, the British decision to invade Egypt in alliance with France and Israel was a decision about their relationship with Egypt. The demand on the information services was then to persuade others to accept this choice. The communications issue is the second-order set of consequences that follow from this initial choice. How do publics, other than the primary target of the "policy" decision, react? Do the consequences of these reactions justify or undermine the original decision? Thus, the usual discussion about policy and communication can be understood as a debate about the relative priority of one relationship over others. The question then arises about the extent to which this prioritization was justified. Skillful communication (or diplomacy) may then be able to adjust the reaction to this decision. Diplomatic relationships and public diplomacy relationships, however, have to be treated as part of the same universe and affect each other.

The consequences of public diplomacy actions very much depend on the context. Therefore, pure communications considerations—relevance of message, truthfulness, sincerity, cultural awareness, language—while important, are only part of the picture.

THE MISSING DIMENSION OF POLITICS OF PUBLIC DIPLOMACY

In examining the practice of public diplomacy, the political environment in which it takes place defines a large part of the context. Politics, however, tends to attract little attention in the discourse of public diplomacy. Why is this?

Practitioners of public diplomacy and related activities such as cultural relations and nation branding often go to great lengths to explicitly or implicitly emphasize the nonpolitical nature of what they do. There are good reasons for doing so. Public diplomacy involves representatives working with citizens of another country in order to modify some aspect of that country. Despite the resemblances to public relations, it is this cross-border dimension of public diplomacy that creates the sensitivity. Thus, minimizing the political dimension of influence is universal. Even the more overtly political parts of public diplomacy, such as policy advocacy, utilize neutral terminology such as "publicity," "information," and "engagement."

In relational activities such as cultural relations programs, this distancing from politics is even more elaborate. If diplomatic relations are poor, cultural relations are a way of maintaining lines of communication. Additionally, if you want to influence someone to support your country's objectives, it might be more effective to be relatively vague about precisely what it is that you are doing. Public diplomacy operates in spite of political difficulties, and by doing so—at least in some cases—ameliorates the underlying causes of those realities.

Three features of public diplomacy scholarship sometimes reinforce the practitioners' de-emphasis of the politics of public diplomacy. First, analysis often treats public diplomacy as essentially an exercise in interpersonal communication. Discussions of deliberation and dialogue advocate truthfulness, honesty, and openness; these same principles can be applied to the construction of public diplomacy relationships.[7] Second, public diplomacy scholarship tends to share the assumption that conflict is a function of misperception, and, hence, is amenable to moderation through better information. Third, an implicit democratic teleology rooted in the familiar ideology of modernization leads to the assumption that technology aids the emergence of democratic forces and, by doing so, removes the sources of conflict.

The organizational politics of public diplomacy organizations similarly leads to a de-emphasis of politics. In instances when independent or quasi-independent agencies are involved in public diplomacy, they tend to distance themselves from their respective ministry of foreign affairs. The British Council, for example, differentiates its work as "cultural relations," distinct from "public diplomacy," a function performed by the MFA. This can be interpreted as an effort to make the organization more acceptable in foreign countries, while simultaneously resisting the efforts of the Foreign Office to exert influence over the organization.[8]

THE POLITICS OF PUBLIC DIPLOMACY

If both practitioners and scholars tend to downplay public diplomacy as politics, where does the politics come from? There are two major sources. First, conceptual accounts of public diplomacy tend to emphasize the role of public diplomacy in building relationships between countries. Hence, the diplomatic relationship between countries is a major source. Second, some countries use public diplomacy to attempt to influence the policies as well as the values and governance practices within those countries. For instance, the embrace of human rights as an objective within public diplomacy is often simultaneously treated as nonpolitical by Western countries and supremely political by others.

Based on the interaction between the objectives of public diplomacy activities and the state of the diplomatic relationship, this section derives five scenarios from recent public diplomacy practice. It shows how different scenarios produce characteristic reactions from the host government. The argument here is that the prospects for the success of public diplomacy activities are intimately tied to the state of the diplomatic relationship. There is a commonly unexamined assumption in current scholarship that public diplomacy can act to influence the overall situation. The following analysis suggests that public diplomacy's capacity to do so is limited. The overall diplomatic relationship is likely to constrain public diplomacy operations; and public diplomacy initiatives may actually worsen diplomatic relationships. The major point is that researchers and practitioners needs to recognize the interdependence between diplomatic relations and public diplomacy both analytically and programmatically.

Theoretical discussions of public diplomacy tend to focus on the potential to improve diplomatic relations. However, this section argues that the history of public diplomacy shows that lines of influence also run in the other direction. Public diplomacy is usually treated as a way of improving diplomatic relationships, but one also needs to consider the inverse possibility. The state of the diplomatic relations has a powerful impact on the nature and effects of public diplomacy. In fact, if we consider the relationship between public diplomacy objectives, the nature of the diplomatic relationship, and the nature of the political system, we can identify numerous situations where the outcome of public diplomacy activities will make the diplomatic relationship worse.

The five scenarios involve situations where the initiating country is interested in achieving one of the following objectives:

1. Reinforcement of the diplomatic relationship
2. Influencing a policy stance
3. Improving a diplomatic relationship
4. Regime change
5. Contributing to the improvement of governance

The inclusion of regime change as a public diplomacy objective may seem less than diplomatic but reflects the origins of the term as a euphemism for propaganda in the context of American Cold War diplomacy. Governance—a major theme in Western diplomacy since the end of the Cold War—is where foreign ministries undertake and or support activities aimed at developing human rights, supporting civil society organizations, and contributing to the support of democracy in target countries.

From the point of view of the public diplomacy initiator, each objective reflects a particular political configuration. Objective 1 (relationship reinforcement) implies a positive or neutral diplomatic relationship and objective 4 (regime change) guarantees a negative diplomatic relationship. Objectives 2 (influencing policy), 3 (improving relations), and 5 (governance development) are more ambiguous political configurations. Efforts to influence particular policies can take place in any diplomatic context. Let us review each of these objectives in turn.

Public Diplomacy as Relationship Maintenance

In the first case, two countries have a positive relationship. Here, public diplomacy activities are aimed at supporting the relationship. For instance, exchange programs seek to build support for the relationship through youth programs or the development of artistic collaborations. These activities may be motivated by the desire to raise the profile of one of the countries. For instance, both the UK and Brazilian governments may view British efforts to raise its profile in Brazil as a positive activity, and thus the Brazilian government is supportive of these activities.[9]

The overall importance of the initiative will vary depending on the broader set of relations. For instance, although activities targeted at particular groups may make sense, the overall impact of U.S. public diplomacy in the UK will probably be marginal, due to the large volume of other relations between the two countries. Given the relatively lower visibility of the UK in the United States, it might be argued that UK activities in the other direction may have more of a rationale.

The politics of public diplomacy here might come from the objection that some people hold to the relationship itself, which for some countries might be considerable. In some relationships, the elite might be committed to a relationship that is largely unpopular with other sections of the population. During the 1980s, for instance, NATO governments supported the deployment of Intermediate Range Nuclear forces, in the face of power opposition. In general, these conditions foster a highly supportive environment for the conduct of public diplomacy with a high probability of support from the host government.

Public Diplomacy as a Policy Influence Tool

In the second scenario, public diplomacy practitioners engage with legislators, the media, and NGOs, as well as with conventional government-to-government contacts, in order to influence policy. This implies a situation where the host political system is relatively open and where groups outside the government have some influence on policy.

The attitude of the host government varies depending on the proposed policy change. If the host government sees the advocacy activity as supporting a favorable policy change, it may welcome the activity. The host government will be more ambivalent if the PD campaign is aimed at modifying its own policy. This mode of action, however, typically takes place in a democracy, where lobbying activity is a normal part of the game. The United States, for example, has lobbied to influence Norway's policy on missile defense.[10]

Public Diplomacy as an Instrument to Improve Relations

The third scenario is perhaps the classic concept of public diplomacy as an instrument to improve relations. The implication here is that two countries have ambivalent or poor relations and that the development of new public diplomacy programs will ameliorate those relations. However, returning to the politics of public diplomacy, it is important to assess the nature of the existing relations. The government-to-government relationship may be poor, for a variety of reasons. It may be poor simply due to neglect; and investment in public diplomacy is a way to signal recognition of the importance of the relationship. Alternatively, the relationship may be one of conflict. When relations are strained, public diplomacy becomes an object of suspicion; is it a way to score points in the ongoing battle? This may be thought of as the terrain of U.S.-Soviet conflict.[11]

Public Diplomacy as Regime Change

The above three scenarios sit within the norms of diplomatic practice. However, we also need to consider an additional perspective—public diplomacy as an instrument of regime change. A classic example of this scenario is the public diplomacy of the Cold War. The United States sought to erode the Soviet bloc, even as they worked through formal diplomacy to improve state-to-state relations. In this respect, the U.S. approach paralleled that of the Soviet Union; the doctrine of peaceful coexistence applied at an interstate level, but did not reflect a cessation of class struggle. Within such a framework, the objective of the public diplomacy activity is to undermine the regime's domestic support while building support for its opponents and critics. Such a position almost guarantees a negative diplomatic relationship, and that there will be measures to constrain public diplomacy activities. This leads toward the reliance on broadcasting as the main communication tool and, in turn, to the prominence of jamming as a counter to broadcasting operations.

Deteriorating diplomatic relations tend to create barriers to relational public diplomacy work. In this scenario, the regime might seek to demonize those who participate in relational activities in order to de-legitimize relations with what is portrayed as a hostile external power. The outcomes depend on the strength and legitimacy of anti-regime forces. The creation of the *Ikhwan al Hurriya* (Brotherhood of Freedom) in Egypt was one of the most elaborate efforts in British relational public diplomacy aimed at regime change. Organized by the British during the Second World War, the Brotherhood of Freedom was a network of discussion groups that met weekly to discuss current events based on a newsletter. The intervention was initially conceived of as a way of mobilizing opposition to the Axis powers and support for the British war effort. The organization continued to operate after the war; by the late 1940s, it was estimated to have more than 5,000 groups and upwards of 56,000 members. The program initiators stressed that its intention was to increase support for democracy rather than for Britain. The organization was incapacitated when conflict between Britain and the regime of Colonel Nasser escalated in the early 1950s. In the end, the relations that tied the Ikhwan's members to Egypt were stronger than those that tied them to the UK.[12]

This negative response to public diplomacy activities is not confined to non-Western states. The surveillance and harassment of communists during the Cold War can be seen as efforts to counter foreign influences. Such efforts lie in the perception of the host country. In recent years, the status and operations of the British Council has proved to be a major source of tension between the UK and Russia. The Russia Authorities have questioned the tax affairs of the Council, an action that the Council has portrayed as politically motivated.[13] OFCOM, the UK's communications regulator, has taken actions against the Iranian external television service *Press TV* for breaches of the British program code. In turn, *Press TV* has portrayed the actions as being politically motivated.[14] Not surprisingly, public diplomacy efforts aimed at regime change are more common and provoke greater backlash when they involve authoritarian or more closed regimes.

Contributing to the Improvement of Governance

Objective 5 (governance development) indicates a range of state activities designed to impact how other states develop. Some of these steps fall within the remit of public diplomacy organizations; others are undertaken by development agencies or NGOs under contract to governments or international organizations. This area includes: support for civil society organizations, media development, human rights promotion and protection, and similar activities. These activities, commonly regarded as nonpolitical by the people conducting them, are inherently political when you consider the fact that they entail pushing modes of governance toward Western models. The receiving country thus views them with ambivalence.

Over the last two decades, Western diplomacy has become increasingly concerned with governance. This transition has its origins in the emergence of foreign assistance as a policy priority after decolonization and the entrenchment of human rights issues in international politics in the wake of the Helsinki Agreement. In U.S. public diplomacy, human rights first became a major theme under President Jimmy Carter (1976–1980). As well as confronting the Soviet Bloc and its allies, the Reagan Administration supported democratic transitions in the Philippines and South Korea.[15] The Third Wave of democratization culminated in the collapse of the Eastern Bloc and the Soviet Union, and in political upheavals in Soviet-allied nations around the world. In succeeding decades, we have seen the emergence of a transformational diplomacy concerned with the development of liberal democratic political regimes and a rules-based international order.

Within this context, the boundaries between public diplomacy, development, stabilization, and related concepts commonly shade into one another. This is a likely consequence of a relational approach. When the development of the relationship is the primary concern and communication is secondary, the relationship needs to be about something and involve some activity. Relationship-building activities range from working with human rights organizations and other civil society groups to promote a certain goal, such as media law and regulation reform, to improving the performance of government institutions.

This type of governance-development activity implies some degree of consent on the part of the receiving country. Such consent, however, may be reluctantly given. Rather than on genuine support for the activity, it may be based on the fear that objections to public diplomacy activities may threaten the provision of associated aid or damage the government's reputation. Any activities that advocate changes in the mode of governance may lead to a redistribution of power away from entrenched government actors. In this situation, host governments may greet public diplomacy work with verbal support and practical obstruction. Under this scenario, the political regime is likely to be semi-authoritarian, but the state of relations with the sending country may actually be quite cordial. Public diplomacy, therefore, becomes a source of disturbance rather than reinforcement for state-to-state relationships.

There are several recent examples of the contradictions between public diplomacy and politics wrought by this scenario. In 2012, the post-revolutionary military regime in Egypt, for example, made headlines by raiding the offices of Egyptian NGOs supported with American funds.[16] In 2011, WikiLeaks released 251,000 unredacted U.S. State Department cables. These cables contain many references to the tensions with U.S. embassies caused by their "democracy programming," or what under the G.W. Bush administration was referred to as "the Freedom Agenda."[17] Indeed, as a telegram from Oman points out, sensitivity to perception forces the embassy to reduce the public profile of its democracy promotion activities.[18]

CONCLUSION

The main conclusion that we can draw from this discussion is that relationships matter for public diplomacy but that, from a practical and theoretical perspective, the context of relationships also matters. Looking at the context in which a public diplomacy activity occurs explains a large part of its successes and failures. Both policymakers and academics must focus on the implications that the relational context has on shaping the parameters and outcomes of public diplomacy.

For the policymaker, diplomatic choices affect the possibilities for public diplomacy. Public diplomacy activities may generate additional tensions with target countries as well as ensure that public criticism or obstruction from the host government may render the activities ineffective or endanger participants.

This indicates that public diplomacy scholarship should turn greater attention to the interaction between the context of communication and the communicative act itself. In focusing on message improvement and delivery, we will often miss the critical role of context in shaping the success or failure of the communicative act, regardless of how it is crafted and conceived.

NOTES

1. Harrison C. White, *Identity and Control: How Social Formations Emerge* (Princeton, NJ: Princeton University Press, 2008), xi.
2. Ronald S. Burt, *Brokerage and Closure: An Introduction to Social Capital* (Oxford: Oxford University Press, 2005).
3. Martin Kilduff and Wenpin Tsai, *Social Networks and Organizations* (London: Sage, 2003), 6.
4. Ibid., 1.
5. Ronald S. Burt, *Brokerage and Closure: An Introduction to Social Capital* (Oxford: Oxford University Press, 2005).
6. Charles Hill, *Both Sides of the Hill*, 1st ed. (London: Heinemann Educational Books, 1964).
7. Kathy R. Fitzpatrick, *U.S. Public Diplomacy in a Post-9/11 World: From Messages to Mutuality*, CPD Perspectives, USC Center on Public Diplomacy, Paper 6 (Los Angeles: Figueroa Press, October 2010), http://uscpublicdiplomacy.org/publications/perspectives/CPDPerspectives_Mutuality.pdf
8. Martin Rose and Nick Wadham-Smith. *Mutuality, Trust and Cultural Relations* (London: Counterpoint, 2004); J. M. Mitchell, *International Cultural Relations* (London: Allen and Unwin, 1986).
9. Foreign Affairs Committee, "UK-Brazil Relations" (London: House of Commons Foreign Affairs Committee, October 11, 2011).
10. U.S. State Department, "Wikileaks Cable: Norway: Missile Defense Public Diplomacy and Outreach," Embassy Oslo: *Wikileaks*, accessed April 30, 2012, http://cablegatesearch.net/cable.php?id=07OSLO248; Suman Lee, "An Analysis of Other Countries' International Public Relations in the U.S.," *Public Relations Review* 32(2) (2006): 97–103.

11. Walter L. Hixson, *Parting the Curtain: Propaganda, Culture, and the Cold War, 1945–1961* (Basingstoke: Macmillan, 1998); Yale Richmond, *Cultural Exchange & The Cold War: Raising The Iron Curtain* (University Park: Pennsylvania State University Press, 2003).
12. Andrew Defty, *Britain, America, and Anti-Communist Propaganda, 1945–53:The Information Research Department* (Abingdon: Routledge, 2004); James R. Vaughan, "'A Certain Idea of Britain': British Cultural Diplomacy in the Middle East, 1945–57," *Contemporary British History* 19(2) (2005): 151–168.
13. "Russia Sends 'Punitive' Tax Bill to British Council," *The Guardian*, June 18, 2008, accessed April 16, 2012, http://www.guardian.co.uk/world/2008/jun/18/russia.foreignpolicy
14. "Iran's Press TV loses UK license," *BBC News*, January 20, 2012, last accessed April 1, 2012, http://www.bbc.co.uk/news/entertainment-arts-16652356
15. Nicholas Cull, *The Cold War and the United States Information Agency: American Propaganda and Public Diplomacy, 1945–1989* (New York: Cambridge University Press, 2008).
16. Los Angeles Times, "Egyptians Raid Offices of NGOs, Including U.S.-based Groups," *Los Angeles Times*, December 29, 2011, accessed April 15, 2012, http://latimesblogs.latimes.com/world_now/2011/12/egyptian-authorities-raid-offices-of-ngos-including-us-based-groups.html
17. U.S. State Department, "Wikileaks Cable: Thoughts on Finland as I Depart Post," Embassy Helsinki: *Wikileaks*, 2008, accessed April 16, 2012, http://www.cablegatesearch.net/cable.php?id=08HELSINKI155; U.S. State Department, "Wikileaks Cable: Embassy Brussels Outreach to Democracy Activists," Embassy Brussels: *Wikileaks*, 2008, accessed April 19, 2012, http://www.cablegatesearch.net/cable.php?id=08BRUSSELS690; U.S. State Department, "Wikileaks Cable: Democracy Promotion Strategies: Burma," Embassy Rangoon: *Wikileaks*, 2005, accessed May 1, 2012, http://www.cablegatesearch.net/cable.php?id=05RANGOON1177
18. U.S. State Department, "Wikileaks Cable: Follow Up on Outreach to Activists: Oman," Embassy Muscat: *Wikileaks*, 2008, accessed April 1, 2012, http://www.cablegatesearch.net/cable.php?id=08MUSCAT351

4 Taking Diplomacy Public

Science, Technology, and Foreign Ministries in a Heteropolar World

Daryl Copeland

INTRODUCTION

Contemporary Western diplomacy is facing a perfect storm. For the past few hundred years, high-level statecraft has focused mainly on balancing power in an ever-changing world. From the age of European empires through to the end of the Cold War, the statistical indicators of national power—armies, navies, missiles, warheads, economies, populations, and territories—were carefully calculated, codified, and notionally balanced in an attempt to secure stability. Alliances and treaties were forged to express or extend these balances. When inevitable imbalances arose, negotiations re-opened. If the negotiations failed, wars usually ensued. And so were fashioned efforts to craft security and world order.

Since the end of the Cold War, the nature and distribution of global power and influence have been on the move, both geographically, from the North Atlantic to the Asia Pacific, and institutionally. The latter shift has been multidirectional: upwards, to central agencies and supra-national institutions; outwards, to other government departments—especially defense—and various new actors, and; downwards, to other levels of government.

Diplomacy matters now more than ever, but it is struggling, beset by crises of image and substance. Foreign ministries most everywhere are under severe stress: disconnected, change-resistant, inadequately resourced, and without a domestic constituency. Western diplomacy especially is seen as having failed to deliver the expected peace dividend at the end of the Cold War. The militarization of foreign policy after 9/11 and the prosecution of an undifferentiated and ill-defined "war on terror" compounded this problem. The Cold War, it seems, simply morphed into the Long War, featuring endless "overseas contingency operations," stabilization programs, counterinsurgency campaigns, and now worldwide special operations, selective assassination, and drone strikes.[1]

While diplomacy appears to be on the decline, the phenomenon of heteropolarity is on the rise. International power and influence have become highly dispersed geographically; and crucially, the sources and vectors now vary enormously. The mainstream view is that world politics have returned to some kind of a multipolar dispensation. Unlike in previous eras, however, differences among and between major actors now outweigh similarities. The *heterogeneous* nature of the competing poles renders comparison difficult and measurement even more so. Clearly delineated empires are no longer colliding, the specter of world war and thermonuclear annihilation has receded, and deterrence has lost its luster.

If diplomacy is going to work, then the basis of security will have to be re-imagined, and foreign ministries will need to be fixed. In our globalization age, many of the most profound threats and challenges to human survival—public health and pandemic disease, food security and resource scarcity, diminishing biodiversity and climate change to name a few—are transnational, and rooted in science and driven by technology. Given these circumstances, the time is ripe for nonstate actors and civil society acting in concert to take the lead by forming new partnerships. This chapter examines the problems facing contemporary diplomacy; highlights the role of science and technology; and outlines how foreign ministries can and should establish crosscutting, public-private, and independent networks to advance thinking on diplomacy and international policy.

ESSENTIAL REFORM

Three inter-related issue clusters are the principal drivers behind the need for change in foreign ministries and diplomacy.[2]

Globalization and Power Shift

Globalization is best understood as a totalizing historical process that compresses space and accelerates time, determining outcomes across a huge swathe of human activity worldwide. Intimately related to the embrace of neoliberal economics and the revolution in information and communication technologies, globalization finds expression in integrated markets, financial and monetary interdependence, and increased levels of trade and investment, travel, and migration. It generates wealth and productive efficiency but is inherently unstable and tends to polarize and widen inequality at all levels, producing winners and losers, social ferment and political fragmentation. Increasing connectedness has many benefits, but globalization is very much a double-edged sword. Careful handling and constant attention are essential.

With the advent of globalization, power is once again migrating. Much has been made of the rise of the Asia Pacific, largely at the expense of the North Atlantic, as the dynamic center of the world economy.[3] Less celebrated has been the impact of this evolving world system upon the apparatus of the state, which virtually everywhere finds itself under siege. Most diplomats work for states, and these days, states are of diminishing importance, only one actor among many on a world stage now crowded with multinational corporations, NGOs, think tanks, and celebrities.[4] Foreign ministries, for their part, have lost a good deal of their turf to executive branches, central agencies, and other government departments. Power is migrating upwards, to supranational institutions, outwards, to business and other civil society actors, and downwards, to other levels of government. Foreign direct investment, offshore remittances, and private philanthropy are displacing official development assistance as exogenous engines of development.[5] With the state's reduced resources and receding clout, globalization and power shifts mean that creative, deliberate adaptation is no longer just an option, but a necessity.

Heteropolarity and World Order

When the era of bipolarity ended unexpectedly with the implosion of the USSR, it was preceded by a brief period of American unipolar dominance.[6] With costly wars in Iraq and Afghanistan, corporate excess, political dysfunction, and the financial crisis—leading to the Great Recession—this interlude crashed to a halt.[7] Most commentators believe that the world is now reverting to some kind of multipolar dispensation, not unlike the case of Europe in the nineteenth century.[8] But nineteenth-century dignitaries such as Prince Klemens von Metternich and Lord Castlereagh would not recognize this tableau. This time around, the sources and vectors of international power and influence are *heterogeneous* rather than comparable; diplomats now function in a world of *heteropolarity*.

The emergence of a *heteropolitan*[9] world in which the drivers and goals of power and influence are no longer easily meshed will inevitably cause friction. In the interstices surrounding these highly differentiated poles, edges will be sharp, competition fierce, objectives divergent, and interests difficult to align. In areas such as trade, investment, and environmental protection, finding basis for bargaining has already become difficult.

While the United States will remain the Praetorian, or "hard power"[10] pole, for the foreseeable future, its economic position is slipping. China has become the world's largest manufacturer and importer of energy and raw materials. India is the globe's English-language back-office, call center, and software incubator. Brazil is a resource and agribusiness powerhouse and the voice of the Global South at multilateral negotiations. Europe's comparative advantage resides in its still abundant "soft power," the appeal attached to its culture, history, and lifestyle. The list continues.

Heteropoles are forming in all shapes and sizes. Certain countries, such as Turkey, Iran, South Africa, Egypt, and Mexico, as well as regions, such as Southeast Asia and perhaps the Gulf states, will almost certainly figure in this new dispensation. Some poles may take the form of international organizations, others may be corporate, and a few, after the likes of Bill Gates, will be individuals.

Despite a profusion of spirited denials,[11] this is a very different horizon than the one imagined by the framers of the Atlantic Charter, or the triumphalists so prominent during the first decade after the end of the Cold War. That world has passed, rendering its international organizations, dominant doctrines, and leadership in the realm of thinking and ideas increasingly anachronistic. The G8 has given way to the G20, the U.S. dollar to a basket of reserve currencies, the Bretton Woods agencies to a new development bank controlled by the BRICS, NATO to the Shanghai Cooperation Organization (SCO), the Trilateral Commission to INSouth, and the Washington Consensus to the Beijing Consensus. This reorganization of the world system is mirrored in state governance institutions. While some of this movement has been more symbolic than substantial, the general direction is clear. Market democracies are not the end of history, after all.

Post-Iraq, post-Afghanistan, post-Kyoto, post-Arab Spring, post-WTO, suggest that we are witnessing a whole new order in the making, one that is not converging around Western ideals. In this emerging, heteropolar order, direct connection on issues of mutual concern, such as trade, the environment, and intellectual property, will become even more trying than at present. Gone are the days when well-acquainted negotiators came to the table with similar cards in their hands. Look instead for new players, new rules, and a whole new game. In such circumstances, finding the basis for bargaining will be tough, the identification of trade-offs elusive, and consensus rare. Sparks will fly, and established forms of dispute resolution will be of marginal relevance. That said, and perhaps most significantly, because these sorts of issues cannot be settled by the threat or use of armed force, the utility of militaries will be highly circumscribed.

Science, Technology, and the New Security

Defense departments have a place in international relations, but at this point in the twenty-first century, it should not be at center stage. The fundamental threats that imperil the planet have little to do with organized violence. Few states threaten others, and political and religious extremism, the animus behind the launch of the ill-starred *global war on terror*, should never have been placed on the A-list.[12] Instead, the most profound global challenges[13]—climate change, environmental collapse, management of the global commons—are rooted in science and driven by technology. So, too, are the solutions, which will flow from research and development, collaboration and information sharing. As instruments of international policy, defense departments are both too sharp, and too dull, to provide the kind of security required. As the Cold War exemplified convincingly, militaries work best when they aren't used. The best army cannot stop pandemic disease. Air strikes and extraordinary rendition are useless against hunger. Alternatives to the carbon economy cannot be acquired through special operations or by the dispatch of expeditionary forces. You can't kill, capture, or garrison against these kinds of threats.

It is talking rather than fighting that offers the best hope. In the heteropolar world, or *heteropolis* now under construction, durable security will not flow from defense, but from diplomacy integrally linked to broad-based development.[14] It is the underdevelopment of human potential rather than conventional or irregular aggression that breeds insecurity. People rather than states have become the primary referent in the search for a safer, more prosperous world.[15] Fear, want, and unmet needs give rise to anger, resentment, and alienation. These symptoms are best treated directly and interpersonally using knowledge and understanding. This is precisely why diplomacy is going public most everywhere, including in conflict zones.[16] Yet to get at the deeper causes of insecurity, such as distributive injustice, resource scarcity, and diminishing biodiversity, ways will have to be found to bridge the divide. Specialized skills and expertise, extending well beyond traditional disciplines such as political science and international relations, and often delivered through imaginative forms of cooperation such as science diplomacy will be essential.[17]

Foreign ministries are the institutional home of diplomats. In a fluid and fraught operating environment, network development, strategic communication, and reputation management are critical for diplomatic effectiveness. Contemporary diplomacy tends to take place openly—in the media and at conferences, in a barrio or a souk, in an internet chat room or on a blog, along Main Street or in a Quonset hut set astride the wire in places such as Afghanistan. The terrain may be unfamiliar, even dangerous. It is certainly replete with challenges.

Foreign ministries provide a strategic nexus connecting national governments and national interests with the world. Inherently rigid and risk averse, and often populated by those with an interest in the status quo, very few foreign ministries, however, are making the most of their connective position. Change has come slowly and fitfully, if at all. There is a yawning performance gap that must be addressed.[18]

In the age of globalization, because development has become the foundation of security, diplomacy rather than defense must find its way to the center of international policy. For that to occur, reforms are needed to ensure that foreign ministries are vested with a capacity for scientific understanding, knowledge-based problem solving, complex balancing, and real cross-cultural exchange. The way forward is by embracing innovation, acting pre-emptively, and reaching out to new partners.

HOW CHANGE CAN HAPPEN

The ends of diplomacy, and hence the writ of its institutions, have remained more or less constant since the emergence of the state-centric, Westphalian system of international relations in the seventeenth century. The search for the nonviolent resolution of differences through dialogue, negotiation, and compromise, and engaging in international political communication for purposes of promoting cooperation for mutual gain, thankfully are with us still. No matter how immutable the ends, the means of diplomacy must evolve in tandem with changes in the world system. Unless foreign ministries find ways to successfully adapt, they face a bleak future. With planning, foresight, and sufficient resources, however, they will not merely survive, but prevail in the face of these steep challenges.

Vision and Mission: From Foreign Policy to Global Issues

While states and relations between them remain important, in the twenty-first century the profusion of new actors and forces has created the need for an *entrepot*, a docking mechanism between national governments and all aspects of the widening world beyond. If re-imagined as a catalyst, or central agency for the management of globalization, foreign ministries can assume a new role as the nation's international policy broker, guide, and storyteller.[19] This would involve transferring, or otherwise dispensing with, many lower-level, and even some more highly specialized, functions to focus instead on regional priorities and thematic clusters where the foreign ministry brings comparative advantage and a unique perspective to the table. As other government departments assume line responsibility for the steward-ship of particularistic files best suited to their field of expertise, the foreign ministry will be able to redeploy resources to more elevated and emerging priorities.

By raising the level of activity up a couple of notches and taking the lead on whole-of-government, whole-of-country international policy development and integration, foreign ministries can get out of the weeds, end duplication, resolve counter-productive turf wars, and concentrate on providing interpretation to their citizens and strategic advice to decision makers. Critical, cross-cutting issues that are not the responsibility of other agencies or levels of government could include public administration and governance; trade policy; rule of law; promotion of human rights and democracy; and the range of broad-based international challenges like climate change, the energy-environment-economy cluster, and management of the global commons. Formal bilateral and multilateral relations will remain part of the mix, but for diplomats, there is now much more to be done—and done differently.

Headquarters Structure and the Representational Footprint Abroad

Foreign ministries are often the oldest of the various organs that constitute the machinery of government. Consequently, more than a few have become

ossified and sclerotic, relying heavily on established procedures and com-
mand- and control-style social relations. Brittle and highly stratified, such
agencies are almost always characterized by a profusion of internal silos.
Their outward orientation—backs to the capital, face to the world—has
frequently resulted in domestic isolation. Foreign ministries are rarely models of modern public management. But that need not be so. Managerial and
administrative overheads can be lowered through de-layering, offloading,
and outsourcing. Technology can be substituted for labor through the embrace of social media platforms and the adoption of innovations such as the
virtual desk.[20] Job design, career management systems, and the terms and
conditions of employment can be overhauled. An organization that functions as an international network node and focal point for policy analysis
and development can be smaller, flatter, and more nimble, and thus a more
rewarding place to work.

Where appropriate, diplomatic representation abroad should take the
form of portable brass plaques on hotel room doors, secure mobile communications, and concentrate on a results-oriented business model rather
than simply waving the flag and maintaining a presence through chanceller-
ies and official residences. In some places—major capitals and world cities,
for instance—investing in visibility may well make sense. In other locations,
a more fleet-footed approach will be superior, and not produce the long
shadow of lingering financial and personnel liabilities. When it comes to
representation, cookie-cutter formulas and preconceived notions about
standards and norms, however dear, no longer obtain. The future favors
clicks over bricks, hubs and spokes over universal replication, and new approaches generically.[21] To cope with the *heteropolar* world order, flexibility
and adaptability are essential.

Bureaucratic Culture and Building a Better Diplomat

A foreign ministry's culture and values are generally conservative and risk
intolerant, turning more frequently on convention than originality. While
ministers and deputy heads come and go, the main body of the workforce,
due mainly to the career nature of most foreign services, tends to turn over
much more slowly than is the case elsewhere. This can be a strength in
terms of accumulating knowledge and experience; but when the nettle must
be grasped, familiarity can breed constraint. When ideas—the lifeblood
of diplomacy—are judged according to their provenance rather than their
quality, there is a problem. Refined manners, deference, book learning, and
an Ivy League education still have a place in diplomacy. But in the roil-
ing badlands associated with underdevelopment and insecurity, it is life
skills—problem solving, improvisation, cross-cultural communications, and
agility—that are now in increasing demand.

Today's ideal recruit is less an international policy bureaucrat than a renaissance polymath, a street-smart, tech-savvy, likely well-traveled policy

entrepreneur with natural curiosity, a sense of adventure, and a keen interest in both people and places. Part activist, part analyst, part alchemist, she or he is instinctively able to swim with comfort and ease, never flopping around like a fish out of water, in the sea of the people beyond the embassy walls. Unlike all too many serving envoys, this candidate prefers mixing with the population to mingling with colleagues, making contacts and generating intelligence to exchanging hearsay about what might be going on outside. The work environment must be made supportive and conducive to the care and nurturing of this new variety of diplomat.

Ways of Work: Rethinking Diplomatic Practice

Because governments will always have official business to transact, traditional, state-to-state interaction performed by designated envoys will not disappear anytime soon. Still, making formal calls, leaving diplomatic notes, writing reports, and awaiting instructions are no longer enough. With the wholesale transformation of the operating environment described above, diplomatic practice must evolve. This will, at times, mean working to resolve complex emergencies in conflict zones; operating from storefronts instead of leafy suburbs or high-rise towers; managing issues and networks rather than pushing paper; and spending more time doing domestic outreach and constituency development.

Consequently, many countries, especially those who face capacity limitations and lack hard-power alternatives, increasingly rely upon public diplomacy. Diplomacy's new frontier involves perfecting the practice of persuasion through public diplomacy and engineering a positive predisposition through branding.[22]

Foreign ministries are not cathedrals, and the foreign service is not a priesthood. Getting around entrenched perceptions will require a determined and systematic effort to turn the inside out, and bringing the outside in. Participation in secondments and exchanges, not just with other government departments, but with private sector businesses, think tanks, universities, or NGOs, could be made a pre-condition for advancement or assignment abroad. If diplomats are to use their judgment, tact, discretion, and local knowledge, and act with greater self-sufficiency and self-reliance, then they must be assured that their superiors will tolerate a wide range of occupational hazards. Executives must be willing to learn from the occasional misstep rather than punish the intrepid. Empowering employees to shape their own futures implies an organizational culture that is less top-down and authoritarian, more supple and lithe, and more confident, trusting, and respectful.

Success in diplomacy—and hence, ultimately, in the reform enterprise—will flow directly from the understanding of, and connection to, *place*. This is the major benefit associated with the staffing and operation of diplomatic missions abroad, whether temporary or permanent. When it comes to delivering on critical responsibilities such as the promotion of economic relations or the generation of political intelligence, the foreign ministry's competitive advantage is its connection to place. Although unique, this aspect is typically undervalued by governments, and regarded as something that can be acquired by other means or for less. That conclusion is incorrect. It is no one else's job to make sense of the world through the unique prism of national interests, policies, and values, and to convey that understanding to ministers and populations. The case for diplomacy rests upon this value proposition. Before a credible bid for reinvestment can be made, however, governments and opinion leaders must be convinced that foreign ministries and diplomats are prepared to do the necessary. In short, they must not only change, but be seen to be changing.

TAKING DIPLOMACY PUBLIC

Deliberate action on the proposals set out above will be necessary if foreign ministries and diplomatic practice are to narrow the performance gap and achieve something approaching their potential. Given the transformed operating environment and myriad constraints associated with state structures, even the most sweeping and progressive reforms will not be sufficient, however. For that to occur, the epicenter of *thinking* about diplomacy must be liberated—at least in part—from the confines of government.

I am a fan of the progressive state, but with the role of public sector receding and the foreign ministry in many countries shrinking,[23] important aspects of a country's diplomatic future and potential may now reside beyond existing political or institutional structures. To that end, civil society organizations, and other levels of government can, should, and almost certainly will play a larger role. In that respect, science diplomacy—which is by nature collaborative and partnership based—and the provision of high-level scientific and technological advice to decision makers, provide an ideal starting point.

Given the absence of creative thinking on international policy, due in significant part to the unfortunate condition of so many foreign ministries, it may be time for nonstate actors and popular forces to take the lead. A university, think tank, foundation, or several organizations operating in concert could champion the construction of a standalone national entity dedicated to the exploration of diplomatic alternatives—and alternative diplomacy—that would not suffer from the diffuse objectives, debilitating administrative overheads, or political controls associated with government departments. Such an enterprise, perhaps (un)structured along the lines of a Silicon Valley-style entrepreneurial "skunk-works," could adopt values such as innovation, flexibility, adaptability, teamwork, continuous learning, and risk tolerance. The engagement of diasporic communities, use of new media, and the creation of virtual networks in addressing the globalization suite of scientific and technological challenges would all figure centrally.[24] This kind of approach would extend well beyond current musings on "citizen diplomacy."[25] Indeed, it may already have begun.[26]

The establishment of crosscutting, public-private, and independent network nodes for the promotion of diplomacy and international policy would burnish nation brands and serve as a conduit for a country's comparative advantage.[27] A whole-of-country "Institute for Diplomatic Alternatives/Alternative Diplomacy" could, for example: develop new diplomatic strategy and tactics; identify and advocate approaches and solutions to global issues and problems, with an emphasis on those rooted in science and driven by technology; generate creative ideas on crisis remediation and conflict resolution; conduct research and analysis, propose policy and provide advice; undertake continuous outreach to journalists, attentive publics, and opinion leaders; reach out to strategic partners on all sides of key issues; organize events (conferences, symposia, round tables); edit and publish an e-journal of alternative diplomacy; and design and deliver training and professional development programs. As with so much else in the age of connectivity, showcasing the use of digital, and especially social, media would be central, not least, to offer one promising example, in providing services to citizens traveling or working abroad through the development of facilities such as a consular "app" for smart phones.[28]

When it comes to science diplomacy and to the design of a more sophisticated approach to the management of international science & technology (S&T) issues more generally, several countries have achieved significant gains.[29] The British and the Swiss, for instance, have for some time been nurturing purpose-built networks through the assignment of dedicated embassy or consulate staff to designated hubs of science, technology, innovation and education, globally.[30] The United States has enlarged its cadre of science counselors, upgraded the position of Science Adviser, and expanded the Jefferson Fellows program, which appoints scientifically trained postdoctoral specialists to term positions throughout the State Department in the U.S. missions abroad.[31] This is a very effective way to embed S&T almost instantly, although major weaknesses remain.[32] European governments have been collaborating on high-energy particle physics research since 1954 under the auspices of the European Organization for Nuclear Research (CERN). This collaborative focal point for the work of some 10,000 scientists internationally counts among its many achievements the launch of the World Wide Web.[33]

Science and technology issues provide an ideal focus for efforts aimed at bridging differences, bringing people together, and taking diplomacy public. Scientific endeavor is by nature open, interactive, bottom-up, and evidence based. It is a global enterprise and possibly the closest thing we have to a universal language. During the Cold War, apolitical and nonideological international science research proved an effective channel for communications when state-to-state relations were otherwise strained or difficult. Today, the need, and the potential, is perhaps even greater.

CONCLUSION

If diplomacy is going to work, the basis of security must be re-imagined, and foreign ministries must be fixed. They need to be more relevant and less isolated domestically, more effective in their operations, and more responsive to today's challenges, especially those driven by science and technology. The requirement to manage globalization and *heteropolarity* peacefully and in a manner that addresses the issues associated with growing polarization and inequality will be germane.[34]

As we move inexorably into the messy, dynamic, asymmetrical world order that is heteropolarity, governments will need diplomacy, and especially science diplomacy, more than ever. The analytical bottom line comes out something like this: If human-centered, long-term development is the key to the new security, then diplomacy must displace defense as the core of international policy. There are simply no military solutions to the vexing range of transnational issues that constitute the globalization threat set. Only diplomacy privileges talking over fighting. To address challenges associated with heterpolarity, complex balancing, knowledge-based problem solving, and genuine dialogue remain the best tools in the shed.

NOTES

1. Tom Engelhardt, *The American Way of War* (New York: ReadHowYouWant, 2012).
2. On need to reform foreign ministries and diplomacy: Daryl Copeland, "Bureaucratoxis," *Professional Association of Foreign Service Officers Occasional Paper*, 1:2 (Ottawa: PAFSO, 1992); Shaun Riordan *The New Diplomacy* (London: Polity, 2003); Brian Hocking and David Spence, eds., *Foreign Ministries in the European Union: Integrating Diplomats* (Basingstoke: Palgrave Macmillan, 2002).
3. "Rising to Meet the Asia Challenge," *Canada 2020* (2011), http://www.asiapacific.ca; Ashley Travis Tanner and Jessica Keogh, eds., *Strategic Asia 2011–12: Asia Responds to Its Rising Powers—China and India* (Seattle, WA: National Bureau of Asian Research, 2011).
4. On new international actors: Andrew F. Cooper, *Celebrity Diplomacy* (Boulder, CO: Paradigm, 2007); Ann-Marie Slaughter, *A New World Order* (Princeton, NJ: Princeton University Press, 2004).
5. "Transformative Power of Partnerships," *Africa Progress Panel* (2011), http://www.africaprogresspanel.org/files/7713/0441/3939/APP_APR2011_FINAL.pdf
6. Francis Fukuyama, *The End of History and the Last Man* (New York: Free Press, 1992).

7. See Fareed Zakaria, *The Post-American World* (New York: Norton, 2008). For a survey of the "declinist" arguments, see Gideon Rachman "Think Again: American Decline—This Time It's for Real," *Foreign Policy* (January/February 2011): 59–63; Johnson, *Nemesis: The Last Days of the American Republic* (New York: Metropolitan Books, 2007).

8. Some analysts, however, believe that the world is entering a period of "nonpolarity": Richard Haas, "The Age of Nonpolarity," *Foreign Affairs* 87:3 (May–June 2008): 44–56. For additional conceptions of contemporary world order models; see also, Charles Kupchan, *No One's World: The West, the Rising Rest, and the Coming Global Turn* (New York: Oxford University Press, 2012); Ian Bremmer, *Every Nation for Itself: Winners and Losers in a G-Zero World* (New York: Portfolio Books, 2012); Parag Khanna, *How to Run the World* (New York: Random House, 2011).

9. James Der Derian of Brown University introduced me to the term "heteropoloar" about a decade ago. I was struck by its intuitive force, and have been developing that concept and the related idea of the *heteropolis*. Daryl Copeland, "Heteropolarity, Security and Diplomacy," *Embassy* (January 19, 2012), http://www.embassynews.ca/news/2012/01/18/heteropolarity-security-and-diplomacy/42168?absolute=1; "Heteropolis Rising: World Order in the 21st Century," *Embassy*, (February 2, 2012), http://www.embassynews.ca/news/2012/02/02/heteropolis-rising-world-order-in-the-21st-century/42176; "Heteropolarity, Globalization and the New Threat Set," *Embassy* (February 16, 2012), http://www.embassynews.ca/news/2012/02/16/heteropolarity-globalization-and-the-new-threat-set/42185

10. Daryl Copeland, "Hard Power vs. Soft Power," *The Mark* (February 2, 2010), http://www.themarknews.com/articles/895-hard-power-vs-soft-power/#. UMKJB6UXKs4; James Der Derian, "The 'Virtuous' War," *Canadian International Council*, (June 14, 2012), http://opencanada.org/features/the-think-tank/comments/the-virtuous-war/

11. See: Robert Kagan, *The World America Made* (New York: Knopf, 2012).

12. Gwenne Dyer, *Crawling from the Wreckage* (New York: Random House, 2010); Adam Curtis, *The Power of Nightmares* (London: BBC, 2005), http://archive.org/details/ThePowerOfNightmares/; Tom Engelhardt, *The United States of Fear* (New York: Haymarket Books, 2011).

13. Chris Abbot; Paul Rogers, and John Sloboda, *Beyond Terror: The Truth about the Real Threats to Our World* (London: Rider, 2007).

14. Expressed and contextualized slightly differently, a similar conclusion was reached in 2010 by the U.S. State Department in its first *Quadrennial Diplomacy and Development Review*.

15. Referring to freedom from want and fear, UNDP launched the concept of "human security" in 1994. Although heavily contested, it gained traction in the late 1990s, but has declined in visibility since 9/11.

16. Daryl Copeland and Evan Potter, "Public Diplomacy in Conflict Zones: Military Information Operations Meet Political Counterinsurgency," *The Hague Journal of Diplomacy*, 3 (2008): 277–96; Kurt Amend, "Counterinsurgency Principles for the Diplomat," *Small Wars Journal* (July 19, 2008), http://smallwarsjournal.com/jrnl/art/counterinsurgency-principles-for-the-diplomat

17. For more about science diplomacy, see Daryl Copeland, "Science Diplomacy: What's It All About?" (University of Ottawa *CIPS Policy Brief*, November 11, 2011), http://cips.uottawa.ca/wp-content/uploads/2011/11/Copeland-Policy-Brief-Nov-11-5.pdf; *Report on Wilton Park Conference 1037: Science Diplomacy: Applying Science and Innovation to International Challenges*, (Steyning, UK: Wilton Park, 2011), http://www.wiltonpark.org.uk/en/reports/?view=Report&id=23157983

18. Problems faced by the U.S. State Department are typical, but better documented than most. See Kori Schake, *State of Disrepair* (Stanford, CA: Hoover Institution Press, 2012); and John Dorschner, "Revamping the Foreign Service," *Diplopundit* (June 20, 2012), http://diplopundit.net/tag/revamping-the-foreign-service/

19. Daryl Copeland, "The Role of the FCO in UK Government," *UK Parliament*, 2010, http://www.publications.parliament.uk/pa/cm201011/cmselect/cmfaff/writev/fcogov/m04.htm

20. Daryl Copeland, "Diplomacy, Technology and International Political Communications in the Digital Age," in *The Oxford Handbook of Modern Diplomacy* (London: Oxford University Press, forthcoming).

21. The U.S. State Department has taken this line of thinking to its logical conclusion through the creation of customized "Virtual Presence Posts" that exist *only* in cyberspace. For other eDiplomacy initiatives, see http://www.state.gov/m/irm/ediplomacy/c23840.htm, and visit the U.S. cyber-mission to Somalia (http://somalia.usvpp.gov/) or Gaza (http://gaza.usvpp.gov/).

22. Simon Anholt, *Places* (Basingstoke: Palgrave Macmillan, 2009); Anholt, *Competitive Identity* (Basingstoke: Palgrave Macmillan, 2007); Daryl Copeland, "Public Diplomacy, Branding, and the Image of Nations: Part III A Pair of Aces," The Center on Public Diplomacy Blog, 2012, http://uscpublicdiplomacy.org/index.php/newswire/cpdblog_main/author/Daryl_Copeland/

23. Alex Himelfarb, "Going, Going, Gone: Dismantling of the Progressive State," *Alex's Blog*, April 17, 2012, http://afhimelfarb.wordpress.com/2012/04/17/going-going-gone-dismantling-the-progressive-state/; Daryl Copeland, "In Defense of DFAIT: Diminished Diplomatic Capacity Damages Canadian Interests," *iPolitics* (July 4, 2012), http://www.ipolitics.ca/2012/07/06/daryl-copeland-in-defense-of-dfait-why-diminished-diplomatic-capacity-damages-canadian-interests/

24. Daryl Copeland, "Virtuality, Diplomacy and the Foreign Ministry," Canadian Foreign Policy, 15:2 (2009): 1–15.

25. Christine Dal Bellow, "The Power of Citizen Diplomacy," *DipNote* (February 22, 2012), http://blogs.state.gov/index.php/site/entry/power_citizen_diplomacy/

26. For example, *Independent Diplomat* is an NGO started by former UK Foreign Service Officer Carne Ross to provide diplomatic services "to those who need them most." See http://www.independentdiplomat.org/. The *Dubrovnik Diplomatic Forum* is an innovative joint venture between the Croatian foreign ministry and several universities and international organizations. See http://www.emuni.si/en/strani/424/Diplomatic-Forum.html. The *London Academy of Diplomacy* hosts an annual "International Symposium" that brings together practitioners, researchers, and graduate students. See http://london.uea.ac.uk/international-symposium. *DiploFoundation* is a broadly supported Geneva-based part training institute, part think tank. See http://www.diplomacy.edu/

27. In Canada's case, by way of illustration, this advantage might be based not on deliberate policy, but on the country's success in integrating immigrants, and the resulting presence of burgeoning and diverse diaspora communities. See *Tapping Our Potential: Diaspora Communities and Canadian Foreign Policy* (Toronto: The Mosaic Institute, Walter and Duncan Gordon Foundation, 2011); Jennifer Welsh, *At Home in the World: Canada's Global Vision for the 21st Century* (Toronto: Harper Collins, 2004). *Canada's World* was an ambitious three-year (2007–10) civil society–led effort to raise Canadian

awareness about major issues in international policy development. See http://www.canadasworld.ca/. The Canadian International Council, whose *Open Canada* project was based on national research and consultations, has taken a leadership role in diverse and interactive engagement. See http://www.opencanada.org/ and http://www.opencanada.org/features/reports/opencanada/

28. Such an application could include detailed consular contact information, a direct phone link to a hotline for nationals in distress, and a panic button incorporating software to permit the immediate geo-location of the user. See Ali Fisher on tracking the development of digital networks, "Smarter Networks and Collaborative Approaches Underpin the Response to 21st Century Challenges," *USC Blog*, July 20, 2012.

29. One country that has not, however, is Canada. There, a leading position in PD has been squandered; see Daryl Copeland, "A Future for Public Diplomacy?" *The Mark* (January 14, 2012). Federal scientists and their representatives complain of being "muzzled" (see open letter to Prime Minister Harper, dated February 16, 2012, available at http://www.ipolitics.ca/2012/02/16/prime-minister-please-stop-muzzling-scientists-and-researchers-open-letter/) and have demonstrated against the demise of evidence-based decision making (see Megan Fitzpatrick, "Death of Scientific Evidence Mourned on Parliament Hill," *CBC News*, July 11, 2012). There is no international S&T policy, strategy, or plan; budgets for science-based departments and agencies have been slashed, and the DFAIT S&T division has been directed to spend considerable time increasing Canadian widget sales abroad (see Paul Dufour, "Becoming a Northern Minerva," *Science and Diplomacy* 1(2) [June 2011]: 2). An exception has been DFAIT's highly successful Global Partnerships Program, which includes science diplomacy around a major nuclear security initiative in the former Soviet Union.

30. On the UK Foreign and Commonwealth Office's Science and Innovation Network, science advisor and activities in science diplomacy, see http://www.fco.gov.uk/en/about-us/what-we-do/working-in-partnership/working-with-stakeholder-groups/science-innovation/. On Switzerland's public-private "Swissnex," an innovative form of representation in international S&T hubs, see http://www.swissnex.org/

31. For the Jefferson Fellows program, see http://www.state.gov/e/rls/rmk/2012/182545.htm. For the Office of the Science and Technology Adviser, see http://www.state.gov/e/stas/index.htm

32. Bill McKibben, "Smoggy Bottom: Hillary Clinton's Environmental Failure," *The New Republic* (July 13, 2012).

33. On CERN's recent "God particle" discovery, see Paul Rincon, "Higgs Boson-Like Particle Discovery Claimed at LHC," *BBC News* (July 4, 2012).

34. For a full elaboration of this argument, see Daryl Copeland, *Guerrilla Diplomacy: Rethinking International Relations* (Boulder, CO: Lynne Rienner, 2009), http://www.guerrilladiplomacy.com

5 Diaspora Diplomacy and Public Diplomacy

Kishan S. Rana

INTRODUCTION

Diaspora diplomacy is a fairly new term that has gained currency at a time when the activity of cultivating external relations is a multidimensional process open to many participants.[1] This particular sub-branch of diplomacy is about engaging a country's overseas community to contribute to building relationships with foreign countries. A migrant community becomes a diaspora if it retains a memory of, and some connection with, its country of origin. Without that memory or connection, migration simply becomes one more footnote in the movement of people that has occurred throughout history since the first groups migrated from what scientists regard as humankind's original home, Africa, perhaps 150,000 years ago.

Diasporas have gained increasing prominence in international relations due to their distribution and growing size. The International Migration Organization estimated that, in 2010, some 214 million people were first-generation migrants, and resided outside their countries of birth; this represents a sharp increase over the 2000 figure of 150 million.[2]

Within diplomacy, diasporas are mainly relevant in bilateral relations, but they also play a wider role in relation to regional or global issues. For the most part, it is the original country that takes advantage of diaspora connections, but, as we shall see, sometimes the process works in reverse. A host country to diaspora communities can mobilize them to advance its ties with their particular country, or more generally, to burnish its own global profile as a country practicing enlightened policy. By their very nature, most of these activities come under the rubric of public diplomacy.

While we may segment and scrutinize diplomatic activities under different labels (political, economic, cultural, consular, educational, public, etc.), the actual process of building relations is a single, holistic, and seamless activity. Each step that is taken has multiple consequences that go beyond the immediate objective. Also noteworthy is the idea that diaspora communities, in forming connections among members in their home and host cultures, create transnational networks and exemplify global connectivity and the functioning of multidimensional networks.

This chapter looks at the role of the diaspora in the public diplomacy of the home and host countries. The first section provides a taxonomy of the different types of diaspora communities based on migration patterns and time periods, as well as conditions in the receiving countries. The second section discusses methods used by home countries to build connections with the diaspora, including specific policies and economic, political, and public diplomacy practices. Discussion on "reverse diplomacy" surveys some of the practices host countries use to engage diaspora communities within their borders. The chapter concludes with thoughts on how social media is transforming communication with diaspora public diplomacy.

UNDERSTANDING THE GLOBAL DIASPORA

Among the oldest migrating communities to retain its memory and connection is the Jewish diaspora, which has held on to its identity for two millennia. Other more contemporary diasporas have emerged from migrations over the past two hundred years. When, why, and where migrant communities move affects their capacity to act as contributors to external relations. Not all migrating communities retain their memory or connection to their country of origin. By segmenting these movements on the basis of the date and principal cause of migration, we can build up a taxonomy that provides insights into their relations with both their home and host countries.

Origins of Diaspora Communities

One prominent migrant group consists of those who embarked on the historical journey to the New World. The descendants of Europeans who moved to North, Central, and South America after the sixteenth century lost most of their familial contacts with the countries of origin, even while retaining their linguistic, cultural, and religious heritage. They are today seldom viewed as diaspora communities by their origin countries, even when they enjoy cultural, linguistic, and other ties with them.

Another group consists of slaves and indentured laborers: Those taken from Africa as slaves in the fifteenth to the nineteenth centuries retained only sketchy memories of their origin, culture, and language. They, too, are not seen as diasporas, even though some have attempted to trace their roots; this offers African states, especially in West Africa, a potential source for connections.[3]

Among the oldest group of migrants that retain vivid memory of their original homelands are the descendants of indentured laborers taken by the British from the undivided India of the nineteenth century into different colonies in East and South Africa, the Caribbean, and the South American mainland. These places became today's Guyana, Fiji, and Mauritius. In contrast, those from India taken by the French and the Portuguese to Africa, whether the island of Reunion (which adjoins Mauritius) or Madagascar, or to the West Indies, retained very little of their original cultural connections to their places of origin, no doubt owing to the assimilative nature of French and Portuguese colonial rule.

The movement of traders constitutes another group. Across Southeast Asia, the descendants of Chinese traders can be found in virtually every country, their migration having begun in the seventeenth century. They have retained their cultural identity and the regional dialects of their ancestors. The same is true of the Indian migrants, mostly from the south, who migrated mainly to what were then Burma and the Malay Peninsula. A common feature of trader migrants of both ethnicities is that they are now firmly rooted in their countries of adoption, despite cultural insularity vis-à-vis the host country.

The trader migration has continued. The influx of Chinese businessmen, entrepreneurs, and shopkeepers in Africa in the past several years has been subtle and pervasive; there are now more than one million Chinese in Africa, and more pour in each year.[4] That situation is replicated in parts of Latin America.

Migration of professionals and technicians followed specific policy changes in some host countries. The Hart-Celler Act of 1965 in the United States eliminated restrictive "national origins" quotas, permitting those that came for advanced studies in fields ranging from medicine to engineering and the liberal arts to settle if they found jobs. This permitted skill-based migration. Australia, Canada, and the UK implemented their own versions of similar policies. In the name of family reunion, relatives were also permitted to migrate. This has created large groups of Chinese, Indians, Koreans, Vietnamese, and others in the United States, and similar ethnic clusters elsewhere.

Other migrant communities emerged through labor demands. The oil boom of the 1970s in the Persian Gulf and North Africa created widespread movement of labor, mainly into Arab states, but even after living there for fifteen or twenty years, such laborers, semi-skilled and skilled, do not qualify for long-term or permanent residence permits, much less citizenship. Their situation remains fragile, and they are liable to repatriation anytime if they transgress the regulations of these states.

Foreign students make up a rapidly increasing demographic. Of the tens of thousands of Chinese, Indians, Koreans, Taiwanese, and other Asians who go to North America to study, a sizable percentage stay on as migrants. A significant proportion may eventually return, bringing with them advanced skills and technologies, while others become investors in their home countries. Special programs run by the United Nations and by individual countries capitalize on this "brain gain," and this, too, becomes part of a set of global, diaspora-oriented networking connections.[5]

Increased globalization has contributed to the migration of mobile professionals. This migration consists of today's bankers, business and investment advisors, and top corporate managers, in demand in many advanced countries, some of which, like Singapore, offer special inducements, particularly to the graduates of top management, technology, and other professional schools. They have high potential as participants in global networking.

Several of the above categories overlap, or morph into one another. For instance, when Idi Amin drove out Uganda's "Asians" in 1972, sizable numbers migrated to the United Kingdom, the United States, and Canada, becoming even more successful as traders and entrepreneurs.

The diaspora profile varies greatly in different locations, and that conditions their interest and engagement capacity regarding the home country. Workers and technicians on permits that need continual renewal will not undertake activities, especially political ones, that expose them to risk, especially in authoritarian countries. This applies to the workers from Asia or Africa that serve in oil-rich states in the Gulf and North Africa, as well as the ill-paid maids from Indonesia and the Philippines who work in wealthy Singapore and Hong Kong. The descendants of historical migrants often have dim recollections of the homeland, and insufficient interest in its politics. That holds true of diasporas in South and Central America, and the Indian migrants in former British colonies. One also finds an interesting paradox in the separation of distance and many generations: communities retain cultural, religious, and linguistic memory, but no personal or familial links. In contrast, the new professional migrants often retain sharp interest in their homeland, but it is the environment of the receiving country that affects their public diplomacy profile.

Host or Receiving State Environment

Where the diaspora are located also influences the level of migrant activities. Conditions in the host or receiving state can shape the contour of what activities are permitted or discouraged. The United States and Canada are countries largely composed of migrants, apart from the original inhabitants of those sprawling lands that now constitute a small minority. It is not surprising that these nations offer a generally hospitable environment to migrants, notwithstanding a new hostility they exhibit toward undocumented foreign nationals.

African, Asian, and Latin American migrants to North America do encounter local prejudice with racial overtones, but they are visible at the apex of their professions to a depth and degree that is unique for diaspora populations, compared to other countries. This facilitates their public diplomacy role. For instance, the number, diversity, and political activism reflected in the "ethnic" publications of such diasporas, whether they belong to Chinese, Indian, Korean, Mexican, or Vietnamese groups, has no parallel elsewhere. Typically, such publications carry stories of their engagement in the local, state, and federal politics of the adopted country, as well as detailed news of important developments in the homeland. They serve as instruments of public diplomacy, and often of citizen diplomacy, as well.

Britain, and to a lesser degree Australia, also offers a hospitable environment. Britain features diaspora representation in its Parliament and in local elected offices that is far ahead of any other country, including Canada and the United States. All British political parties field candidates from migrant communities, and at any point in time, fifteen to twenty members of the House of Commons are descendants of migrants. It is also ahead of the curve in *reverse public diplomacy*, as we see below.

On the continent of Europe, the role played by diasporas is much more modest, and the environment less enabling than in Anglo-Saxon countries. The reason for this deserves reflection. For instance, the Turkish community in Germany, descendants of the *gastarbeiters* of the 1950s, won limited access to citizenship only in the late 1990s. At present, perhaps two serve as members of the *Bundestag*, as do two persons of Indian descent. However, the nearly 3 million-strong Turkish diaspora and the 100,000-strong community of Indian origin do not take a high public profile, much less engage in political activity locally or vis-à-vis the original homeland. But they are strong supporters of cultural cooperation, especially through the network of around thirty branches of the Deutsche-Indische Gesselshaft, the official friendship societies.

The situation of the population of Arab and African descent in France, which consists of several million, is similar, though politicians of diaspora descent are more active there than in Germany. French insistence on conformity by migrants to French cultural norms is hardly capable of real implementation, except through selective prohibitions, as visible across the *banlieu* of Paris and Marseilles. That, too, makes a public diplomacy role problematic for some of these communities.

In other parts of the world, be it in Fiji or in Malaysia, Indian diasporas face local political complexity that restricts their engagement in, or even deep interest toward, the homeland. Often, be it for the Chinese in Southeast Asia or for Indians in the Caribbean, there is a relative lack of interest in the political concerns of the original homeland that makes a public diplomacy role almost irrelevant, except in the sense of retaining residual interest in the well-being of the homeland. The governments of India and other concerned home countries tread warily, not wishing to rouse antipathy for their diasporas from the main community in these countries. Often, education in the home country is a source of connection, and sustains long-term interest. Thailand's situation is probably unique for Chinese descendants in its submersion into the local ethnicity, to the point where it becomes almost impossible to identify a distinct diaspora. Everywhere, though, the Chinese diaspora plays an economic role in the homeland that is discreet, pervasive, and unparalleled in comparison with other such groups.

HOME COUNTRIES: REACHING OUT TO DIASPORAS

While the connections of the diaspora to the home country provide a critical spark for engaging diaspora communities, home countries can facilitate and strengthen those connections through their policies. Enhancing these connections can expand the role that diasporas play in public diplomacy.

Israel is the arch-practitioner and inventor of diaspora diplomacy. The near-global spread of Jewish communities and the horrors of the Holocaust give Israel strength and legitimacy to mobilize ethnic–religious connections. Because of Israel's unique history and its strong claim on the loyalty and political support of the Jewish diaspora, it can be said that everything in this essay applies to the intense, largely uncritical, and pervasive support that Israel enjoys from the Jewish diaspora communities. Much as other countries trying to mobilize their own diaspora might envy Israel, many simply do not have such ironclad linkages to "their own" people.

What are the ingredients that make for an effective outreach or public diplomacy to the diaspora community by the home country? How can the home country recreate and strengthen its connections to the diaspora?

Home Country Policies and Practices

One of the first critical ingredients is a coherent policy by the home country for managing the affairs of their diaspora. On April 15, 2012, Indian External Affairs Minister S. M. Krishna told a conference of Indian envoys in the United Arab Emirates that they must roll up their sleeves and pay as much attention to the welfare of Indian expatriates working overseas as they do to hard diplomacy. He also urged that special attention be given to the blue-collar workers among them, as they are the most vulnerable segment. Some have called this emphasis on the diaspora a "Krishna doctrine."[6]

China has long had its Overseas Chinese Commission as a state agency, and has cultivated these connections assiduously. When overseas Chinese faced a crackdown and subsequent massacre in Indonesia in 1976, China broke relations with Jakarta. Since then, it has worked with concerned states in Southeast Asia and elsewhere to support these communities, while also accommodating the concerns of states regarding their loyalty. Some African states have recently begun to develop a diaspora policy, and others are considering the steps they need to take. Kenya established a unit in its Foreign Ministry to reach out to the 1.8 million Kenyans estimated to be living abroad.

Mexico has more than fifty consulates in the United States to service its huge diaspora, which numbers over 30 million, including nearly 10 million who are undocumented. Consulates are especially useful as connectors with diaspora communities. Unlike embassies that operate in the national capital and deal with a clutch of weighty high-diplomacy issues, consulates are "on the ground," more closely attuned to a local ethos. If consulates run their visa and other services well, they gain a strategic advantage in connect-ing, especially with diasporas who depend on such services.[7] As a Mexican colleague put it, for the consulate, communication with local authorities is more direct—otherwise, the job could not be done. In an embassy, official channels must be strictly observed. Also, prevention, as well as reaction, dominates the daily work. *Prevention* is achieved through campaigns directed to the diaspora in matters ranging from health to labor rights. *Reaction* is carried out through quick responses by highly professional con-sular officers in the Protective Service Department.

Interestingly, unlike in many emerging and developing countries, virtually no Western foreign ministry has a special unit or agency charged with han-dling its diaspora abroad. Clearly, there is room for some learning by these countries.

Building Financial Links

Another initial step of home governments toward their diaspora is to entice them to invest at home. According to the World Bank, the remittances that such migrants send to their countries of origin have grown exponentially, from $132 billion in 2000 to $440 billion in 2010.[8] The main remittance recipients in 2011 were India, $55 billion; China, $51 billion; Mexico, $26.6 billion; and the Philippines, $21.3 billion. Moldova, with a popula-tion of 4.3 million, earns one-third of its GDP through the money sent back by its diaspora, which mainly works in Europe.

Diaspora investment can be via bank deposits, purchase of bonds, acqui-sition of property, and portfolio and foreign direct investment. For develop-ing states, this taps into a useful source for funds and embeds the diaspora more firmly into the home country as a friendly agent. Special facilities are offered as inducements not available to the general category of foreign in-vestors. In general, wealthy potential investors are savvy, and beyond a cer-tain point, such inducements work only when they offer clear economic gain, say in the shape of arbitrage between prevailing international rates of return or the interest rates on deposits in the countries of residence, vis-à-vis the inducement offered by the home country. Sentiment works only up to a point.

Political Links

There are various avenues and goals associated with facilitating political links. Since 2002, India has held an annual jamboree, a *"Pravasi Bharati Conference,"* attended by up to 1,000 overseas Indians; this event ro-tates between different Indian cities, and is co-hosted by the government and a major business association. It provides a platform for both public discourse and for serious confabulation on issues affecting the overseas community.

Mexico has a "Consultative Council of the Institute for Mexicans Abroad"; their 120 members are Mexicans or Mexican-Americans residing in the United States, and are elected by Mexican community in the United States for three-year periods. Its members come from diverse backgrounds, most of them from citizen-based organizations, and sometimes they have found it difficult to achieve agreements. Their successful actions include, for instance, a student scholarship fund. Mexico has also used this group in its public diplomacy in the United States, in relation to dealing with local authorities, though some observers are critical that this diaspora is not sufficiently active in lobbying U.S. policymakers. Overall, it is an interesting experiment to use a truly representative elected body to advocate diaspora public affairs, which works for both the home country and the diaspora.[9]

India and Pakistan have mobilized their diasporas to project national viewpoints in the plural U.S. political process, particularly through constituency persuasion aimed at Congress members. The communities engage in fund-raising efforts during elections at local, state, and federal levels. India openly used its diaspora after its 1998 nuclear tests to counter U.S. sanctions, mandated under its law, holding out the attraction of the huge Indian market. This effort was repeated during the negotiations leading to the 2008 Indo-U.S. civilian nuclear agreement. In a coordinated public diplomacy effort, Indian industry bodies invited up to fifty U.S. congress members to Delhi.

Political activity with diaspora communities should be approached with caution. Often, designated embassy officials keep close contact with community leaders, but sometimes these efforts transgresses diplomatic norms and result in allegations of improper action and adverse publicity. In 2011, the U.S. authorities publicly charged Pakistan's Inter-Services Intelligence (ISI) of gathering intelligence from among its diaspora and intimidating those who opposed the Pakistani government. On the other side, Nigeria has occasionally felt that some of their diaspora attempt to interfere with home politics, and that, too, becomes a diplomatic issue.

As a former high commissioner to two countries that host sizable diaspora communities, Kenya and Mauritius (in the latter, the majority of the population is of Indian origin), I have experienced firsthand the discretion with which diaspora relations must be handled. It is a natural tendency at such places to counsel these communities to submerge their factional and sub-ethnic differences and act together, but at the end of the day, each diaspora is autonomous and knows its own situation well. Official representatives are no more than informal, friendly advisors. In Mauritius, in particular, India has experienced occasional over-involvement of its representatives in community affairs, which results in backlash and political embarrassment.[10]

Dual citizenship is another facility that is increasingly offered to the diaspora. For many Western countries, permission to citizens to claim rights nationality of two or even more countries has long been in existence. For some former colonies that gained independence and retain a narrow construct of sovereignty, dual citizenship has not been easy to swallow. Yet some African states are actively considering this option to better connect with their diaspora.

Given the nature of familial, ethnic and "nationalist" sentiment, welcoming policies in home countries are obviously attractive. What the diaspora often does not broadly favor is involvement in home country partisan politics, even while some "community leaders" set up branches or entities abroad that are allied with home political parties. Sometimes, theses leaders act as fund-raisers for the home parties, though this seldom has large impact. In the case of Nigeria, it has been argued that the diaspora has played a small role in the restoration of democracy at home. Conferences of the diaspora reveal that the majority has little interest in such politicking. On the other side of the fence, it is difficult to identify any country where the diaspora is a factor in domestic politics.

How well does home-country outreach serve the diaspora? Operational circumstances vary greatly in the ways in which different countries reach out to and mobilize their diaspora. We may note a progression in the way home countries reach out to diasporas: the first step is *exploitation*, where they are used in activities of direct advantage to the home country (e.g. bank deposits, investments, and the like); a second step is *accommodation*, where the home country begins to understand the motivation and real interests of the diaspora (e.g., granting dual citizenship, or easing visa regulations); a third step is *two-way networking*, where it interacts with them with sensitivity, using them as its public agents, to the extent that they are capable of, and accept, being used in this manner. This step also serves to give these communities a primacy and importance at home, as feasible.

Home Country and Diaspora Public Diplomacy

We may also look more closely at the political, economic, cultural, educational, societal, and other connections that the diaspora offers. For some countries, be it Armenia, Cyprus, or Malta, the diaspora may be equal to or significantly larger than the population in the home country. That can mean, besides sizable inward remittance, that there are also possibilities for using the connections of the diaspora to advance home-state objectives in the target country. This works especially well in the United States, where the tripartite constitutional structure offers levers for such diaspora power in Congress. It may also mean caution in handling the diaspora, to ensure it does not to project too much of the external perspectives or agendas into that home state.

As economic actors who have access and clout in their countries, the diaspora becomes an instrument of outreach for the home state. In Kenya, and later in Germany, I found that key diaspora members could be used to provide access to high political personalities.[11] Elsewhere, diaspora figures become key contacts in advising diplomatic mission on how to tackle complex markets, as narrated in an essay I wrote for a collection of case studies on Indian economic diplomacy.[12]

In the culture arena, the diaspora are natural ambassadors of the country of origin, and can play a special role in the development of its soft power in the target country. Again, this is borne out by practical examples. For instance, in relation to the Indian and the Chinese cinema, the large diaspora, spread virtually throughout the world, acts as a captive audience, which gives the film-makers of each country a first platform to reach a global audience. Similarly, the diaspora helps in building up a following for the music and dance of the home country.

There is hardly any musician of repute in India or Pakistan, classic or popular, who does not thrive on the oxygen of overseas support, which has led to a situation where much of such cultural expression overseas is now autonomous, not requiring official sponsorship. They also provide a support base as purchasers of paintings and other art from the home country, in effect creating new markets for such art objects. For the home country, it makes sense to factor in the diaspora in the cultural offerings it makes to countries where they are to be found in sufficient concentration. The same applies to satellite TV channels from the home country, now rendered even more ubiquitous thanks to internet-based broadcasts.

Diaspora members have also provided assistance to their consulates in emergencies and for disaster preparation, as volunteers or with payment of a small honorarium. At times of mass evacuation of citizens, be it at the time of the First Iraq War of 1992 or during the Libya civil uprising of 2011, hard-pressed embassy staffs of different countries have used this method. This has a salutary public diplomacy dimension, in that it exposes the community to the complexity of such evacuation; in effect, wins their support. The simple principle: it is better to have potential critics inside the tent as helpers than outside throwing stones at a faceless bureaucracy.

REVERSE DIPLOMACY: HOST COUNTRIES AND DIASPORA

The countries where diaspora groups are installed have begun to use them to build connections with the original home country, as also to embellish their own public profile. In effect this is "reverse" diplomacy, another variant on established techniques. This is best illustrated through examples.

Australia, the UK, and the United States have appointed immigrants and their descendants to high-profile diplomatic positions in their countries of origin. Shortly after the Second Iraq War ended, the United States sent an ambassador of Iraqi origin to Baghdad. In 2004, the UK picked a senior official of Bangladeshi origin working in another department as its high commissioner to Dhaka. The limited nature of similar appointments underscored the deliberate nature of that British gesture. Australia's current High

Commissioner in New Delhi is of Indian descent. Uganda's High Commissioner to India has been a woman, Nimisha Madhvani, and a member of one of the country's leading business families; the appointment is doubly innovative against the background of the country's efforts to attract back to Kampala the "Asians" that had fled under Idi Amin's misrule. The underlying assumption in all such appointments is that the receiving state will feel flattered by receiving back its diaspora exemplars.

Diplomatic services belonging to the same cluster of Anglo-Saxon countries now select a wide ethnic mix in their intake of young entrants. It seems as though priority is given to assigning them to their country or region of origin. Besides the domestic advantage of such affirmative action, officials that straddle two cultures also usually find themselves at ease at these appointments.[13]

For this cluster of countries (Australia, Canada, New Zealand, the UK, and the United States), the diversity in public service appointments serves both domestic and external public diplomacy objectives. For instance, appointing ethnic minority figures to high visibility jobs nurtures a multiethnic self-image the countries wish to project. Political parties in Britain and Canada lead in appointing ethnic figures to cabinet and ministerial office. For some years, Lord Swaraj Paul, a leading entrepreneur, co-chaired the prestigious Indo-British Forum, and has been succeed by another prominent Indo-British businessman, Karan Bilimoria.[14]

In 2011, the U.S. State Department launched an initiative, "The International diaspora Engagement Alliance" (IdEA), which promotes and supports diaspora-centered initiatives in entrepreneurship, volunteerism, philanthropy, diplomacy, and social innovation.[15] The Caribbean region has been one of the targets, and it cultivates diaspora giving in areas of education, health, nutrition, and disaster relief in countries of origin. This is public diplomacy in the best sense: engaging ethnic communities as agents of change vis-à-vis home countries. One may expect other countries to emulate such reverse diaspora diplomacy.

As we observed under the rubric of "enabling environment," countries on the continent of Europe tend to be more conservative with such appointments. For instance, in France, one sees the emergence of minority ethnic figures in ministerial and other official appointments, but relatively few are in the diplomatic services. We seldom hear of Arab-, African-, or Turkish-origin officials in the foreign ministries of France or Germany.

DIASPORA AND SOCIAL MEDIA

We cannot leave our discussion of public diplomacy and the diaspora without looking at the role of the new media. As mentioned earlier, the many "ethnic publications" one finds in countries illustrate the desire of diaspora communities to connect and enhance communication among its members. The advent and proliferation of advanced communication technologies greatly reduced the costs, while enhancing the means, of communicating on a global level. The social media has added an interactive dimension that not only facilitates communication between a government and its diaspora populations around the globe, but also enhances communication within diaspora communities.

Diaspora groups, especially those based in advanced countries, tend to be avid users of social media, and post the largest number of messages on Twitter, YouTube, and Facebook, especially in relation to issues relating to the home country that "go viral," with hundreds of thousands of posts on anything that catches their fancy. In relation to home countries, they are driven by a volatile mix of emotive sentiment: pride in the home country's heritage, culture, and ethos, and embarrassment bordering on shame at its contemporary failings, be they failures in governance, corruption, or societal disabilities. This has a frequent public diplomacy dimension, in terms of shallow understanding of the real situation at home, and a normative, prescriptive attitude. From the perspective of the home country, it becomes vital to engage them on their own turf, use Web 2.0 tools, and reach out to them in "smart" ways, in an idiom that they understand.

At the time of the evacuation of Indian technicians from Libya in 2011, India used the social media to reach out to the scattered pockets of these workers, who were for the great part unregistered, with numbers and whereabouts unknown.[16] Twitter and social media networking contacts with families and friends around the world overcame these information gaps.

A Kenyan example illustrates innovative use of modern communications technology, with a diaspora angle. At the time of post-election civil riots in that country in which lost their lives, one problem was to locate the villages and clusters where losses were at their worst. A Kenyan based in the South Africa, Ory Okolloh, who had gone back to Kenya to vote and observe the election, applied phone call cluster tracking to identify the trouble spots, calling this *ushahidi*, which means "witness" in Swahili. This method was used subsequently in Haiti and Chilean earthquakes to locate main disaster spots.

Diaspora diplomacy also carries some risks. From the perspective of countries host to a diaspora, the main danger is that a foreign country may use the diaspora to play politics with them, or to interfere in its internal affairs. When such incidents take place, they are settled through discussion and quiet withdrawal of officials that have transgressed.[17] Table 5.1 summarizes the intervention of different diaspora groups in public diplomacy.

Table 5.1 Typology of Diaspora in Public Diplomacy

Diaspora character	Receiving country attitude	Home country policy	Consequence	Comments
Historical migrants who outnumber the home-country population	Mostly well integrated, yet retaining cultural and linguistic roots	Finds it useful to rekindle old connections, for benefit of home-country development	Can produce new source for economic connections, and for PD	Home state must not over-use them for own objectives
Old migrants (e.g., descendants of indentured labor, workers; as with Indians in Africa, Caribbean, Fiji, Mauritius)	Usually well embedded in local environment, retain cultural links with old country	Respect their situation, work for close relations with that country, limited PD role	Gives home country permanent stake in good ties with migration state, plus broad PD platform	
Professionals that went to rich countries 1960s onwards (Australia, Canada, UK, United States)	Many at top rungs of society, keenly aware of home country, look to linkages; often break through glass ceilings (but this does not happen in continental Europe, with their traditional mindsets)	Reach out to them, cultivate connections, use as PD agents	Encouraged as investors, venture capitalists and technology sources; powerful PD contributors, increasingly in both directions	Bilateral and international connectors; often loudest claimants for benefits and recognition from home state
Contract workers in Arab and other states, house maids, pursuing economic opportunities	No long-term residence rights, no citizenship	Look after welfare, strive to reduce exploitation, aid during crisis (e.g., Libya in 2011)	Biggest source of inward remittances, but do not receive due recognition; limited PD role	Home states need to give them more attention

Students from developing states in advanced countries, many hoping to take up jobs and migrate	Increasing restrictions on post-graduation work, or circumscribed with rules	Assist them during education phase, ambivalent about their migration hopes	Sometimes home country spurred into improving own education facilities; strong PD agents both ways	Some among them will return when home conditions improve, producing "brain-gain" (e.g., as in Taiwan, South Korea, China, India)
Undocumented migrants, lured by dreams of rich economic prospects	Tight restrictions, imprisonment for those caught, push back to countries of origin	Attempts to check outflow, usually not successful (as in South Asia, Africa)	Paradoxically, some "illegals" become successful entrepreneurs; this shifts them from a PD liability (for the image of home country) to assets	Home countries can do more to look after them, the more so as target countries often unmindful of their rights
Professionals with scarce skills (doctors, nurses, top-end specialists), actively targeted by rich states	Offered jobs, residence and eventual citizenship (e.g. Canada, Singapore, US)	Often view this as "brain-drain", apply exit fees and bonds, which seldom reduces outflow	Important actors for PD, increasingly in both directions	Again, key to future connections between state
Businessmen, often belonging to communities with traditional commercial aptitude	Always able to rise to the top, even when migration may have taken place in adverse conditions ("Asians" from Uganda), highly valued	Valuable connectors, rich source for PD connections of the broadest kind	Source for FDI, technology transfer; contribute to positive image for home country, build networks that contribute to PD and familial links	Many are "international" families with multiple passports, and global interests

CONCLUSION

We now see awareness in many countries of the role that diasporas can play in building good international relationships between pairs of countries and in enhancing the country brand. It is fascinating for me that this is one area in which it is the countries of the Global South that have mainly taken the lead. Western states are now playing catch-up in using these communities as allies and empowered agents.

Diaspora diplomacy is a niche activity that contributes to relationship building between states. It is likely to gain in importance in the years ahead, for the reasons detailed above. Many developing and emerging states are now alive to its potential. I imagine Western states will also look to weaving these non-state actors into their outreach systems. Given their character, diasporas are a natural instrument for improved public diplomacy, also contributing to image enhancement. My study of the role played by the Indian diaspora also suggests that when persons of Indian descent face crisis, regardless of whether they are Indian citizens or not (as in Burma in 1962, Uganda in 1972, and Fiji in 1987), New Delhi has marshaled its diplomacy.[18] For the home country, this means a permanent stake in the welfare of the country of emigration and special care in managing that relationship in order to avoid a situation that might rebound on the diaspora. Leaving aside such worst cases, the diaspora is a hugely worthwhile asset.

NOTES

1. K. Rana, "India's Diaspora Diplomacy," *The Hague Journal of Diplomacy* 4 (2009): 361–372.
2. International Migration Organization, http://www.iom.int
3. Liberia came into existence as home to many descendants of former slaves that returned to Africa.
4. *The Economist*, April 23, 2011.
5. This term "brain gain" is deliberately chosen by the authors of such programs to provide a counterpoint to the notion of "brain drain." U.N.'s TOKTEN program is one example of such multilateral activity.
6. *Hindu*, April 16, 2012.
7. These come from personal experience as a consul general in San Francisco (1986–1989), and observations offered by Mexican participants in the distance learning courses I have taught at DiploFoundation.
8. *The World Bank, Migration and Remittances Factbook 2011*, http://econ.worldbank.org/WBSITE/EXTERNAL/EXTDEC/EXTDECPROSPECTS/0,,contentMDK:21352016˜pagePK:64165401˜piPK:64165026˜theSitePK:476883,00.html (accessed on 26 May 2012).
9. See Gustavo Cano and Alexandra Délano, "The Mexican Government and Organized Mexican Immigrants in the United States: A Historical Analysis of Political Transnationalism (1848–2005)," *Journal of Ethnic and Migration Studies* 33(5) (2007): 695–725.
10. K. Rana, "Island Diplomacy," *Indian Express*, New Delhi, June 7, 2003.

11. A leading member of the diaspora helped me establish direct contact with President Daniel Arap Moi in 1984 when I served as high commissioner in Kenya. See Rana, *Inside Diplomacy* (Manas, New Delhi, 2000), 62–63. Indian newspapers reported in the past that in the late 1980s major diaspora businessmen had helped the Rajiv Gandhi government to reach out to U.S. and UK leaders.

12. At San Francisco, when in 1986–1989 we attempted for the first time to organize marketing of Indian software services, young Indian software engineers became our voluntary advisors; this and other details are in: K. Rana, "Networking with Local Partners: Experience in Silicon Valley, Mauritius and Germany," *Economic Diplomacy: India's Experience* (CUTS, Jaipur, 2011), 197–208; http://www.cuts-international.org/Book_Economic-Diplomacy.htm

13. This comment is based on personal observation, and discussion with such diplomats.

14. For an examination of the utility of such eminent person groups, please see K. Rana, "Building Relations through Multi-Dialogue Formats: Trends in Bilateral Diplomacy," *Journal of Diplomacy and Foreign Relations*, Kuala Lumpur, 10 (December 2008).

15. See U.S. State Department, International Diaspora Engagement Alliance, http://www.state.gov/s/partnerships/diaspora/index.htm

16. *The Japan Times,* June 18, 2012.

17. Rana, "Island Diplomacy."

18. Rana, "India's Diaspora Diplomacy."

6 Relational Dimensions of a Chinese Model of Public Diplomacy

Yiwei Wang

INTRODUCTION

In an age of global awakening and information expansion, increased interest in public diplomacy has become a worldwide phenomenon. Similar to development models and cultural diversity one finds around the globe, public diplomacy reveals distinct national characteristics. These distinctive features are rich and colorful, not only in practice, but also in their meaning and conceptualization.

China's public diplomacy features are related to the contemporary context of its cultural awareness as well as cultural confidence.[1] Despite major investments by the Chinese government in public diplomacy, China still has a soft power deficit.[2] Some foreign media commentators called Chinese public diplomacy irrelevant and doomed to fail.[3] Questions about the viability of China's public diplomacy may arise from the fact that it has not been able to keep up with the rapid pace of its emerging economy. It may also be that the long-term effects of public diplomacy have not yet materialized.

Whatever the explanation, there has been an urgent need for China to formulate public diplomacy strategies on the basis of local conditions, the objective reality of its rise, and the changing world. The current situation has shown clearly that with the development of public diplomacy, it is time to explore its origins and probe into its essence. Remaining in the phase of studying and imitating is not advisable. Theoretical breakthroughs and innovation can play a particularly significant role in advancing China's public diplomacy.

In pursuit of a theory, several basic questions need answering: Is public diplomacy a global or national phenomenon? Is there a universal theory of public diplomacy? Are there differences between China's public diplomacy and that of Western countries, in concept, goals, and cultural origin? If so, what are some of the distinguishing features of China's public diplomacy?

China's rise as a world power has paralleled the expansion of the study and practice of public diplomacy. Therefore, this chapter argues that it is critical to understand the implications of China's public diplomacy model both for theory and practice. In order to explore the contributions of the

Chinese model of public diplomacy, this chapter proceeds in four sections. First, it explores how national hues may influence the practice and theory of public diplomacy. Second, it discusses some of the underlying relational dimensions of Chinese public diplomacy found in Chinese perspectives of soft power and worldviews. Third, it identifies how the relational dimensions of Chinese public diplomacy are mirrored in Chinese models of practice and theory building. The concluding section ends with thoughts on the development of a Chinese theory of public diplomacy.

NATIONAL HUES OF PUBLIC DIPLOMACY PRACTICE AND THEORY

Public diplomacy is the art of communication between countries in the information age. Public diplomacy bears the stamp of its national brand in addition to distinct historical characteristics. In this regard, public diplomacy is more an art of practice than a science or theory.

Generally speaking, public diplomacy has three main sequential functions, each bearing distinct national characteristics. The first function is to improve the national image. A country's national image is not only closely related to its current policies, strategies, and actions, but also shaped by its culture. Few people show aversion to a certain culture. Their sentiments are frequently displayed in their perceptions of the image of a corresponding state. Cultural image is often exemplified in national image. For example, the charisma of India lies in its cultural and religious diversity. People from any country can find traces of their affinity with India and identify with India to such an extent that India's nation-branding campaign chose "Incredible India" as its theme.

The second major function of public diplomacy is to enhance a country's situation or stature. As the saying goes, "constrained by an unfavorable situation, we had better accept reality as the only choice." The stage on which a nation develops is directly connected to how it is perceived by international public opinion. Western developed countries claim that China, as the largest beneficiary of globalization, should undertake more international responsibilities. This perspective is the source of China's "responsibility theory."

The third function is to convey the intent of the state. As evident in China's promotion of Chinese culture to the world through the Confucius Institutes or the United States' promotion of its own values globally as universal values, public diplomacy entails looking back on a nation's history and culture and discovering commonalities between its national will and the general will of humankind.

While these functions are apparent in the practice of public diplomacy, public diplomacy theory still lags behind practice. Some have suggested that there is no public diplomacy theory. The international community lacks consistent criteria with respect to the concept of public diplomacy. Actually,

Table 6.1 Concept of "Soft Power" among China, the European Union, and the United States

	China	European Union	United States
Underlying premise	• Peaches and plums do not have to talk, yet the world beats a path • One can be modest if one has no selfish desires	• Empire by example • Empire by example • Cosmopolitan mission	• City upon the hill • American Exceptionalism
Outreach approach	• Confucius: If rural people are not submissive, all positive influences are cultivated to attract them; and only when they have been so attracted will they be bent and accepted. • Change oneself, change the world	• Normative power • "Soft imperialism" (Hetten & Soederbaum, 2005)	• Carrot and Stick Public diplomacy
Implementation approach	• Confucius: Do not do to others what you don't want others to do to you • Substantive democracy: reach people's hearts; accept a multipolar world	• Promoting EU values around the world • Procedural democracy: Effective multilateralism	• Unilateralism; Do what is in national interest, pre-emptive • Pragmatism: bilateralism and multilateralism
Objectives	• Art of dealing with differences: accept the beauty of your civilization and others; share beauty and create the world's great harmony	• Art of seeking common ground: EU standard • Civilian power	• Art of seeking common ground: U.S. values Assertive (Aggression)

I would suggest that different countries have different understandings of basic terms related to public diplomacy; these include ideas about publics, diplomacy, power, and soft power.

Based on my previous research on the national identity of international relations theory,[4] current public diplomacy theory reflects in particular the American national features, because the United States holds a near monopoly in the public diplomacy field. In this regard, the national features of public diplomacy theory have been largely related to "Americanization" and "Universalism." The American mode of thinking, political culture, national mission, and national character shape the intention and extension of public diplomacy theory. As a result, existing public diplomacy "theory" may only be applicable to the U.S. model or perspective.

There are also distinctive differences in how the concept of soft power is viewed by different countries. The U.S. concepts of soft power and public diplomacy are strongly related to American Exceptionalism and Manifest Destiny. China's and the European Union's understandings of soft power differ from each other and from that of the United States, as Table 6.1 indicates.

RELATIONAL DIMENSIONS OF THE CHINESE VIEW OF SOFT POWER

Chinese history and culture help shape its understanding of soft power and public diplomacy, just as the history and experiences of other countries have shaped their understanding of the concept. In looking closer at the Chinese perspective, one can see the strong relational dimension that serves as a foundation for Chinese understandings of soft power. This is in contrast with the individualism found in the European and, particularly, American views.

The premise of soft power in China stresses the ability to attract or appeal to others by one's nature rather than by words or actions. This concept is aptly summarized by the Chinese idiom: "Peaches and plums do not have to talk, yet the world beats a path (to them)." This idiom means that even though peach trees and plum trees cannot talk to attract attention, their sweet fruits and fragrant flowers attract people anyway. People would like to walk beside the trees to appreciate their beauty and taste their fruits. As many people walk toward the trees, a path forms.

This idiom indicates a method of communication. Once people possess abilities or do good deeds, they do not need to boast. If they are low-key and sincere, people can see their virtue and contributions, which will then help to gain more support from the public. By contrast, those who are bombastic easily trigger aversion.

The idiom also reflects Chinese culture. In China, people are encouraged to be low-key and restrained. Tanina Zappone, in her study of Chinese public diplomacy, noted this feature: "many Chinese scholars notice that the behaviour of Chinese politicians is traditionally introvert (*neixiang*). While Western culture tends to be open and communicative, the Chinese cultural tradition considers humbleness as a value, and prefers the "resounding of a silent victory" (*wusheng sheng yousheng*)."[5]

The method of implementation of soft power from the Chinese perspective emphasizes attraction through "a managed system and social harmony." The words of Confucius here refer to a method that a governor should use to manage the country. Poverty will not damage a country if the governor can equally distribute the wealth and make the society stable. This benevolent method of governance will help to attract more people to move to the country. In order to encourage obedience, the governor can use favorable policies or present the advantages of living in the country. The way the governor manages the country directly affects the stability of society and the psychology of its citizens.

The implementation of soft power, from the Chinese perspective, is captured by Confucius's version of the Golden Rule, "Do not do to others what you do not want others to do to you." The main concepts of this idiom are forgiveness and self-restraint. When people communicate or governors manage the country, they should use strict rules for themselves and be tolerant of others. Society will become harmonious and people will demonstrate strong values. "Change oneself; change the world" is another popular idiom.[6] Ancient Chinese thinkers advocated the "rule of virtue" as the key political value. Chinese people prefer self-examination and look for self-transformation in attempts to convince others. Traditional Chinese culture is a learning culture.

The objective of soft power stresses diversity. The art of dealing with differences is key to harmony. Here another prominent saying from Confucius applies: the exemplary person seeks harmony, not conformity, while the small person seeks conformity.

The Chinese concept of harmony (和谐) has two parts: 和:禾+口, 人人有饭吃 (grain + mouth, everyone has enough to eat), 谐:言+皆, 人人能说话 (speech + all, everyone is able to speak). The former part highlights well-being, and the second highlights civil rights. These sayings are similar to European values but with the strong mark of an agricultural civilization. The two aspects provide key pillars for the harmonious world, common prosperity and lasting peace. In Confucius's eyes, harmony proceeds from self-cultivation to family-regulation to state-ordering, and finally the entire world is at peace (修身、齐家、治国、平天下).

The relational premise in soft power can also be found in the Chinese understanding of power. In Western politics, the term *power* refers to the ability of one actor or organization to influence the attitude and behavior of another actor or organization. Such a definition is related to the logic of Charles Darwin, focusing on those with power as the subject and those without power as the object. Actually, the definition of power should take into account not only the ability of the power subject, but also the extent of acceptance in the power object. This is the important difference between the ancient Eastern "tribute" system and the modern Western international system.

In reality, in China, there is no such dichotomy of soft power–hard power. In traditional Chinese, power, or *quanli* (权力), has two basic meanings: "steel yard" (noun) or "to be against scripture but for principle" (verb). In practice, *quanli* (power) is always connected with *quanshu* (tactics or strategy). So, historically, although there was balance of power in the period of Warring States (475–221 BC), it was not a system but a strategy (*junshi shu*).

In philosophy, a Chinese understanding of power is always related to ethics. Different schools of Chinese traditional philosophy explained the connection differently. Xunzi or Hsun Tzu (313–238 BC) argued that power is contrary to morality (君子以德, 小人以力;力者, 德之役也), while Confucius (551–478 BC) claimed to "become a sage from inside and an emperor from outside," or "ruling others and cultivating himself" (内圣外王). In other words, morality cultivated from the inside brings power on the outside. Confucius famously said, "Do not impose upon others what you do not desire yourself" ('己所不欲, 勿施于人,' 《颜渊》). Lao Tzu (854–770 BC) taught, "Govern by doing nothing that is against nature" (无为而治), meaning power comes from nature. In essence, traditional Chinese thinking about power is that power comes from morality and morality comes from nature. The traditional Chinese tributary system integrated power and morality.

This relational view of power finds parallels in the China construction of the world. The West views China primarily as a nation-state. The Chinese perception of China favors China as a cultural community, an ancient civilization or culture. In Chinese traditional thinking, there is no concept of nation, nation-state, sovereignty, or international system but the ideas of "all-under-heaven" (*tianxia*). "Heaven" was used in the traditional Chinese concept before Han Dynasty instead of "world." Heaven has the meaning of virtue and final judge, as the saying "Heaven has eyes" (苍天有眼) indicates. The Western notion of "world" only has the sense of geography. Chinese philosopher Zhao Tingyang has pointed out that the concept "all-under-heaven" has a triple meaning—as the land of the world, as all peoples of the world, and as world institutions—combined in the single term, indicating a theoretical project of the necessary and inseparable connections among these three elements.[7] The "all-under-heaven" concept emphasizes a unity of the physical world (land), the psychological world (the general heart or sentiment of peoples), and the political world (a world institution). As Zhao Tingyang adds, "all-under-heaven" is a deep world concept; it introduces a political principle, "worldness," that transcends the principle of "international."[8]

Chinese intellectuals pursue "unity between the heaven and human" (天人合一), while European thought highlights the division between paradise and hell. In international relations, the Chinese perspective tends toward monism, preferring a harmonious world over a dualism or dichotomy rooted in Christianity, a culture prone to dividing the world between good and evil. Christianity adopts the idea of the absolute. God is identified as the source of creation; others, especially heathens, are affirmed as irreconcilable enemies. Chinese thought supposes that there is always a method by which "otherness" can be changed into harmonious co-existence.[9] In other worlds, all non-harmonious things can be changed from Other to Us. Western political discourse first thinks about "who are you?" It is an identity problem based on the need to distinguish friend and enemy, us versus other. It is a divisive world outlook. The premise of Chinese political thinking is "who are we?" based on the idea of the whole world as one family.

EMERGING CHINESE MODELS OF PUBLIC DIPLOMACY PRACTICE

With China's dynamic identity, its particular stage of development, and the uncertainty of the world, China's public diplomacy practice promotes the formulation of a Chinese model of public diplomacy. China's foreign minister Yang Jiechi has summarized five characteristics of China's public diplomacy as follows:

> First, China's public diplomacy is guided by socialist theories with Chinese characteristics, and in particular, by the unique theories that China has developed on diplomacy. Second, the objective of China's public diplomacy is to promote common development and prosperity around the world. Third, we approach public diplomacy from both domestic and international perspectives. Fourth, we emphasize the integration of Chinese culture with elements from other cultures in our public diplomacy. Fifth, China's public diplomacy is moving forward with the times while carrying on the traditions of the past.[10]

Because one finds a strong relational orientation in the basic elements associated with public diplomacy, it is not unexpected that one also finds a relational orientation in the emerging Chinese models of public diplomacy. The characteristics identified above are particularly relevant to collaborative and relational models.

Another example that illustrates the relational orientation is the view through China's dynamic national identities. Liang Qichao, a great scholar at the end of the Qin Dynasty, has classified Chinese history as "China's China," "Asia's China," and "the World's China," which also exemplifies China's three identities.[11]

In today's world, "China's China" refers to socialism with Chinese characteristics. As a socialist country under the leadership of the Chinese

Communist Party, China's public diplomacy is imprinted with distinctive characteristics of a system: upholding fairness and justice in the international community, opposing hegemony, acknowledging the superiority of the socialist system, and acknowledging that the government drives the people, while the people facilitate government. Constructing socialist core values is the focus of China's public diplomacy, not only to let the international community know "who China is," but also to provide the universal values that eliminate the capitalist system's crisis and failure.

"Asia's China" refers to Eastern civilization (East Asian civilization). If we look around the world, ancient civilizations, such as Egypt, Babylon, and India, were essentially intermittent. Today's Egypt and ancient Egypt are not the same. Only the Chinese and European civilizations demonstrate the greatest continuity, having been modernized and secularized. In today's world, we need to go back to initial civilizations to find answers rather than rely on technology. Providing a new idea or conception of China is increasingly becoming a project that goes beyond "Made in China" and follows Chinese society's transformation as well as China's rise. China is the cradle of Eastern civilization, but is also a secular and modern civilization. As an Eastern ancient civilization, both China's soft power and its hard power are rising rapidly. The rise of China's public diplomacy demonstrates the civilization's awareness and confidence.

"The World's China" refers to China as a developing country and emerging power. As one of the biggest developing countries in the world, another historical mission of China's public diplomacy is to increase the discourse power of developing countries in the global arena. For this purpose, developing China's public diplomacy must be incremental and pragmatic. As a developing country that has only recently become an emerging power, China feels more deeply with regard to the injustice of international norms that other countries experience. So, China's public diplomacy shoulders the historical mission of building a new international order that is fair, equitable, inclusive, and well managed. However, considering an emerging country's position in the international system, fulfilling this historic responsibility and mission will need to take place through constructive cooperation.

China's four national identities define public diplomacy along four Chinese dimensions. "China's China" emphasizes fairness and justice. "Asia's China" emphasizes the priority of culture. The "World's China" stresses defensive cooperation and an incremental and pragmatic approach. In practice, the traditional China Model in public diplomacy is relationship building.[12] The Chinese understand public diplomacy by emphasizing the importance of *minjian waijiao* (people-to-people diplomacy).[13] In recent years, three sub-models have emerged. The first is an External Publicity Model. In this model, the State Council Information Office takes a leading role in coordinating the media and internet on external publicity. The second is the Olympic Model. This model has three dimensions: (1) traditional culture as national image contest; (2) contemporary high-profile public display; and (3) Chinese international celebrity figures convey and share culture abroad.[14] The third model is the Confucius Institute Model. This model has two major dimensions: (1) seeking the unity of politics, culture, and business; and (2) promoting a joint venture between Chinese Hanban and foreign universities. Culture has been another distinctive feature of Chinese public diplomacy. Whereas the West views China primarily in political terms as a nation-state, the Chinese perceive their country as a cultural community that prefers to be recognized as an ancient civilization rather than as a modern state.[15] China's emphasis on culture is why its public diplomacy tends to be closer to the French approach, emphasizing a cultural exchange and cultural diplomacy, rather than advocacy or discourse as found in the American-style media diplomacy approach.

These models share three distinctive features. First, the models are government driven. Under the central government's coordination, there is a division of labor among the ministries. The Ministry of Foreign Affairs is charged with public diplomacy and public affairs. The Ministry of Education oversees the Confucius Institute initiative, People-to-People Exchange, and Dialogue programs. The Ministry of Culture conducts cultural diplomacy, such as with the Chinese cultural centers, national year, or cultural year with other countries. Other ministries act in close coordination.

At the central level, the Chinese Association of Public Diplomacy was established in December 2012. Besides the Ministry of Foreign Affairs, the CPPCC National Committee played a unique role. Traditionally, the CPPCC does not have the authority in diplomacy, but public diplomacy is an exception since it stresses the communication with foreign civil society, and CPPCC is the organ that represents Chinese civil society. Under the leadership of the Chairman Zhao Qizheng and Vice Chairman Han Fangming of the Foreign Affairs Committee of CPPCC, the Charhar Institute was founded in 2010, along with the first professional journal in public diplomacy of China, *Public Diplomacy Quarterly*.

Besides the central government, local governments are taking actions in public diplomacy to promote the Chinese image. For instance, the Shanghai Association of Public Diplomacy, the first of its kind in China, was established in 2011 and was soon followed by associations in Gangzhou, Tianjin, Huizhou, Nanjing, Hangzhou, and Wenzhou. Another example is the recent Shanghai-Houston Exchange and Broadcast Promotional Videos initiative, an example that may be followed by other cities.

Another shared feature is that of social mobilization. For instance, NGOs such as Oxfam played a very active role in explaining Chinese policy and improving the Chinese image in Copenhagen and Durban.[16] The World Buddhism Forum has made significant strides in promoting religious or faith public diplomacy. A final shared feature is commercial operation. For example, Xinhua news agency, CCTV, and other media are busy telling China's story and informing the world about China's news and opinions.

Overall, there are two trends for the China model in public diplomacy. The first trend is a shift from defensive to offensive; for instance, strategic communication has been the highlight in Chinese public diplomacy. The second trend, combining cultural and political contexts, official and civilian approaches, and public and commercial operations, has been the mission for Chinese public diplomacy.[17]

TOWARD A CHINESE PUBLIC DIPLOMACY THEORY

We need a theory to explain the practices in the field of public diplomacy based on the characteristics of China's public diplomacy. It is first necessary to cultivate a Chinese perspective that avoids American influence. China's goal for the twenty-first century is to build a new relationship with the rest of the world. Such a theory also requires a connection with traditional Chinese culture. This section will address these two aspects.

China's Public Diplomacy Theory Must Be De-Americanized

After being overshadowed by the United States for years, China's public diplomacy today is eager to venture out on its own. Theory starts by reviewing the nature of U.S. public diplomacy. First, the ideological hues of U.S public diplomacy should be exposed. The strategy of "peaceful evolution"[18] contributed to America's success in winning the Cold War. After the end of the Cold War, the introduction of the theory of "soft power" not only enhanced the legitimacy of public diplomacy, but also finally dispelled "peaceful evolution" and justified its contemporary status. In this respect, public diplomacy has always been tied to ideology.

Second, the religious nature of U.S. public diplomacy cannot be ignored. The original intention of "soft power" advanced by Joseph Nye was to counter the iron law of the rise and fall of great powers and, in particular, to discredit the decline of the United States and preserve the legitimacy of American hegemony. Unfortunately, though, when the Americans cheered the abrupt end of the Cold War, one may find that the soft power theory led to historians' interpretation that the United States was on the right side of history, and the Soviet Union on the wrong side, after the collapse of the Soviet system. I argue against this interpretation, which indicates that American public diplomacy was virtually given the religious complex of "Manifest Destiny." With Americans' intention to command others, U.S. public diplomacy values the idea of forcing its own views upon others. The United States calls on other nations to adhere to its policy, ideological system, and ideas, because they believe that American policies, systems, and ideas are right.

China's traditionally secular society will act to reduce the influence of American ideology in China's public diplomacy. China's public diplomacy theory does not contain the dichotomy (us vs. other/them), a keystone of American society. Another moderating influence that will act to de-Americanize the theory and practice of China's public diplomacy are China's traditional culture and fundamental national realities.

Theoretical Mission of China's Public Diplomacy

China's public diplomacy struggle is related to China's three identities: "China's China" (Traditional China), "Asia's China" (Modern China), and "the World's China" (Global China). China's public diplomacy must answer the following questions.

First, how is China developing and what does it mean to other countries? When China was isolated from the rest of the international community, the mission of China's public diplomacy was to speak out and define "who China is." After the reform, emphasis was on clarifying "how China would develop." In other words, the goal of peaceful development precipitated a change from "minding one's own business" during the Cold War period to adopting a more engaged "harmonious yet different" posture in the interdependent age of globalization. The long-term mission for China's public diplomacy is to explain to the world in a universal language what China will do with her rising power and how China will contribute to the world's peace and welfare.

A second question is how can an increasingly powerful China get along with the rest of the world? When China emerged as the second-largest world economy, people began to compare China with the United States, the largest world economy. China has to convince the West that visible differences are not so important. For example, Chinese eat with chopsticks while the Westerners use knives and forks. We cannot infer that chopsticks symbolize peace. Similarly, the West should not deny the existence of democracy in China because it is developed within the Chinese political system. China should persuade the West to consider strategies beyond governmental systems and to return to cultural standards in order to establish faith in the idea that the "China model" and other development models can legitimately develop together and coexist.

A final question is what will China be in the future and what kind of world does China prefer? China's rise as a world power indicates an urgency to predict its future identity, its vision of the world, and the responsibilities China will assume. However, what worries the international community is that Chinese traditional culture cannot fulfill its mission in an age of globalization, because the so-called "all-under-heaven system" (*tianxia system*) is confined to East Asia. However, China's public diplomacy provides a more expansive vision of China with three identities: Traditional China, Modern China, and Global China. It also clarifies the essential difference between the multipolar world promoted by China and the one that easily caused wars in history and contributed to the concept of systematization, policy-orientation, and universalization.

The theoretical missions of China's public diplomacy help provide answers to the three questions above: to implement altruism and offset the "eagerness for instant success and quick profits" found in Western public diplomacy; to surpass the "invisible influence" of Western diplomatic strategies; to overcome the Western definition of democracy by adhering to Chinese faith and reconcile the conflict between the world's idea of China and the Chinese idea of the world with the "Great Harmonious Universe." Thus, we may reach the perfect harmony realm of "China is the world and the world is China."

The Constructing Path of China's Public Diplomacy

There are several features that we can point to in laying a conceptual path for China's public diplomacy. First, the philosophical base of Chinese public diplomacy is objectivity. Different from the public diplomacy of the United States, which emphasizes unilateral output, China's public diplomacy lays stress on mutual respect, objects to self-congratulation, and doesn't impose its views on others, but lets others find identification from China's development on their own.

Second, mutuality (or reciprocity) is the idea behind the process of Chinese public diplomacy. It emphasizes interactive learning, and mutuality of impression and emotional construction. One listens to and respects others' feelings while sharing his or her own feelings. Implementation of public diplomacy leads to inclusiveness. China has, therefore, put effort into emphasizing the inclusiveness that public diplomacy inspires.[19] National harmony is the goal that Chinese public diplomacy is pursuing. A person should accept differences instead of imposing his or her views on others.

In summary, China's public diplomacy theory seeks the road of de-Americanization and combines theoretical missions with traditional culture. It contains Chinese characteristics and provides for China's contribution to the world, without neglecting the inputs from other countries. This theory is based on the philosophical value of objectivity, uses mutuality as its ideology, and considers inclusiveness as an approach to turn public diplomacy theory into reality while pursuing harmony as the goal.

CONSTRAINTS OF CHINA'S PUBLIC DIPLOMACY MODEL

There is always a gap between the reality of "what is" and the ideal of "what should be," which is reflected in the obvious constraints in both practical and theoretical aspects of China's public diplomacy.

On an international level, changes in attitudes lag behind changes in the power equation. Time is needed for China's rising hard power to be transformed into relevant soft power. Regarding the relationship between China and the world, the reform and "opening up" of China also follows the logic of globalization dominated by Western norms and values. These factors have shaped and will continue to shape the development of Chinese public diplomacy.

On the domestic level, there are three components of constraints on public diplomacy. First is the constraint of society. Traditional Chinese culture is a learning culture and secular society. These two characteristics lead to a lack of aggressiveness in public diplomacy. Second is the constraint of traditional culture, which seeks inclusion over conversion. For instance, Zheng He, the great navigator in the Ming Dynasty, made the royal gifts famous during his seven voyages to the Indian Ocean but did not actively promote China or seek conquest or missionary conversion. Third is the constraint of discourse and the philosophical system. As mentioned previously, traditional Chinese culture favors self-cultivation and pragmatic action to convey its intention over trying to persuade others through discourse. However, because of the vigorous discourse in the global arena, China's public diplomacy should begin the cultivation of its international discourse power or global voice. It will be a great test to build public diplomacy from traditional secular society and express the international spirit through a "Chinese model" of public diplomacy.

A country's soft power depends on how much it has represented the requirements of the advanced productive force, how much it has represented the popular will of most countries, and how much it has represented the shared value of humankind. Correspondingly, the public diplomacy of a country also largely depends on the understanding of the nature of age and the reflection of the people's universal will. It will take time to surpass the constraints of home and abroad in order to construct China's public diplomacy theory.

NOTES

1. Research for this article was sponsored by the Chinese Ministry of Education's Program on Humanities and Social Sciences (2012–2014), titled "Study on the Mechanism of China's Public Diplomacy towards Europe" (12YJAZH148).
2. Joseph S. Nye Jr., "China's Soft Power Deficit," *Wall Street Journal*, May 9, 2012.
3. David Pilling, "Why China's Charm Offensive Is Doomed to Failure," *Financial Times*, February 23, 2011, http://www.ftchinese.com/story/001041765/en
4. Yiwei Wang, "On National Identity of International Relations Theories: A Chinese Perspective," *ICFAI Journal of International Relations* 1 (2007): 7–24.
5. Tanina Zappone, "New Words for a New International Communication: The Case of Public Diplomacy," *Europe China Research and Advice Network* (2012): 22, http://www.euecran.eu.
6. Zhang Baijia, "*Gaibian ziji, gaibian shijie*" ("Change Oneself, Change the World"), *Zhongguo Shehui Kexue (China Social Science)* 1 (2002).
7. Tingyang Zhao, *Tianxia System (All-under-Heaven): Introduction to the Philosophy of World Institutions* (Nanjing: Jiangsu Higher Education Publishing House, 2005); Tingyang Zhao, "Rethinking Empire from a Chinese Concept 'All-under-Heaven' (Tian-xia)," *Social Identities* 12 (2006): 29–41.

8. Zhao, *Rethinking Empire.*
9. Yiwei Wang, "China: Between Copying and Constructing," in *International Relations Scholarship around the World*, eds. Arlene Tickner and Ole Weaver (New York: Routledge, 2009).
10. Yang Jiechi, "China's Public Diplomacy," *Qiushi Journal* 3, 3 (July 1, 2011), http://english.qstheory.cn/international/201109/t20110924_112601.htm
11. Liang Qichao, "Introduction to Chinese History," *Yinbinshi Heji* (Complete Works of Liang Qichao) 1 (1988): 11–12.
12. Han Fangming, ed., *Introduction to Public Diplomacy* (Peking: Peking University Press, 2012), 223.
13. Yiwei Wang, "Public Diplomacy and the Rise of Chinese Soft Power."
14. Zhou Qing'an and Hu Xianzhang, "Change of Chinese Public Diplomacy Models," *China Social Sciences Today*, July 9, 2009.
15. Yiwei Wang, "Is Chinese-European Cultural G2 Possible?" *Marco Polo Magazine*, February 17, 2011, http://marcopolomagazine.wordpress.com
16. Zhang Zhongkai, "Analysis on Oxfam Model in Public Diplomacy " *Duiwai Chuanbo* (International Communications), 4 (2012).
17. Li Defang and Li Weihong, "An Analysis on China's Public Diplomacy Model," *Journal of Liaocheng University (Social Sciences Edition)* 1 (2012), http://en.cnki.com.cn/Article_en/CJFDTotal-VOUS201201019.htm
18. U.S. Secretary of State Dulles was a proponent of this concept.
19. Yiwei Wang, "Beyond Peaceful Rise: The Necessity and Possibility of China's Inclusive Rise," *World Economy & Politics* 8 (2011).

Part II
Conflict & Culture
Connectivity in Practice

7 Building and Measuring Sustainable Networks of Organizations and Social Capital

Postwar Public Diplomacy in Croatia

Maureen Taylor and Michael L. Kent

INTRODUCTION

The 1995 Dayton Peace Agreement between the Republic of Bosnia and Herzegovina, the Republic of Croatia, and the Federal Republic of Yugoslavia was the product of several years of diplomatic negotiations. It marked the formal end of war in the Balkans and heralded the beginning of an ambitious public diplomacy initiative to build a democratic foundation and civil society. What made the task particularly daunting was that the former communist nations had few if any organizations that were not government sponsored. Nonprofit civil society organizations were needed, and needed quickly; a stipulation of the peace agreement called for parliamentary and presidential elections for the newly created nations.

Both the United States and the European Union (EU) started immediate programs of humanitarian aid and interactive public diplomacy in the Balkan countries. How successful were these public diplomacy efforts? This chapter argues that the Croatian public diplomacy efforts were among the most successful U.S. public diplomacy campaigns. Public diplomacy, enacted by foreign aid to civil society groups, helped to create a network of advocacy organizations that brought the values of human rights and democracy into the everyday public discourse of Croatian society. Not only did the Croatian NGOs play a pivotal role in the first democratic elections after the war, but the public diplomacy efforts also created a "network of organizations" and social capital that enabled them to continue their mission long after foreign assistance ended.

Successful public diplomacy means building up communication "networks of networks" consisting of people who share common values. This chapter explores U.S. public diplomacy efforts in postwar Croatia through the relational lens. The first part provides a conceptual foundation for a relational approach to public diplomacy based on network theory and social capital.[1] The second section discusses public diplomacy efforts in Croatia from 1998 to 2000 by tracing public perceptions of civil society topics in Croatia after the aid ended. The third section tackles the question of measurement and presents an approach for assessing the long-term relational dynamics of the public diplomacy initiatives. The final section features conclusions, recommendations, and ethical considerations for public diplomacy practitioners as they work to increase international understanding and build relationships with publics across the world.

BUILDING NETWORKS OF ORGANIZATIONS

Writing during the Cold War, Gifford D. Malone called public diplomacy "direct communication with foreign peoples, with the aim of affecting their thinking and, ultimately, that of their governments."[2] But those days have passed. One-way image cultivation campaigns intended to "win the hearts and minds" of the people have proven ineffective. Many nations—Ethiopia, Malaysia, and Haiti, for example—have strong relations among the media, government, and business. Reporters and station managers often hold very different values about appropriate topics for reporting, and image cultivation efforts by foreign nations to influence the media are met with suspicion and enmity.

Benno Signitzer and Carola Wamser have called for a generic approach that involved multiple theories, multiple systems of analysis, and multiple media channels as a way to better understand both public relations and public diplomacy.[3] The scholars argue that in modern public diplomacy, "relations are becoming more and more closely connected with actors other than national governments.[4] There is a shift away from the traditional, state-level diplomacy and toward public, citizen-level diplomacy." Nongovernmental organizations (NGOs), international nongovernmental organizations (INGOs), multinational corporations (MNCs), and even the entertainment industries now have more influence over how citizens in one nation view another nation than governmental strategic communication campaigns.

Additionally, public relations and public diplomacy are generally more effective and most ethical when they promote relationships among citizens and organizations. Public diplomacy efforts in the form of humanitarian or development assistance can have lasting impact. For instance, some public diplomacy efforts train journalists in how to report on public information and health campaigns.[5] More public diplomacy success has come from community-based efforts than from one-way, top-down image cultivation strategies. We believe that understanding the networks of relationships that are the outcomes of public diplomacy efforts will help academics and diplomacy professionals move forward in understanding an evolving public diplomacy process.

The shift from mass communication to interpersonal and group communication has had a big influence. If we move away from a focus on images and messages and instead focus on organizations, or what Signitzer and Wamser termed "systems," then public diplomacy efforts can extend beyond cultivating an image about the United States or another country. Instead, efforts should be devoted to building relationships among national governmental organizations and local NGOs across the world.

We suggest that public diplomacy's most important assets lie in networks of organizations with shared values. Interactions between organizations are unique ways to understand relationships. Such a focus moves the level of analysis in public diplomacy away from messages and directs it toward inter-organizational relationships that build social capital. Social capital, as highlighted in this chapter, provides critical insights for public diplomacy scholarship that have to this point been under examined.

Social capital is created by a system of trusting and supportive interconnected organizations.[6] Social capital "consist[s] of some aspects of social structures, and they facilitate certain actions of actors-whether persons or corporate actor-within the structure."[7] Social capital is enhanced by certain organization actions such as collaborative networks, cooperation, information sharing, and resource mobilization.

As Peter Monge and Noshir Contractor suggest, social capital is created when organizational members communicate and enter into relationships with others.[8] The outcome of these relationships includes new opportunities, information, and access to a variety of resources. Thus, social networks based on communicatively constructed inter-organizational relationships create social capital.[9] Activist organizations, for example, cooperate to fight for animal rights legislation; religious and social groups work to provide food and shelter to the poor; and governmental health and aid efforts (USAID, PEPFAR, etc.) all build social capital and contribute to soft-power public diplomacy.

Governmental efforts like USAID or PEPFAR provide resources to train journalists in better health and social reporting. In the process, these programs also spawn and strengthen relationships among and between journalists, health specialists, and governmental officials. Many observers tend to focus on the achievement of objective tasks in such programs and overlook the public diplomacy implications of how providing training and interacting with the public on health projects can help build social networks and create social capital. Indeed, the synergistic power of collective group activities is often underestimated as a public diplomacy outcome and tool.

Organizations not directly related to the U.S. government can also enact programs that support U.S. values every day. Organizations such as the Habitat for Humanity work to make affordable housing a basic human right. Similarly, organizations like the U.S. Chamber of Commerce, the Rotary Club, and different membership organizations such as the Kiwanis Club International also advocate on behalf of U.S. values of education, community engagement, service, open markets, and participatory government to people across the world.

If the goal of U.S. and Western European public diplomacy efforts is to build social capital, then fostering relationships with local organizations that share their values may be the best way to accomplish public diplomacy outcomes. The relationships among U.S. and Western European donor organizations and their local counterparts are another example of coordinated strategic communication.

The next section provides a longitudinal case study of Croatians' evolving perceptions of civil society. The data from three points in time (2000, 2002, and 2004) are used to assess the outcomes of public diplomacy efforts of the international community as they worked to strengthen Croatian media institutions and civil society.

PUBLIC DIPLOMACY STRATEGY: FOSTERING RELATIONSHIPS WITH LOCAL NGOs

After the Dayton Peace Agreement, both the United States and the EU started immediate programs of humanitarian aid and interactive public diplomacy in Croatia. The Dayton Peace Agreement between the leaders of Bosnia, Croatia, and Yugoslavia marked the formal cessation of hostilities. But the agreement was only a first step; nationalist political leaders controlled both Croatia and Yugoslavia. In Croatia, Franjo Tudjman and his nationalist HDZ party ran all aspects of the government. In Yugoslavia, Slobodan Milosevic similarly controlled activities in his nation. Tudjman and Milosevic, however, were the elected leaders of their nations, and no amount of world pressure was able to unseat them from power.[10] However, the United States and the EU recognized that peace in the region would not last if nationalist politicians continued to lead the nations.

After the Dayton Peace Agreement, the governments in the United States and Europe wanted to ensure that democratic elections would be held in Croatia.[11] Significant amounts of international humanitarian assistance were devoted to Croatia and Bosnia. An important part of that assistance was to help establish civil society organizations and independent media in these nations to facilitate democracy building.

In Croatia, both government affiliated and international humanitarian organizations such as the United States Agency for International Development (USAID), the British Department for International Development (DFID), the Soros Open Society Institute (OSI), and the Norwegian People's Aid (NPA) started to fund civil society initiatives. These international organizations helped to prepare newly formed local grassroots nongovernmental organizations (NGOs) for the much anticipated (but unscheduled) democratic elections.

Building up a network of NGOs was not easy. Before 1990, the existence of non-state organizations was foreign throughout much of Eastern and Central Europe. In communist nations, there were few, if any, civil society organizations that existed outside of the state. The Western governments' funding of public diplomacy efforts in Bosnia, Croatia, and Yugoslavia sought to reinforce, create, and sustain nongovernmental organizations (NGOs). Efforts also focused on helping independent media outlets work for voting rights, peace, women's issues, and political reforms. Many Western governments believe that media independence is a foundation for democracy building.

One can look at these public diplomacy efforts through a relational lens. When the Western governments and humanitarian NGOs provided technical and financial support for local media, NGOs, and activist groups that shared their values, they were enacting a relational approach to public diplomacy. The civil society transition in Croatia is considered a success story for international donors.[12] During the late 1990s, the U.S. and European governments dedicated approximately 16.5–19.5 percent of their total aid budgets in Eastern Europe to NGOs and democracy-building efforts.[13] The social capital built up within the networks had financial benefits; Croatian NGOs often cooperated with each other to maximize the financial assistance and expertise offered by international donors.[14] Their actions had significant implications in 1999 and 2000. These civil society organizations, run by Croatians, for Croatians, created a grassroots movement—effectively expanding their relations into a network of organizations. When the calls for democracy, free and fair elections, and women's issues grew louder, they were no longer coming from foreign governments. The calls originated from within the network; they were from Croatians.

CROATIA'S DEMOCRATIC TRANSITION

The lead-up to the 2000 elections in Croatia showed dozens of NGOs, supported by Western donors, working within their network of organizations to communicate information about the upcoming elections. The 2000 parliamentary election campaign was important to the future of Croatia because it was the end of the Tudjman regime, and, thus, the first time a democratic election was possible.

Looking in the rearview mirror to study the civil society network in Croatia is important for several reasons. First, foreign donors facilitated relationships among domestic Croatian organizations and supported coalitions to amplify NGO efforts. Second, at the time, the exact dates of the pending Croatian parliamentary and presidential elections were unknown. In Croatia, when the parliament announced the election, candidates and parties had a very short period to mobilize public support for change. This was a common practice in nations where the government seeks to weaken the opposition by allowing them little time to prepare for an election.

On November 27, 1999, acting president Vlatko Pavletic announced the parliamentary election would take place on January 3, 2000. On December 10, 1999, Franjo Tudjman died, suddenly shifting the political dynamic in the country. The pro-democracy movement had five weeks to communicate their messages, reassure voters that this would be a fair election, and educate the public about the major issues facing the nation. Because of the strong network of activists and media organizations that had been built in Croatia, there was reservoir of social capital. With this social capital, the network of organizations was able to cooperate, to create a non-partisan movement, and to ensure that accurate information and fair elections took place.

In January 2000, Croatians elected a new parliament, and the nationalist HDZ party lost much of its power. With the election of reformist parliament and President Stjepan (Stipe) Mesic, Croatia started on the path to democracy. Soon after the election, Croatia entered into discussions with the EU and applied for membership in 2003. Croatia is now set to become the twenty-eighth member of the European Union on July 1, 2013.

TACKLING THE QUESTION OF MEASUREMENT

Croatia's successful transition to democracy and EU membership provides the opportunity to study the outcomes of public diplomacy efforts. If we accept that public diplomacy should be based on systems or networks, then the time period from 1998 to 2004 in Croatia may be a valuable example to illustrate the outcome of public diplomacy efforts that built networks of NGOs and created social capital.

Maureen Taylor and Marya Doerfel studied the Croatian NGO and media network that operated before, during, and after the 2000 elections and outlined a methodology for measuring features of that network that are applicable to other public diplomacy actors.[15] Their research found that this pro-democracy network was primarily supported (both financially and technically) by Western governments. Croatian NGOs, such as Citizens Organized to Monitor Elections (GONG), Helsinki Human Rights (HHO), and the environmental group Green Action, all received large amounts of training and financial support from international donors.[16]

For our task here, we are interested in assessing the long-term impact of the development efforts of the initial public diplomacy efforts. The immediate and early results of the network of organizations had been a success, but would the network and the core values be sustainable? And, more important for the donors, would the network continue without foreign support?

In the former Yugoslavia, Croatia was one of the wealthiest republics. However, Croatia's economy had suffered since independence, and unemployment has ranged from 12 to 17 percent. Croatia will officially join the EU in 2013 after a long acceptance process that required changes in the political, economic, legal, and social systems.

The research team selected the capital city, Zagreb, as the site for the study. There are approximately 4 million Croatians, and 25 percent of them live in Zagreb. The city of Zagreb is the cultural, economic, and media capital of Croatia. Croatians have traditionally had a high literacy rate, and

Zagreb has a saturated media market with dozens of television stations, radio stations, daily papers, and weekly papers vying for limited advertising revenue. As the capital, Zagreb is also home to the nation's parliament, and it is the county seat of government for the surrounding towns. There is a vibrant NGO sector in Zagreb, with most of the international and national organizations headquartered there.

For the six-year period 1998–2004, we wanted to examine how public attitudes evolved on the issues that the network originally had advocated. These issues included the importance of civil society groups in Croatia, NGOs cooperation with government, and citizens' desire to participate in civil society activities. We were also interested in whether the local NGOs that had been originally financed (in 1998–2000) and trained by foreign governments were still perceived by the Croatian public to be active and influential in building social capital in Croatia in 2002 and 2004. It is important to point out that the surveys were collected during the summers of 2000, 2002, and 2004, two and four years *after* the United States and EU had withdrawn most of their donations to the NGO network.[17] We asked two research questions, noted below, designed to assess the impact and provide evidence of lasting outcomes of the public diplomacy efforts.

Our first general research question was: "How has the Croatian public's understanding of the role of non-governmental organizations in civil society evolved over time?" This question was based on the assumption that the network of NGOs supported by public diplomacy efforts generally share the same values as the EU and the United States, and played an important role in Croatia's political transition. Just because there are NGOs in a country does not necessarily mean that there will be civil society. The existence of NGOs is *necessary* for the potential for civil society, but their presence is not *sufficient* for civil society development.[18]

For this first question, we asked respondents to indicate whether (1) civil society organizations are important for improving the situation in Croatia; (2) civil society organizations should cooperate with the government to improve the situation in Croatia; and (3) the person surveyed wants to participate in civil society. Responses were based on 5-point Likert scales with 5 meaning "strongly agree" and 1 meaning "strongly disagree." The questions were asked over four years, in three time periods (2000, 2002, 2004).

After we had gauged respondents' knowledge and attitudes toward NGOs, survey participants were asked to identify which specific NGOs had emerged as leaders of civil society in Croatia. We asked this question to probe deeper into the public's perceptions of NGO groups, and their awareness of group activities.

Our second general question was, "In what ways has the Croatian public's understanding of the leaders of the NGO movement evolved over time?" This second question assumes that the general public's view of the quality and value of civil society activities is a better indicator of their overall social value than is asking members and leaders of the groups themselves to rate their social value. All members of groups and organizations are self-interested, and stepping outside of one's comfort zone is difficult. Since the NGOs naturally claim in their annual reports and public relations materials that they have achieved their goals, an outside assessment from the publics served was a necessary step to measure real impact. Open-ended questions were used, and interviewees were asked to identify the specific NGOs in Zagreb that were (1) most active, (2) most trusted, and (3) most influential in civil society in Croatia. Since the groups were quite new in 2000, the three questions were only asked in 2002 and 2004.

In order to locate evidence of the outcome of the network approach to public diplomacy, we drew upon primary and secondary data. The primary data came from the survey responses and the open-ended questions. The use of open-ended questions allowed respondents to name as many or as few organizations as they desired. Open-ended question also minimized the chances that respondents would merely select the names of organizations from a list of NGOs provided to them. Based on the responses from survey participants, a roster of key organizations was developed. This secondary data identified the major recipients of foreign assistance from 1998 to 2000 and compared the names mentioned by the Croatian citizens with the names of recipients of public diplomacy assistance before the 2000 elections.

The assumption guiding the research was that organizations originally supported by the public diplomacy efforts from 1998 to 2000 would continue to be leaders in Croatian civil society in 2002 and 2004. The research questions sought to provide data to show if there were lasting outcomes from U.S. and EU public diplomacy efforts to support pro-democracy groups in Croatia from 1998 to 2000.

CROATIAN FINDINGS INFORM AN EVOLVING
PUBLIC DIPLOMACY MINDSHIFT

One of the larger looming questions in public diplomacy and foreign assistance has been about measurement. The effectiveness of assistance, whether agricultural, educational, health, or social development aid, is often difficult to assess. Indeed, it often takes years to see measurable outcomes for the targets of the aid: the citizens living in the recipient countries. Yet this study suggests that there are long-term implications for the outcomes of Western assistance to the civil society sector in Croatia.[19] In fact, the findings from this Croatian study inform an evolving public diplomacy mindshift.

One important finding of the study was to show that by 2002, the NGOs had emerged as independent actors in Croatian civil society efforts. Prior to 1996, Croatians had little experience with NGOs, but less than a decade later, random people on the street were familiar with local civil society organizations. Clearly, the values of NGOs, and an interest in civil society that had been an objective of the donor agencies, appear to have made an impact on Croatians.

Figure 7.1 shows that Croatians had become aware of civil society organizations. The results of the three survey questions suggest that Croatians generally believe that civil society organizations should cooperate with the government to improve the situation in Croatia. Croatians also believe that NGOs are very important for improving the situation in the nation. Yet Croatians do not appear as willing to participate in civil society. There seems to be gap between the perceived value of civil society organizations and an individual's willingness to participate in them.

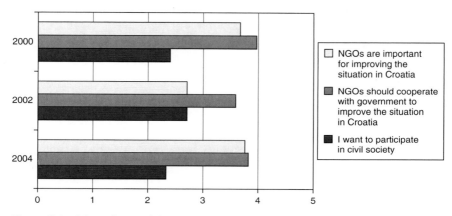

Figure 7.1   Mean Score of Croatians Agreeing to Civil Society Questions

Answers calculated on five-point Likert scales with 1= strongly disagree and 5= strongly agree. Sample: 373 residents of Zagreb in 2000, 401 residents of Zagreb in 2002, and 406 residents of Zagreb in 2004.

The second research question asked which NGOs were the most active, influential, and trusted over the two time periods (2002 and 2004). Figure 7.2 shows that two NGOs—GONG ("a non-partisan citizens' organization founded in 1997 to encourage citizens to actively participate in political processes") and the Croatian chapter of Helsinki Human Rights (HHO) ("dedicated to "support, promote and implement the principles of the Final Act of Conference of Security and Co-operation in Europe, signed in Helsinki in August 1975")[20]—account for 40–50 percent of the total responses to reputational questions.

Although there are thousands of NGOs registered with the Croatian government, only GONG and HHO emerged as national leaders in the 2002 and 2004 open-ended answers of Croatians. GONG "conducts nonpartisan monitoring of the election process, educates citizens about their rights and duties, encourages mutual communication between citizens and their elected representatives, promotes transparency of work within public services, and manages public advocacy campaigns." The Croatian Helsinki Committee for Human Rights (HHO) "support, promote and implement

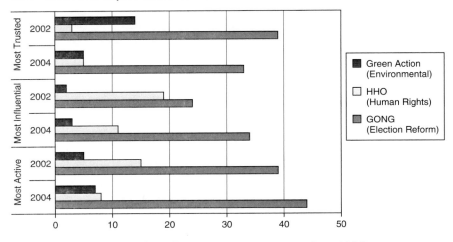

Figure 7.2   Percentage of Total Responses to Statement about NGOs

principles of the UN relating to human issues, and implement in practice the documents of the Council of Europe, support the development of democratic institutions, and promote the rule of law, human rights, and education for these values." HHO also organizes research and documentation regarding human rights in Croatia, and helps victims of violations of human rights and those whose rights are threatened.

To look for the long-term, sustainable impact of public diplomacy efforts, our research team tried to determine if the NGOs that had received significant financial and technical assistance from the United States and the EU before 2000 would continue to be trusted, active, and influential in civil society development as Croatia moved toward EU accession. Although countries do provide aid simply for humanitarian purposes, aid is often linked to outcome objectives and public diplomacy activities. Public diplomacy is measured according to public opinion about the sending country—but it should be measured in terms of the values—and the nature of the cross-national networks. Building social capital can lead to the growth of democratic principles and when this happens, it fulfills public diplomacy goals.

Of the five most frequently mentioned NGOs, three had been recipients of USAID support (GONG, Croatian chapter of HHO, and Green Action) in the past, but no longer required U.S. support to remain viable actors. Croatian NGOs were fulfilling civil society functions on their own and had found donors and supporters to offset large amounts of Western European and American assistance. The organizations were on their way to sustainability. For instance, a look at GONG tells a very compelling story: The year 2000 annual report of GONG indicates that the U.S. government donated over 1.3 million Kuna (about $25,000) to support election-monitoring activities. In 2001, however, donations from the U.S. government totaled only $10,000. By 2002 and 2004, *there were no recorded donations from the American government or any U.S. government-affiliated organization.*

The relatively small amounts of financial and professional support provided to Croatian NGOs in the early years of the political transition were able to build a network of organizations, which in turn created social capital and strengthened the capacity of Croatian aid organizations, and ultimately generated not only short-term but also long-term public diplomacy results.

OUTCOMES OF PUBLIC DIPLOMACY

What conclusions, recommendations, and ethical implications can we draw from the Croatian experience for public relations scholars and public diplomacy practitioners as they work to increase international understanding and build relationships with people across the world? Public diplomacy efforts from the United States and Europe to Croatia attempted to create and sustain a network of organizations that shared similar values. In doing this, foreign governments trained and financially supported election-monitoring organizations, human rights organizations, and environmental groups in Croatia. The data from the last two surveys suggest that even though the public diplomacy efforts that provided money for NGOs were short lived, the NGO partners continued in 2002 and 2004 to be viewed as influential, trusted, and active organizations in Croatian society.

Respondents in the three time periods leaned toward agreement that NGOs were important for improving the nation. Moreover, people surveyed agreed that they wanted NGOs to work with their government to improve the situation in Croatia. The response to the question about people's willingness to participate in civil society showed that only one in five people said that they wanted to participate in civil society organizations. We believe that one in five people off of the street is a reasonable response rate for such a question.[21] The numbers suggest there is a stable interest in civil society that previously did not exist.

Moreover, public diplomacy efforts built sustainable organizations that enact civil society today. Though the creation of sustainable like-minded organizations in other countries may not be a routine public diplomacy activity, it is a valuable outcome of public diplomacy efforts. The data from this study suggest that the NGOs that shared American and European values during the 1998–2000 transition are indeed continuing to advocate for issues that are building the social capital of the nation in 2004. The Croatian organizations were originally selected as partners because of their values: election reform, human rights, environmental protection, and voter education. Indeed, achieving success at building social capital and enacting public diplomacy activities like those in Croatia requires careful selection of like-minded partners.

GONG has evolved to a level that they now train NGOs in other nations in election monitoring and government reform. GONG has conducted training in Albania, Armenia, Belarus, Bosnia and Herzegovina, Bulgaria, Georgia, Iraq, Kosovo, Macedonia, Montenegro, Russia, Serbia, Ukraine, and several Central Asian countries. Such a level of cooperation further extends the initial public diplomacy impact by having GONG build the capacity of other organizations that share its value of election reform and transparency. Because of a modest public diplomacy effort to help the transition in Croatia, a dozen other nations have benefited from the capacity built.

The Croatian chapter of the Helsinki Human Rights organization (HHO) is part of an international network for human rights and cooperates with chapters throughout Europe. Its projects were also once funded by foreign governments, and now the Croatian HHO has worked on such issues as a Croatian Freedom of Information Act (FOIA), refugee returns, public right-to-know legislation, Roma rights, and media reform. All of the issues were topics of the public diplomacy efforts after the Dayton Peace Agreement. They are clearly important elements of civil society development and mirror the values of EU and U.S. public diplomacy activities.

Recommendations for Future Public Diplomacy Efforts

A network approach to public diplomacy is premised on the assumption that inter-organizational relationships should be a foundation for theorizing about and practicing public diplomacy. Public diplomacy efforts, like public relations efforts, are most effective and most ethical when the activities create and extend relationships among people and organizations.

The authors would be remiss not to suggest that there are limitations to this study. First, a causal link cannot be established between the public diplomacy efforts and the attitudes of the Croatians who participated in the survey. Although the research team is confident that there is a link between the public diplomacy efforts and the sustainable capacity of the NGOs, there could be other factors that affected their development. Second, the findings of this research are a "lesson learned" for the U.S. government. Public diplomacy efforts need to extend beyond cultivating an image about the United States. Instead, efforts should be devoted to building relationships among American governmental organizations and local NGOs across the world. The same lessons also extend to other nations and countries interested in public diplomacy. Many cultural/diaspora groups only provide assistance to their own group's members. By branching out, and supporting groups that have a broader civic reach, assistance can build relationships with a broader segment of targeted communities.

In terms of U.S. interests, building relationships with civil society organizations, NGOs, INGOs, etc., creates social capital and enacts the values of participation, democracy, and tolerance the United States hopes to share. If

U.S. public diplomacy professionals want people in other nations to think favorably about the United States, and to understand its ideological and political positions on global issues, then the goal of American public diplomacy should be to help sustain organizations that share U.S. values, including freedom of speech, human rights, and tolerance.

At the same time, public diplomacy scholars and professionals in every nation have more to learn about generating support for civil society initiatives, and more to do in terms of supporting public diplomacy via what might be described as modeled behavior. As mentioned at the beginning of this chapter, many nations put their public diplomacy eggs into an expensive one-way communication basket in an effort to use persuasion and propaganda to build support and trust.

Public diplomacy assistance that empowers local NGOs has long-lasting outcomes. The NGOs listed by the Croatian citizens are no longer dependent on U.S. or even European assistance. They have diverse funding sources and have become localized change agents. This is the real impact of those of who work in public diplomacy: building networks of organizations that share common values leaves a lasting effect that has local and global implications.

NOTES

1. Marya Doerfel and Maureen Taylor, "Network Dynamics of Inter Organizational Cooperation: The Croatian Civil Society Movement," *Communication Monographs, 71* (2004): 373–94; Maureen Taylor and Marya Doerfel, "Another Dimension to Explicating Relationships: Network Theory and Method to Measure Inter-Organizational Linkages," *Public Relations Review, 31* (2005): 121–29.
2. Gifford D. Malone, "Managing Public Diplomacy," *The Washington Quarterly, 8* (1995): 199–213, para 2.
3. Benno Signitzer and Carola Wamser, "Public Diplomacy: A Specific Government Public Relations Function," in *Public Relations Theory 2*, eds. Carl Botan and Vincent Hazelton (Mahwah, NJ: Lawrence Erlbaum, 2006), 435–64.
4. Signitzer and Wamser, *Public Diplomacy*.
5. The President's Emergency Plan for Aids Relief, a multi-part, multi-country effort by the U.S. government to combat AIDS, malaria, TB, infant mortality, and other health-related issues in developing nations is one means to share cultural values and impart international views, without directly interfering in a nation's media or government.
6. Ronald S. Burt, "The Contingent Value of Social Capital," *Administrative Science Quarterly, 42* (1997): 339–65; Doerfel and Taylor, "Network Dynamics"; Robert Putnam, *Bowling Alone: The Collapse and Revival of American Community* (New York: Simon and Shuster, 2000); Elizabeth L. Toth, "Building Public Affairs Theory," in *Public Relations Theory 2*, eds. Carl H. Botan and Vincent Hazelton (Mahwah, NJ: Lawrence Erlbaum, 2006).
7. James S. Coleman, *Foundations of Social Theory* (Cambridge, MA: Harvard University Press), 98.

8. Peter Monge and Noshir Contractor, "Emergence of Communication Networks," in *The New Handbook of Organizational Communication*, eds. Fred Jablin and Linda Putnam (Thousand Oaks, CA: Sage, 2000), 440–502.

9. Doerfel and Taylor, "Network Dynamics"; Taylor and Doerfel, "Building Inter-Organizational Relationships That Build Nations," *Human Communication Research, 29* (2003): 153–81.

10. Richard Holbrooke, *To End a War* (New York: Random House, 1999).

11. Holbrooke, *To End a War*.

12. USAID, *An Evaluation of USAID/OTI Political Transition Grants in Croatia and Bosnia and Herzegovina*, research report published by the United States Agency for International Development (Office of Transition Initiatives, Washington, DC); Susie Jasic, "Monitoring the Vote in Croatia," *Journal of Democracy, 11*, 4 (2000): 159–68.

13. Sarah Mendelson and John Glenn, *The Power and Limits of NGOs* (New York: Columbia University, 2002).

14. Susie Jasic, "Monitoring the Vote in Croatia."

15. Taylor and Doerfel, "Building Relationships"; cf. also Doerfel and Taylor, "Network Dynamics."

16. USAID, *An Evaluation of USAID/OTI Political Transition Grants*.

17. The study piggy-backed on a USAID-funded media project's final evaluation. The researchers also cooperated with the International Research and Exchanges Board (IREX) on a media survey. The surveys were translated into Croatian and then back-translated to improve readability. Members of a national NGO with experience in survey research administered the surveys. The researchers conducted a pilot study to fine-tune the instrument. The surveyors were given detailed instructions, and they collected the surveys during different times of the day in various high-traffic locations around Zagreb. Questions used a five-point Likert scale, and are discussed below.

18. Mendelson and Glenn, *The Power and Limits of NGOs*.

19. The survey was administered to 373 residents of Zagreb in summer 2000; 401 residents of Zagreb in 2002; and 406 residents of Zagreb in 2004. In total, 1,180 surveys were usable, and used for analysis in the longitudinal study. The participant demographics closely matched demographic data on Croatians.

20. For a background on these two organizations, see their websites (http://www.gong.hr) and (http://hho.hr).

21. As a comparison, in the United States, one in four Americans volunteered or participated in civil society activities in 2011 (26.8 percent). See http://www.bls.gov/news.release/volun.nr0.htm.

8 New Frontiers in Relational Public Diplomacy
Collaborative Cultural Initiatives in Peace Building

Tadashi Ogawa

INTRODUCTION

Public diplomacy is often viewed from national lens and focuses solely on the interests and relations of a nation. However, as the world becomes more interconnected on many levels, a more expansive, global view of relations is necessary.

The accelerating interconnectivity of the world, or globalization, challenges diplomacy in three ways. First, domestic policy agendas often become diplomatic issues, as in the case of the environment, energy, economic policies, and human rights issues. One nation, even a superpower, cannot solve such issues without international cooperation. Second, innovations in communication technology, especially social media, have created instant "online public opinions" across borders. Online trans-border voices have the power to change policies of nations, and even to overturn established regimes. National leaders must anticipate how online international opinion will respond to their decisions. Third, in some cases, the social identity crisis caused by globalization can trigger ultra-nationalism, religious fundamentalism, or racism. The spread of these grassroots movements based on negative sentiments can minimize the options of diplomatic policies.

These phenomena reflect the decrease of nation-state governance. The increase of civil-war type conflicts in the post–Cold War era demonstrates the incapacitation of nation-states. To sustain peace and stability in the world of interconnectivity, it is essential for state-actors and non-state actors to positively engage in relationship-building activities and promote interstate governance through collaborative relations.

Since 2004, the Japan Foundation (JF) has intentionally been using cultural initiatives to build and re-build relations among people who have experienced conflict, natural disasters, or war trauma. Projects span from postwar Bosnia–Herzegovina, to Iraq, to Indonesia, to tsunami-affected Tohoku, Japan. During conflicts, people often become physically isolated from the outside world. Cultural initiatives can mitigate isolation through exchanges and empower people through networking and cultural collaboration. The cultural initiatives of the JF provide insight into how relational public diplomacy can be used in peace building.

In this chapter, I discuss the organizational approach and activities of the JF. I highlight in particular "Fostering Peace through Cultural Initiatives" as a manifestation of the relational public diplomacy of Japan.[1] Culture is often blamed as a source of conflict. However, as we will see here, culture can be an important tool for reducing isolation and healing the wounds of trauma caused by conflict and war.

The first section of this chapter provides background and philosophy on relationships that underlie the work of the JF approach. The second section examines the different stages of conflict and the types of cultural initiatives that are appropriate at each stage. The final section of the paper introduces the foundation's initiatives adapted domestically for the reconstruction for the 2011 Great Japan Earthquake and looks at lessons learned.

HISTORICAL PERSPECTIVE: FROM IMAGE BUILDING TO MUTUALITY TO PEACE BUILDING

For those unfamiliar with the JF, it is important to provide some historical background. The JF, the flagship institution for Japanese public diplomacy, was established in 1972 to undertake international cultural exchanges. In the early 1970s, Japan, as a rising economic power, faced the emergence of anti-Japanese sentiments caused by economic over-presence. In addition to these economic issues, the unexpected U.S. secret negotiations with China to change confrontation policy, "the Nixon Shock" in 1972, horrified the Japanese diplomatic community. In order to avoid a repeat of the catastrophic isolation of the 1930s and 1940s, Japan decided to enforce cultural diplomacy, mitigating anti-Japanese emotions and consolidating person-to-person dialogues throughout the world.

When the JF was established in 1972, the Japanese Diet guaranteed its autonomy by allowing the JF to maintain its own funds in order to stabilize its finance. While the JF works in close coordination with the Ministry of Foreign Affairs (MOFA) to carry out public diplomacy goals, the JF is legally guaranteed to maintain a certain level of autonomy from MOFA, in order to play an intermediary role between the government and the private and civil society sectors.

The primary mission of the JF, according to the Japan Foundation Law (1972), was to "deepen other nations' understanding of Japan" by carrying out activities for international cultural exchange. The JF Law also calls for "better mutual understanding among nations" as part of the JF's mission. The Japanese Diet added the supplementary comment, "the Japan Foundation should take into consideration the promotion of the Japanese people's understanding of foreign countries." The Diet resolutions carried a cautionary note that government-sponsored cultural exchange programs had tended to depend on one-way propaganda, and reflected the sensitivity with which Japan understood the relationship between diplomacy and culture.

The Diet resolutions appeared against a lingering historical backdrop of the bitter memories of Imperial Japan's cultural policies in Japanese, East Asian, and Southeast Asian countries. During the prewar and wartime periods, the authorities had strictly controlled cultural expression to the point of eroding freedom of expression domestically, while Japanese intellectuals and cultural leaders were mobilized for the militaristic purpose of producing propaganda for the Japanese colonial and occupied territories.

After the war, Japan sought to establish a new national identity to counter its former image of military power, by including "Culture Nation" (*Bunka Kokka*) and "Peace Nation" (*Heiwa Kokka*) in the national agenda. The successive prime ministers of Japan repeatedly assured Asia, where anti-Japan sentiments prevailed, that Japan would never again seek military hegemony in the region. The best example of this is the Fukuda Doctrine, asserted by Prime Minister Takeo Fukuda in 1977. On a tour of the ASEAN countries, he set out basic principles for Japan's public diplomacy toward Asia, which included consolidation of bilateral and multilateral relations based on mutual trust and "heart-to-heart" understanding with the nations of Southeast Asia.

In 1994, just before the fiftieth anniversary of World War II, Prime Minister Tomiichi Murayama, expanding on the diplomatic approach of the Fukuda Doctrine, spoke of "Peace, Friendship, and Exchange Initiatives." These initiatives included 100 billion-yen dialogue projects and mutual understanding programs based on two goals. The first consisted of historical research and documentation programs focused on promotion of Asian regional joint research in twentieth-century history. The second pillar, future-oriented cultural exchanges, included young Asian artist collaborations and forums for Asian leaders of civil society and public intellectuals. The "Independent Administrative Institution Japan Foundation Law" (2003), revised from the 1972 version, also included "promoting better mutual understanding among nations and contributing to the world in culture and other fields," along with "deepening other nations' understanding of Japan."

The above activities illustrate the traditional use of cultural initiatives in public diplomacy that focuses primarily on the goals of the sponsoring nation to create a better national image among foreign publics. Japan has also moved to fortify its vision of mutuality in public diplomacy by seeking to improve the image of other nations within its own domestic public. This can be seen in the JF's activities in the Middle East.

After 9/11, Japan extended this postwar tradition of mutual understanding in public diplomacy toward the Middle East. In addition to promoting a better understanding of Japan in the region, the JF initiated new projects and grants, such as the Arab Film Festival, the Iraq Theatre, and the Japan–Iraq friendship soccer match to introduce Middle Eastern culture into Japan.

The JF's initial projects sought to provide rehabilitative treatment for the wounded pride of populations in war-damaged countries. The JF gave a travel grant to the Japan Football Association (JFA) to invite the Iraqi national soccer team to play. With this assistance, the JFA organized a match between Japan and Iraq in 2004. Broadcast worldwide, the game was the first international game for the Iraqi soccer team since the Iraq War. The Iraqi people applauded their team's good performance, and the event helped heal their trauma and wounded national pride.

The JF programs with Iraq represented a move to a new frontier: the use of cultural initiatives to heal the wounds of conflict and rebuild relations and peace. In March 2008, Ambassador Kazuo Ogoura, JF president, referred to the important role that culture plays in promoting global peace, improving political governance, and reducing economic disparities: "Clearing up misperceptions and misunderstanding, and dispelling distrust between the disputing parties is essential for peace building."

In April 2008, the JF and Aoyama Gakuin University established the Joint Research Institute for International Peace and Culture (JRIPEC). Working with JRIPEC, Dr. Akiko Fukushima, a Senior Fellow at the JF, organized, coordinated, and further promoted joint research on the new role of culture in peace building. JRIPEC also held a symposium co-organized with the Goethe Institute, conducted field research in East Timor and Aceh, held a series of roundtable discussions with the British Council, and published several reports. JRIPEC research has resulted in changes in JF grant-making policies. Since the 2010 fiscal year, the JF has taken further steps by adding "peace building and culture" to the priority areas for the Intellectual Exchange Conference Grant Program.

The "relational approach" within Japanese public diplomacy practices can also be called "mutual understanding" (*sogo rikai*) or "two-way dialogue" (*sohoko taiwa*), because, in order to build deeper relations, one nation should hear other nations' voices and try to understand other nations more deeply by learning others' language, literature, history, or other social sciences. Combining *sogo rikai* and *sohoko taiwa* is an effective method for communicating and understanding each other by correcting bias of both sides.

MODELS OF CULTURAL INITIATIVES IN CONFLICTS

The challenge of culture-based public diplomacy requires understanding both the positive, constructive use of culture, as well as the negative or potentially divisive and destructive use of culture in human relations. Traditionally in public diplomacy, the focus has been on the positive use of culture.

Analysis of the peace-building roles of "culture"—as broadly defined—cover music, dance, art, and films, as well as thought, philosophy, religion, customs, traditions, and way of life. Culture can create understanding among individuals and facilitate social networking, national integration, and international solidarity through the sharing of common knowledge, emotion, sympathy, and communication. However, culture can also become an excuse for negligence, exclusion, and hostility toward those who exist outside of these commonalities.

Even though a culture or civilization may not crush others, in certain circumstances, culture has been abused consciously or unconsciously as an instrument to foster hostility in political rivalry and economic competition. Some argue that political or economic structures, such as oppression of human rights by authoritarian powers, corrupt administrations or economic divides are integrated with cultural symbols to foster antagonism.

Taking into account these dual functions of culture, the JF categorizes cultural programs within the sphere of three phases:

(1) Cultural initiatives pre-conflict: conflict prevention
(2) Cultural initiatives during conflict: prevention of escalation
(3) Cultural initiatives post-conflict: peacekeeping, reconstruction, consolidation

In practice, it is almost impossible to differentiate clearly among these three phases, because the boundaries are ambiguous. The transitions from one phase to another are not regular as in (1)→(2)→(3)→(1). Reverse processes, as in (3)→(2), have occurred frequently throughout history.

CULTURAL INITIATIVES DURING THE PRE-CONFLICT PHASE

The pre-conflict phase can be differentiated into two sub-phases: "peace-time" and "confrontation." In peacetime, cultural exchanges oriented toward mutual understanding can help prevent conflicts from escalating by enhancing mutual trust and the recognition of others as "partners."

For example, in 2002, Japan and Korea co-hosted the FIFA World Cup. The governments designated 2002 as the Year of Japanese–Korean National Exchange. A wide variety of cultural events, including traditional art performances, pop music concerts, animated and feature film screenings, sports competitions, and people-to-people exchange activities were organized throughout the entire year. The JF played a role in facilitating the flow of information and orchestrating grants for grassroots exchanges. The Year of Japanese-Korean National Exchange was arguably an epoch-making diplomatic decision in the history of bilateral Japan–Korea relations. Prior to 2002, the intense anti-Japan sentiment of Korean society stemming from Japan's colonial rule in Korea had been an obstacle in developing cultural exchanges.

The 2002 Exchange helped established people-to-people networks between Japan and Korea. These multi-track networks extended into Tokyo and Seoul, as well as smaller cities and communities throughout both countries. Before 2002, there was speculation in Korea that Japanese culture would flood the Korean society once the gates were open. Instead, the reverse occurred; a rapid penetration of Korean mass culture flooded Japanese society after 2002. Even more important from a diplomatic standpoint was how the variety of citizens' networks acted to stabilize Japanese–Korean relations when political frictions stagnated formal, governmental diplomatic channels during Japan–Korea territorial disputes in 2005.

In the pre-conflict phase of confrontation, confidence building through the fostering of understanding, tolerance, and trust among opposing parties is essential for easing tensions and preventing escalation to armed conflict. Fukushima shares two examples:

> In 2004, JF invited authors of children's books from the Indian and Pakistani sides of Kashmir to come together in Nepal and write a picture book about their home region that could be enjoyed by children on both sides. Despite the sharp difference in their perspectives, the authors cooperated together produce a single book that was read by children on both the Indian and Pakistani sides of Kashmir. This instilled an awareness of their common foundations."[2]
>
> In 2004 and 2005, JF gave a grant to the Peace Kids Soccer project organized by a Japanese NPO. Israeli and Palestinian children played goodwill soccer matches in which each team was comprised of both nationalities. The children also took part in musical and other cultural activities. They became friends and continued to exchange letters and e-mails after their return home.

CULTURAL INITIATIVES IN THE CONFLICT PHASE

Practical experience suggests that once a conflict breaks out, especially in the early stages, physical or military power can be a determining factor in resolving it. In such situations, the role of culture in peace building is unavoidably limited. Even so, cultural exchange can enhance the educational activities in conflict areas and facilitate introduction of conflict-area culture from conflict to other regions.

In conflict areas, local people can become isolated from the outside world. In the midst of an ongoing conflict, communication and public transportation can shut down, while lack of media coverage robs those affected of a voice to inform the world of their plight. In such desperate situations, people become traumatized, frustrated, and hostile toward the outside world, a response that exacerbates rather than alleviates the conflict. One of the objectives of cultural exchange, pointed out Ambassador Ogoura, is to protect people in conflict areas from psychological and cultural isolation by providing links between them and outside societies.

One example was when Japan invited the Iraqi drama troupe Al-Murwass Folklore and Modern Arts Group to Japan for a performance in October 2004. Even though the primary purpose was to promote better understanding of Iraq among the Japanese people, the experience also helped to provide a voice for the Iraqis. Their performance, titled "A Message Carried by Ship," was based on folk dance and music from the era of the Arabian Nights tales in the Basra region of southern Iraq. At the time, despite the U.S. declaration of an end to major combat in Iraq, skirmishes continued, along with terrorist activity. The situation remained so dangerous that one of Al-Murwass's performers was killed in a blast while they were rehearsing their performances planned for Japan. The performances of the twenty-member Al-Murwass troupe in Tokyo, Osaka, and Nagoya provided the Iraqi performers the opportunity to share with their audiences the realities in Baghdad and to convey the difficulties they had faced under the Saddam Hussein regime and the U.S.-initiated war in 2003. The performers also helped to dispel the general perception in Japan that art and entertainment had not survived in chaos-ridden Iraq. As one Al-Murwass member said, "The collapse of the Hussein administration liberated artists, allowing them to perform creative activities as they wished. It also allowed them to go overseas freely and see different types of art." I believe this project affected the people of Iraq and enabled them to understand that Japan, and the world, will never abandon them.

CULTURAL INITIATIVES IN THE POST-CONFLICT PHASE

The post-conflict phase can be divided into two sub-phases: peacekeeping and reconstruction. The JF identified four roles that cultural exchange can play in peace building during the post-conflict phase: facilitation of reconciliation, mental healing, restoration of cultural and ethnic pride, and passing down reminders of the impact and anguish of conflict.

Facilitation of Reconciliation

One of the best examples of "facilitation of reconciliation" is a conductor's challenge to establish the Balkan Chamber Orchestra. Maestro Toshio Yanagisawa, who had survived on his own in conflict-ridden Kosovo, dreamed of establishing a chamber orchestra consisting of musicians from the various ethnic groups that had strong antagonistic feelings against each other. In 2007, he managed to establish the Balkan Chamber Orchestra, whose members are Macedonians, Albanians, and Serbians. The orchestra sought to build trust among the ethnic communities toward greater prosperity for all through music. The JF and UNDP supported their concert in Kosovo.

Bunji Yokomichi, JF Director in the Performing Arts section, discussed genesis of this project during the JF/Goethe Institute bilateral meeting on

Fostering Peace through Cultural Initiatives. Yokomichi confessed that the JF Performing Arts section did not have any concrete image of the concept for "Fostering Peace through Cultural Initiatives" when they met Maestro Yanagisawa in 2007. However, impressed by the maestro's bravery and passion, they decided to support his activities as part of the JF's peace-building projects.

Yokomichi said he learned two things through this project. First, Maestro Yanagisawa never took sides with any ethnic group represented by the individual musicians in the orchestra and insisted that there should be no political border between musicians. He was well aware that it would be impossible to integrate cultures or reconcile the ethnic differences through one single music project. However, without Maestro Yanagisawa's persistent efforts, nothing would have been accomplished. In the end, the participating members fully appreciated his eagerness and the significance of this project and were willing to take personal risks to see it through. Second, the case still stands as a reminder of how one person—in this case a Japanese man with no conflicting interests related to the ethnic rivalries in the Balkan region—can effectively facilitate interethnic collaboration in a conflict-ridden area.

The key point of Yokomichi's observations about the success of the project is importance of neutrality, which in case of the Balkan Chamber Orchestra existed on the national and personal level. Japan had relatively few political or military commitments to the Balkans. Maestro Yanagisawa himself had no political intentions in connection with the Balkan issues. As a project director, Maestro Yanagisawa consistently took an apolitical position among the various ethnic entities.

This neutrality was also situational and contextual. It is very important to analyze the local situation and context of the project to determine who can function as facilitators in reconciliation before beginning to put peace-building cultural initiatives into action. For the JF, it was necessary to be keenly aware of our limits as external actors in this cultural work. Ronald Graetz, secretary general of the Institute of Foreign Cultural Relations in Germany, noted the promise and limitations of post-conflict contexts: "In extremely polarized societies, frequently, the most constructive role can simply be the creation of forums in which people from different camps can learn and move towards mutual understanding. Sometimes the best that we can do is simply to moderate and provide a safe space ensuring mutual respect."[3]

Mental Healing

In terms of mental healing, cultural initiatives can provide much to people experiencing trauma in the midst of conflict that political or economic assistance cannot address. This is especially true for children who have psychological damage from prolonged conflict. This type of trauma can stay with them throughout their lifetime. Within this context, the JF organized a theater workshop for children in Aceh in order to empower them through psychological care based on artistic methods.

In August 2005, the Free Aceh Movement (GAM) and the Indonesian Armed Forces (ABRI) agreed to end more than thirty years of conflict. Less than a year earlier, areas of Aceh had been severely damaged by the 2004 an earthquake and a tsunami. The international community devoted greater attention to the areas devastated by these natural disasters, and an imbalance in foreign assistance occurred, in which the conflict-damaged areas were barely touched by aid.

In April 2007, the JF sent two veteran Japanese theatrical arts experts to organize a theater workshop in Salley Valley near Banda Aceh. Local children and adults participated in the workshop co-organized by the JF and Komunitas Tikar Pandan, an Aceh-based NGO. The organizers selected ten middle and high school students as workshop participants from the three regencies most devastated by the conflict: Pidie, North Aceh, and Central Aceh. The youth who participated in the program had experienced the deaths of their parents or relatives at the hands of pro-separatist GAM guerrillas or anti-separatist ABRI forces.

For the theater workshop, the participants were randomly divided into groups, irrespective of their origins and backgrounds. The groups played theatrical games, wrote poetry, composed impromptu music pieces, or engaged in other forms of self-expression. At the end of the workshop, the children performed their original plays in front of their guardians at the Aceh Community Center in Banda Aceh.[4]

According to the facilitator, Mr. Azhari, a playwright, the people most affected by the long-lasting conflict were children and women, who had become isolated politically, economically, socially, or culturally from the outside world and the international community. He explained the effects of the workshop within that context:

> The workshop provided the children and their parents with the opportunity to see aspects of Japan, a part of the outside world they had never experienced previously, thus opening up a new world of music, dance, and dialogue for them. This event lessened the sense of isolation experienced by the Acehnese and allowed the children, in particular, to embrace hope for the future. As a result, the children became more willing to work for their villages and Aceh as a whole.[5]

After the workshop, these Acehnese young people became more committed to social-welfare activities after learning how to express their emotions and ambitions through art. As Mr. Azhari explains:

> The workshop allowed the Acehnese children to heal some of the psychological wounds inflicted by the prolonged struggle for autonomy

independence by learning how to forgive. Since the workshop, some of them have joined local children's theater troupes, some have landed jobs with local administrative offices, and others have begun to raise goats for a living.[6]

As follow-up to the 2007 Theater Workshop for Children in Aceh, the JF and the NGO Komunitas Tikar Pandan organized the Aceh Children Conference in 2008 and a second Theater Workshop for Children in Aceh in 2010. The participants of the 2007 workshop acted as assistant facilitators for the 2010 workshop.

Restoring Cultural and Ethnic Pride

The JF considers cultural and ethnic pride a sphere in which international cultural cooperation can make great contributions. Abundant examples worldwide show how conflicts devastate or destroy precious national treasures, tangible and intangible cultural property, and social infrastructures, which have long nurtured the maintenance of historical and cultural heritage.

In terms of psychological impact, the "losers" in any conflict often experience the shock of defeat and an ensuing loss of dignity, as well as feelings of humiliation, frustration, and hostility toward the victor. Mitigating these emotions and reestablishing a sound and healthy individual and national identity can be attained by the victor's efforts to restore and reconstruct cultural and ethnic traditions, which can help create constructive relations with the isolated party.

One example of such an approach was seen in the cultural policy of the U.S. Military Government for Okinawa, which lasted from 1945 after the Battle of Okinawa until 1972, when control reverted to Japan. Encouraging local Okinawa traditional culture may be one of the most successful approaches in U.S. public diplomacy toward East Asia. Even after sixty years, the people of Okinawa continue to appreciate its impact. Okinawa cultural leaders have gone on record saying that the traditional Okinawa music and dance performance held by the U.S. Military Government in the refugee camps were like flames of hope to the desperate people who had lost family and property during the battle of Okinawa. Throughout its twenty-seven-year occupation of Okinawa, the U.S. Military Government undertook various public diplomacy activities in Okinawa, including the founding of the University of Ryukyus.

The JF project in Afghanistan is another strong example. Before the Taliban attack in 1996, the Tajiki village of Istalif north of Kabul had been well known for its centuries-old traditional ceramic industry. The Taliban completely destroyed all houses and kilns in the village, and sent the villagers fleeing to Pakistan and Iran. Most of the villagers did not return until after the collapse of the Taliban regime. Upon returning, they immediately began trying to revive the local ceramic tradition. However, this was not an easy task, because the skilled ceramists had fled to other villages or regions.

In 2005, the JF invited thirteen ceramists from Istalif to Japan. They were all heirs to the family pottery enterprises that had accounted for one-third of the pottery previously produced in Istalif. The group visited various ceramic factories in Japan, where they talked to Japanese ceramists and learned about Japanese ceramic art techniques and skills. The Afghan NGO program coordinator, Sayed Mujib Ahmad L'mar, spoke of the extended benefits of the program beyond the participants: "Cultural reconstruction is very important. Our tour in Japan has reminded us anew of the importance of that perspective."[7]

Sharing Reminders of the Impact and Anguish of Conflict

Culture can also play a role in helping survivors and witnesses share their memories and emotions. According to Ambassador Ogoura, many people who have suffered through periods of conflict are reluctant to talk about their ordeals. Cultural activities can provide ways to help these people acknowledge the impact and anguish of conflict and to express their sorrow, which eases the process of reconciliation and the prevention of future conflicts.

In Japan, peace museums play important roles in cultural exchange for the sake of "passing down reminders of the impact and anguish of conflict." The JF frequently invites foreign guests to visit the museums at the Hiroshima Peace Memorial and the Okinawa Peace Memorial. Both museums are meant to help foreign visitors and Japan's future generations understand the value of peace by reminders of the tragic experiences originating from conflicts. The Okinawa Prefectural Peace Memorial Museum explains its mission in the following way:

> The "Okinawan Heart" is a human response that respects personal dignity above all else, rejects any acts related to war, and truly cherishes culture, which is a supreme expression of humanity. In order that we may mourn for those who perished during the war, pass on to future generations the historic lessons of the Battle of Okinawa, convey our messages to the peoples of the world and thereby contribute to establishing permanent peace, we have hereby established the Okinawa Prefectural Peace Memorial Museum to display the whole range of the individual war experiences of the people in this prefecture.

LESSONS LEARNED: JF DOMESTIC CULTURAL INITIATIVES

In March 11, 2011 (now popularly referred to as 3/11), an earthquake with an unprecedented magnitude of 9.0, known as the Great East Japan Earthquake, hit the east coast of Japan, followed by a massive tsunami, presenting the country with its toughest challenge since the end of World War II. As many as 20,000 people were killed or declared missing, while 6,000 people were injured. These natural disasters led to damage to nuclear power plants that forced hundreds of thousands of people to evacuate their homes.

In remarks, which in hindsight seem prophetic, Tsuyoshi Takahashi, an executive board member of the JF, made a keynote speech at the JF/Goethe Institute Joint Meeting in Sarajevo in May 2010, a year before the earthquake and tsunami, in which he pointed out that public diplomacy cultural initiatives can make significant contributions to restoration efforts after major disasters caused by human conflicts or nature:

> I would like to point out here, that Aceh, in particular, has taught us that public diplomacy culture-based approaches and tools can contribute to the alleviation of trauma after natural disasters, such as earthquakes and tsunamis, which often result in volatile human emotions and reactions that could give rise to ethnic and other social disturbances. Japan's own experience with demagogue-agitated uprisings against ethnic minorities immediately after the Great Kanto Earthquake in 1923 and again, on a smaller scale, after the Hanshin Awaji Earthquake in 1995, show us the importance of preventive cultural initiatives in disaster-ridden areas. In this context, the Japan Foundation facilitated dialogues among the people of Kobe, New Orleans (USA), and Sichuan Province (China). We will continue to execute similar initiatives in other parts of the world when disasters occur.

After 3/11, the JF was instrumental in urging initiatives for developing new projects, based on its accumulated knowledge and practice in "fostering peace through cultural initiatives." In July 2011, four months after the disaster, the JF began requesting proposals for bilateral or multilateral collaborative research projects and dialogue projects related to such themes as disaster prevention and disaster recovery.

The Great East Japan Earthquake drastically changed the external environment of Japan's public diplomacy. Before 3/11, as the Japanese government struggled to reduce its budget due to funding constraints, the JF saw its budget allocation drop by about 20% from 2004 to 2010. Japan's overseas presence had begun to wane, while China, India, and Korea began emerging economically and culturally. The situation was such that the Japanese media lamented that U.S.–Japan relations had gone from "Japan bashing" to "Japan passing" to "Japan nothing." However, immediately after 3/11, global media coverage and detailed analysis on Japan rose sharply. Renewed debate on such critical issues as disaster prevention, nuclear governance for safety, and energy policy garnered worldwide attention. The JF recognized the need to promote similar cross-border discussions and debates in order to empower Japan and foster mutual understanding with the global community:

In that context, JF's request for proposals for its initiative on "International Cooperation in Disaster Recovery and Disaster Prevention in the Global Context" became even more significant. Examples of themes being submitted include: analyses of Post-3/11 Japanese politics, economy, society and culture; roles of media in disaster reporting; global sharing of disaster experience; education and culture programs for disaster prevention; empowerment of disaster victims, especially participatory method by victims themselves.

To that end, the JF has adapted some ideas from "fostering peace through cultural initiatives," such as empowering disaster victims. The JF has learned that cultural exchange, as well as sending relief or donations to earthquake victims, can play a significant role in healing hearts and empowering minds by providing opportunities to express emotion and hope, while sharing their experiences with the global community and the younger generation. Several examples are illustrative of this concept.

One example is the JET (Japan Exchange and Teaching) Memorial Invitation Program for U.S. High School Students. In this program, two American JET participants working as assistant language teachers, Taylor Anderson and Montgomery Dickson, lost their lives in the tsunami-hit prefectures of Miyagi and Iwate. To commemorate their devotion, the JF invited thirty-two U.S. high school students to Japan in July 2011. The students received intensive Japanese-language training at the JF language training center, and were able to speak with Japanese high school students in various places, including Iwate.

Another example is the Kuromori Kagura performance in Russia. In order to convey Japan's "never-give-up" spirit to the world and to help remind survivors of disasters of their self-worth through sharing their local culture with appreciative international audiences, the JF now sends cultural missions from disaster-ridden areas to perform outside the country. As a part of these efforts, the JF organized the first-ever performance in Russia of Kuromori Kagura, a traditional form of sacred dance and music passed down through generations in Miyako, Rikuchu Coastal Region, Iwate Prefecture. Kagura has long functioned as a symbolic ritual ceremony reflecting God's blessing of community unity and local pride in the villages of Rikuchu. During the 2011 tsunami, numerous shrines and religious facilities in Rikuchu were swept away, while the Kuromori Kagura artifacts miraculously escaped serious harm.

CONCLUSION

Cultural connections to human emotion make emotion a powerful force in human relations. Through the presentation of some of the JF's cultural initiative projects, this chapter has shown how culture is communicated and used in relational public diplomacy.

Some may question why the JF engages in this work, when it seems to seek more than solely promoting Japan's image. The JF helps to promote better understanding of other developing nations (Asia and the Middle East). These projects do not seem relevant to Japan's national interest. Some ask whether there are benefits to this policy.

Certainly, there are. One-way-only public diplomacy from developed nations to developing nations, in some cases of lacks in communication processes, exacerbates tensions in relationships. In such cases, targeted developing nations tend to accumulate frustrations over a situation in which their voice is not heard or their sense of self-pride is not respected. Their frustrations erode the credibility of public diplomacy and often turn into hostility toward sponsoring developed nations.

To put it in another way, to promote better understanding of developing nations is to establish a well-balanced flow of culture and pride between developed nations and developing nations. Sensitivity to this balance helps promote mutual understanding by assisting developing nations to express their cultural messages to developed nations. It helps to restore sound self-worth and pride among developing nations. The consequence of mutual understanding is to gain credibility with two-way public diplomacy, to diminish criticism (such as "cultural invasion" or "cultural colonialism") and to promote national images in sponsoring nations.

For example, two-way cultural exchanges and Official Development Assistance (ODA) diplomacy resulted in a steady decline of anti-Japan perceptions in Southeast Asia from the 1970s into the 1990s. A public poll conducted by the Japanese Foreign Ministry in 2008 showed that more than 90% of the ASEAN public embraced a positive image of Japan.

Finally, based on the experiences of the JF shared in this piece, I would like to emphasize that relational public diplomacy has great potential to mitigate the isolation of people affected by conflict or disaster and to empower them through people-to-people networking and cultural collaboration. Rethinking cultural initiatives and relationship building, we take a step forward toward new frontiers in public diplomacy.

NOTES

1. For background, see The Japan Foundation, *The Role of Cultural Initiatives in Peace Building*, Tokyo, 2008; The Japan Foundation, *Conference Report* "*Fostering Peace through Cultural Initiatives: Perspectives from Japan and Germany*," Tokyo, 2009; Fukushima Akiko, ed., *Heiwa no tameno Bunka Initiative no Yakuwari* [Fostering Peace through Cultural Initiatives: Perspectives] (Tokyo: Joint Research Institute for International Peace and Culture (JRIPEC), 2009); and Fukushima Akiko, ed., *Culture, Conflict and Peace: Fostering Peace through Cultural Initiatives: Perspectives* (Tokyo: Joint Research Institute for International Peace and Culture (JRIPEC), 2010).

2. Dr. Fukushima, quoted in "The Roles of Cultural Activities in Peace Building," in *Heiwa no tameno Bunka Initiative no Yakuwari* [Fostering Peace through Cultural Initiatives: Perspectives], ed. Fukushima Akiko (Tokyo: Joint Research Institute for International Peace and Culture (JRIPEC), 2009).
3. Ronald Graetz, secretary general of the Institute of Foreign Cultural Relations, Germany, quoted in The Japan Foundation & the Goethe Institute, *Fostering Peace through Cultural Initiatives: Joint Project of the Goethe Institute and the Japan Foundation*, Sarajevo Session, May 28–29, 2010.
4. Japan Foundation leaflet for the event, titled "The Roles of Cultural Activities in Peace Building," n.d.
5. Japan Foundation leaflet for the event, titled "The Roles of Cultural Activities in Peace Building," n.d.
6. Japan Foundation leaflet for the event, titled "The Roles of Cultural Activities in Peace Building," n.d.
7. Japan Foundation, *The Role of Cultural Initiatives*.

9 The Relational Paradigm and Sustained Dialogue

Harold H. Saunders

INTRODUCTION

For at least three generations, the mantra of U.S. political science has been "politics is about power"—with power defined as the capacity to coerce or control. Among those who study and teach international relations, the prevailing paradigm has been the so-called "realist" paradigm—the "power politics model." Both are essentially state centered, or at least focused on institutions that are seen as possessing power, in the sense of playing a role in some way to influence the course of events.

Yet, these traditional paradigms are insufficient because they do not take advantage of a wealth of resources. I have even gone so far as to say that they are immoral because they leave out 99-plus percent of the world's people.

The greatest untapped resources for meeting the challenges of our time are the energies and capacities of citizens outside government. The vehicles for putting those energies and capacities to work in the public interest are the relationships, associations—to use Alexis de Tocqueville's word—or networks that citizens outside government form for that purpose. To capture these capacities, we need a paradigm for the study and practice of politics large enough to reach beyond states and their institutions to embrace whole bodies politic—citizens both inside and outside government.

This chapter introduces the "Relational Paradigm" and "Sustained Dialogue" as frameworks for capturing the capacity of citizens. These relational tools grew out of my intensive involvement in the Arab–Israeli peace process during the 1970s, and the Cold War dialogues of the 1980s. The tools are particularly apt for helping participants work through conflictive relationships. In this chapter, I first share some of the lessons from these two decades of experience in mediation and dialogue. I then introduce the components of the Relational Paradigm and the stages of the Sustained Dialogue System's dialogue process. I conclude with some final thoughts on the nature of relationships.

LESSONS FROM THE ARAB–ISRAELI PEACE PROCESS

After the 1973 Arab–Israeli war, President Richard Nixon and Secretary of State Henry Kissinger decided to make a major effort to move this protracted conflict toward peace. Kissinger with a small team of four diplomats engaged in an intensive mediation, which the journalists traveling with us dubbed "shuttle diplomacy," as we flew back and forth between Israel and its neighbors, producing three interim agreements in 1974–1975. The effort continued in the Carter administration and produced the Camp David accords in 1978 and the Egyptian–Israeli peace treaty in 1979. From this experience, I learned four lessons.

First, *the power of a continuous political process to transform relationships.* The secretary of state was in the Middle East or foreign ministers of the parties to the Arab–Israeli conflict were in Washington every other month. When we were in the Middle East, we would meet with each of the negotiating parties daily to advance negotiating texts or to define the outlines of an approach to the next agreement. The process was continuous, and it was relentless. When one interim agreement was signed, we moved almost immediately to the next. No agreement was an end in itself; it was the stepping-stone to the next. The strategy was that each agreement would make it possible to negotiate tomorrow what it was not possible to negotiate yesterday.

Second, *the importance of the human dimension of conflict.* One could not deal with the survivors of the Nazi Holocaust in Israel, or the Palestinians who had lost their homes in 1948 when the State of Israel was established, or the Arabs who had suffered the humiliation of defeat in four wars, without recognizing the psychological dimension of the conflict. When Egyptian president Anwar al-Sadat flew to Israel in November 1977—the first Arab leader to set foot in the State of Israel—he did not go to negotiate; he recognized that the real obstacle to movement in negotiations was the deep fear of Israeli citizens that no Arab leader would ever accept a Jewish state in the Middle East. Or, on the Israeli–Palestinian front, one Israeli described the conflict as an "intercommunal" conflict, not an international one.

Third, *the need to think of whole bodies politic rather than only of what governments do.* When we first began the shuttle negotiations, we called what we were doing the "negotiating process." As one agreement followed another, we recognized that each agreement scrupulously implemented was not only moving troops or boundaries, but was beginning to change the political environment. Citizens outside government began to recognize that relationships were beginning to change and to ask themselves whether peace might be possible. We began to call what we were doing "the peace process."

The purpose of Sadat's visit to Jerusalem in November 1977, as I have said, was not to negotiate with the Israeli government but to personify a message to the Israeli people that Egypt was prepared to make peace. I have often felt that, as a result of his visit, the people of Israel "gave permission" to their government to negotiate peace with Egypt.

I am not sure I used the word *relationship* then. But I am sure from a near-verbatim record of the meeting that my first words in 1982 when I participated in founding a Soviet–U.S. task force for dialogue were: "Our purpose in examining Soviet–U.S. interactions in conflicts beyond our borders—conflicts where we competed through proxies as in the Arab–Israeli conflict or in Afghanistan—is to see what we might learn about the 'central' or 'overall' Soviet–U.S. *relationship.*"

Fourth, *the importance of recognizing that a political process unfolds in stages.* During my last year in government, as we turned our attention from the Egyptian–Israeli Peace Treaty to the Israeli–Palestinian conflict, I began to see the importance of unfolding stages. Some challenges must be met before others can be tackled. I particularly recognized, at least in the back of my mind, the importance of the pre-negotiation stage.

At Camp David in September 1978, Egypt and Israel had agreed that, as soon as the Egyptian–Israeli Peace Treaty was signed, the Palestinian issue would move to the top of the agenda. As it did, I realized how different the challenge was. During the shuttles and the negotiation of the Egyptian–Israeli Peace Treaty, the world had come to see the peace process as a series of negotiations, with diplomats meeting to negotiate texts of agreements, soldiers meeting to redraw lines on the map and to schedule the redeployment of troops, and leaders meeting to sign agreements. Journalists began asking when the Israeli–Palestinian negotiations would begin. The answer was, "Not soon. These parties don't formally recognize each other's existence."

After I left government in January 1981, the first thing I wrote was a review of Roger Fisher and William Ury's now classic book, *Getting to Yes.* My message was: This is an outstanding compendium of common sense about principled interest-based negotiation, but it may sometimes be more difficult to get people to the table than it is to get them to "yes" after they get there.

When I wrote my book on the Arab–Israeli peace process in 1985, *The Other Walls: The Politics of the Arab–Israeli Peace Process,* I described it as a political process unfolding through five stages, beginning with a pre-negotiation stage. These stages would later evolve into what I call the dialogue process of the Sustained Dialogue System.

LESSONS FROM THE DARTMOUTH CONFERENCE

While the Arab–Israeli peace process helped lay a foundation for my thinking about the relational aspects of the political process, my ideas were further developed by my participation in the Dartmouth Conference.

When I left government in 1981, before the year was out, I had attended my first meeting of the Dartmouth Conference, the longest continuous dialogue between American and Soviet citizens. It began in 1960 when Norman Cousins, then editor of the *Saturday Review of Literature*, who out of concern for preventing nuclear war proposed to President Dwight Eisenhower that a citizens' channel of communication between the super-powers be established to be available if government relations soured. The president approved, as, we learned only much later, did Chairman Nikita Khrushchev. For the first twenty years, the group met on the average every two years in large plenaries. In 1981—my first meeting—leaders decided to create two task forces to meet every six months between plenaries. One focused on arms control and deployments. The other, as noted above, focused on Soviet–U.S. interaction in regional conflicts—those conflicts in which the superpowers interacted through local proxies. I was asked to co-chair the Regional Conflicts Task Force with Yevgeny Primakov, who after the dissolution of the Soviet Union in 1991 became foreign minister, then prime minister of the new Russia. Together in the 1980s, we co-chaired eighteen meetings of the task force. As of this writing, 135 meetings of three or more days have been held under the Dartmouth umbrella.

In the Dartmouth Conference Regional Conflicts Task Force in its first three years, 1982–1985, I learned four lessons from the relatively new experience of bringing the same people back together over and over again in nonofficial dialogue. This was not just a sequence of meetings; it was a political process that changed the participants.

The first lesson was the opportunity to create a cumulative agenda. Questions left hanging at the end of one meeting could be studied between meetings and become the agenda for the next. A second lesson was the opportunity to develop a common body of knowledge—not just what positions were, but why. A third lesson was that we learned to talk analytically rather than polemically. This was the beginning of genuine dialogue. Fourth, we learned to solve problems together. As a vehicle, we developed the political scenario.

The more we thought about the role of citizens in the conduct of a relationship between two large bodies politic, the clearer it became to me that the traditional state-centered academic paradigm for the study and practice of politics—the so-called realist paradigm or power politics model—was not large enough to allow room for citizens.

In 1986–1987, with one of the first grants from the new U.S. Institute of Peace and in my role as an associate of the Kettering Foundation, I wrote a monograph articulating a new paradigm that I eventually called the relational paradigm: a political process of continuous interaction between clusters of citizens in whole bodies politic across permeable borders. This formulation provided a place for thinking about citizens' politics and the overall relationships between countries.

In 1989–1991, there were three further conceptual breakthroughs. First, I wrote a carefully defined concept of relationship and used it widely as an analytical framework. Second, I began to think of our dialogue experience in the Dartmouth Regional Conflicts Task Force as an experience that had unfolded through a discernable pattern of interaction that could be seen as stages. In 1990, I presented this idea in a paper titled "Thinking in Stages" at the annual conference of the International Society of Political Psychology.

In 1991, I first used the name a "public peace process" in the title of an agreed paper that came out of a week-long dialogue among senior Israelis and Palestinians. I used "public" deliberately to contrast our dialogue to the official peace process. That became the title of the first published article on the process in 1993. Only later, in 1999, did I begin using *Sustained Dialogue*. But my original sense of the power of a continuous *political process* remained central to my thinking.

In 1992 after the dissolution of the Soviet Union, we in the Dartmouth Regional Conflicts Task Force asked ourselves, "What should we do now?" We made three decisions. First, we decided we would conceptualize the process of dialogue we had learned together. Within the task force, we were then calling it "the Dartmouth process." I was well along in the conceptualization, and we published the five-stage process in Harvard's *Negotiation Journal* in March 1993.

Second, we would apply that process in one of the conflicts that had broken out on the territory of the former Soviet Union. Three American and three Russian members of the task force were deputized to explore the possibility of starting a dialogue among combatants in the vicious civil war that had broken out in the former Soviet republic of Tajikistan after independence, over who would govern the country and how. This might be said to have been the first Russian–American citizens' peacemaking mission.

Third, we decided that our task force would focus on the new Russia–U.S. relationship. As our Russian colleagues talked with more than a hundred Tajikistanis, they discovered the convening power of the Dartmouth Conference. They reported that the Tajiks would not come to a Russian meeting, or to an American meeting. But they would accept an invitation from an "international movement"—the way they characterized the Dartmouth Conference.

Between 1994 and 1999, as we experienced the intensity of the Inter-Tajik Dialogue within the Framework of the Dartmouth Conference, as the Tajiks named it, I wrote my book on the dialogue process, revising it after every meeting. This dialogue was the first full test of the five-stage process. *A Public Peace Process: Sustained Dialogue to Transform Racial and Ethnic Conflicts* was published in 1999. Indeed, *sustained* seemed the defining characteristic for a dialogue that, by that time, had held some three dozen meetings of the Dartmouth Task Force and twenty meetings of the Tajik dialogue.

In 1999, when I was a trustee at Princeton University, several students went to the dean of student life to say: "Students of color are not happy on this campus. They feel marginalized. That's wrong. We want to do something about it." The dean sent them to talk with me. The result was the first use of Sustained Dialogue on a university campus. In 2002, we incorporated the International Institute for Sustained Dialogue (IISD). In 2003, what is now the Sustained Dialogue Campus Network was formed as a program within IISD.

In 2005, *Politics Is about Relationship* defined, elaborated, and presented the call for a new paradigm for the study and practice of politics—the relational paradigm. It was presented in the context of a changing worldview that evolved through the twentieth century as citizens began to absorb the import of dramatically changing thinking in the physical and life sciences. As physicist David Bohm, who spent his later years writing and teaching on dialogue, called this post-Newtonian worldview, "A Proper World View, Appropriate for Its Time."[1]

THE RELATIONAL PARADIGM

In our complex and interdependent world, we must think of whole bodies politic in which governments plus citizens as political actors along with nongovernmental political and economic institutions all engage simultaneously. It is not realistic to focus exclusively on states, governments, and institutions or on power defined only in their terms. The human dimension is as at least as important as the institutional or the material. The relationships people form generate their own kinds of power.

My counter to the traditional paradigms is the "relational paradigm." The relational paradigm assumes that politics is a cumulative, multilevel, open-ended process of continuous interaction among significant clusters of citizens in and out of government and the relationships they form to solve public problems in whole bodies politic across permeable boundaries either within or between groups, communities, or countries. The relational paradigm is based on six propositions.

To begin, *we must first see in a body politic a political process of continuous interaction among continuously shifting complexes of citizens, in and out of government, across permeable boundaries, not just a collection of institutions.* Traditionally, the focus has been on intuitions such as the government, political parties, lobbies, or media. The relational paradigm shifts focus to the citizens. Problems and functions draw people together in different, constantly changing interactions. Imagine a continuously shifting kaleidoscope with groups of citizens interacting around common concerns. Each values a number of personal, professional, identity, religious, cultural, family, and other interests. Rather than defining the clusters of citizens in terms of structures, the boundaries are more permeable. Each group is defined only by the pattern created by individuals' interactions. As these clusters of citizens interact, they form networks. We can think of the body politic as the kaleidoscope in which these continuously changing groups interact.

Second, *we must shift our focus from action and reaction to interaction. We are talking about the permeability of boundaries, both of groups and of human beings.* Interaction restores the human dimension to the practice and analysis of politics. Fundamental to interaction is a process of internalizing or integrating the words and actions of another into our picture of the other. Even in distant hostile relationships, both parties develop pictures in their minds about how the other will act. Some of those pictures are misperceptions that can be changed, but for a time they are internalized as the picture of reality from which each acts. Through interaction, one person or group learns about another and internalizes who that other is, what the other needs, how the other conducts interactions, what sensitivities, strengths, or vulnerabilities the other shows, what resources the other draws on. The relationship changes as each conducts the process of interaction that becomes increasingly complex on many levels. As parties grow closer, they interact more directly. They listen, interpret, empathize, understand, respect, agree, or disagree. As they respond to each other in fuller knowledge and feeling, they do not just act and react—they interact. This interaction may not always produce collaborative relationships, but it does produce deeper relationships, whether constructive or distrustful.

Third, *we must focus on the process of interaction.* A process is a progression of steps in which each one includes what has gone before; it is seen as contributing to the next, and it may draw into its orbit a broadening range of resources. It is cumulative. It is open-ended because each step may create new conditions and unforeseen opportunities. The emphasis on a multilevel process of continuous *inter*action among human beings contrasts to the traditional focus on a linear sequence of actions and reactions among institutions as in a chess game. What is important are the interplay and interpenetration between entities—not just the action by one on another.

Though I speak of a "progression," that progression is not only linear; as circumstances evolve, we may circle back to revisit the past and reshape lessons we learn from it. In my work, I observed that citizens in relationships can develop their own political processes for tackling problems systematically. I further witnessed that these political processes could generate the power to solve these problems. Citizens generate power by building relationships. As they involve others, they broaden their base of power.

Fourth, to capture this process of continuous interaction, I have used the human word *relationship.* The concept of relationship provides a tool for analyzing, conducting, and influencing this process of continuous interaction within and among clusters or associations of citizens that make up a whole body politic. I picked the word "relationship" precisely because it is a human word. I am not spinning a grand theory; I am suggesting a conceptual framework for citizens to use in changing the elements in their lives that they believe need changing. The effective conduct of relationships generates what may be called *relational power*; the dynamism of human ties both sustains us and enables us to accomplish what we cannot do alone.

Relationship is not a vague concept; I define it rigorously for analytical and operational use. I see relationship as a complex of five components, or five arenas of interaction in constantly changing combinations within and between the parties interacting:

- *identity*—not just physical characteristics such as size, ethnicity, race, nationality, or religion, but the life experience that has brought a person to the present moment
- *interests*—not just materially defined but what people really care about, what they would die for
- *power*—not just the ability to coerce or control, but the capacity of human beings to come together to influence the course of events
- *perceptions, misperceptions, stereotypes*
- *patterns of interaction*—people habitually interacting confrontationally or collaboratively[2]

Fifth, the concept of relationship is both an analytical and an operational tool. It is analytical because one can analyze observable interactions through this prism and can delve into any of the components to enhance understanding or to change interaction. Someone observing an interaction over time among a group of people with sharp differences can, with the components of relationship in the back of her or his mind, sort what he or she observes under these elements and then put together an accurate description of their relationship. At the same time, in a dialogue, a moderator can get inside each of these elements and change it. For example, the easiest to talk about is stereotypes. When one brings adversaries together face-to-face over time, stereotypes gradually give way to real interaction as individuals hear the other's stories and learn more deeply the other's experience.

An important note also, *relationship* is often seen as a soft—even "namby-pamby"—word out of the 1960s. It is also too often trivialized, as in, "I have a nice relationship with the lady at the check-out counter in the supermarket." Nothing could be further from reality. During the Cold War, the Soviet Union and the United States were locked in a close relationship by a strategy of "mutual assured destruction."

Sixth, relationships can be good or bad, constructive or destructive, mature or regressive, argumentative or cooperative, close or distant. They pervade our lives; the question is how to conduct and change them.

"SUSTAINED DIALOGUE": AN APPROACH TO TRANSFORMING CONFLICTIVE RELATIONSHIPS

After our first decade of experience and experiment in the Dartmouth Conference task force, I finally observed that, when one brings the same participants together repeatedly over time, their relationships evolve through a discernible pattern of interactions. In 1991, I laid that pattern out as a five-stage dialogue process. Coupling that dialogue process with the concept of relationship and what I came to call the "relational paradigm," I have developed a system of thought and practice that I now call the "Sustained Dialogue System."

Whereas classic diplomacy is the instrument of governments for conducting relations between states, Sustained Dialogue is a system of thought and practice for analyzing, transforming, and developing relationships among groups across boundaries of difference.

I define dialogue as one person listening carefully enough to another to be changed by what he or she hears. That openness of one person to another is the beginning of relationship. Dialogue is the essence of relationship. Dialogue when sustained and deepened over time becomes an approach to transforming relationships so that citizens can design social, economic, and political change.

The Sustained Dialogue system includes the relational paradigm, the concept of relationship, and the five-stage dialogue process. That process differs from most other instruments of change in two ways. First, it focuses on the relationships that cause problems, not initially on the problems themselves. Second, because relationships are not easily or quickly transformed, a progression of stages has been designed through which interactions evolve in dialogue.

Let me share, however, a word of caution on the notion of stages in Sustained Dialogue. In 1991, I presented a paper at an international academic conference titled "Thinking in Stages." I sometimes say that I hate myself when I present a five-stage process because it sounds mechanistic: "We have a template; if you just impose this on a problem, the problem will be solved." But the fact is that the stages are a helpful guide for a moderator in a sustained dialogue in assessing the progress of a dialogue group in transforming a relationship from destructive to constructive. It also helps illuminate for a moderator reasons why a group may be "stuck" at a particular point in their dialogue. Below is the observable pattern that formed the five-stage process of the Sustained Dialogue System.

Stage One: "Dialogue about Dialogue"

The first stage, which we call "dialogue about dialogue," is a period in which citizens share their thoughts about an emerging problem that they are concerned about, come to the conclusion that they should try to do something about it, and begin asking themselves what they might do. Sometimes a catalyst organization will talk with individuals in an effort to assemble a group around a particular problem. Or some member of the group may have had experience in dealing with such problems and will offer to help the group pursue that approach. Or perhaps they will approach a citizens' organization that has experience dealing with such problems. In short, the outcome of these informal conversations will be a decision to try to act on the problem, selection of an approach that they might take, agreement on a list of those who need to be involved, and on a time and place to begin.

Stage Two: "Mapping and Naming Problems and Relationships"

This stage is the time when the group first comes together with a moderator or co-moderators. It is also a period of "downloading"—expressing their feelings about the problem and about others involved in it. A Soviet colleague once called this "dumping"—when adversaries first come together, there are certain feelings they have to express. Beyond the need to discharge their feelings about an adversary or their frustrations about a problem, they face three tasks: (1) They will need to overcome resistance to talking openly with those with whom they may disagree vehemently. This is a critical task because the moment when an individual begins to listen to another deeply enough to be changed by what he or she hears is the moment of empathy when a relationship begins to take shape. (2) They will talk about the problem they face in ways that surface the most important dimensions and causes of the problem. (3) Finally, they will name or define the problem in a way that permits everyone to see her or his concerns reflected and readies them to begin working on it together.

Stage Three: "Probing Problems and Relationships to Choose a Direction"

This stage begins when participants have agreed on the nature of the problem as they see it and are willing to begin talking about ways to change the situation. The question for Stage Three is: what might we do? They begin talking about possible approaches to the problem and, as each is raised, what the feasibility and consequences of that approach might be. They are not yet deciding on a specific course of action but rather on a direction in which to move—perhaps we might say a "strategy" for approaching the problem.

Stage Four: "Scenario-Building—Experiencing a Changing Relationship"

At that point, the participants turn to specific actions that they—and others in the community—might take. Their purpose is to develop a series of interactive steps—a scenario—that can gradually change how groups feel about each other. They will:

- List resources available to them for moving in the direction they have chosen.
- List the main obstacles to change.
- List steps to overcome such obstacles.

- List who can take those steps.
- Arrange these possible steps so they reinforce each other and draw more and more actors onto the stage.

For instance, Party A is asked whether it can take Step 1. Party A replies that it could, if Party B would take Step 2 in response. Party B replies that it could, provided Party C would join the action by taking Step 3. And so on until, as in the scenario of a stage play, interactions gradually multiply, engaging a steadily increasing number of actors from across the community.

Stage Five: "Implementation"

In the final stage, "Implementation," participants take their plan into the community to engage a variety of groups in its implementation. As implementation proceeds, members of the dialogue group continue to meet for the purpose of assessing progress and perhaps designing mid-course corrections.

Deeply rooted in the Arab–Israeli peace process of the 1970s and in the Cold War dialogues of the Dartmouth Conference, Sustained Dialogue has been used to address a broad range of deep-rooted human conflicts: the vicious civil war in the former Soviet republic of Tajikistan; the conflict involving Armenia, Azerbaijan, and Nagorno Karabakh; the conflict in Iraq; tension involving political reformers from the Muslim Arab heartland, Western Europeans, and Americans; tensions between Jews and Arabs within Israel; citizens in the diverse community of Oakland, California; students on fifteen college campuses struggling with issues of race, ethnicity, sexual orientation, religion, and other issues that divide communities of young people; employees and leaders in a U.S. corporation around issues of racial discrimination. In each case, the objective has been to enable citizens to form the relationships/associations/networks that will generate the capacity to deal with stubborn challenges that they face.

CONCLUSION

In early 2012, a working group of the Euro-Atlantic Security Initiative, in the most comprehensive study of East–West relations since the signing of the Helsinki Final Act in 1975, called for a new paradigm in dealing with global problems. The approach of relying on traditional diplomacy between governments was not working. The group called for a broader strategy to involve society at large:

> Our most important recommendation is that . . . the vastly changed social, economic, and political landscape brought about by the emergence of new and rapidly expanding forms of civic participation must take a central place in defining our efforts. . . .

There is a clear need to go beyond governments (where formal conflict resolution processes effectively stop) and to find means of building support for peace among elites and the wider publics of conflicting parties. . . .

. . . expansion of traditional diplomacy to include Dartmouth-style Track II dialogue, 'next generation' meetings, and use of social media to prepare the peoples involved for accommodation and development of a non zero-sum narrative should be employed to alter the present dynamic.[3]

This chapter has presented the relational paradigm for engaging citizens. The relational paradigm reaches well beyond the traditional focus on the state and its institutions to see politics in terms of the relationships—the associations—that citizens outside government build to initiate and manage change.

It is my belief that thinking in terms of relationship changes how we act. We are born into relationships; they shape our identities over years. As we go through life, we are nurtured and supported through close relationships. In the five-stage Sustained Dialogue System, citizens can experience and learn a more productive way of relating. Through Sustained Dialogue, one can see hostile relationships transformed into collaboration. Thinking in terms of the relational paradigm enriches our capacity to conduct interactions productively, to manage them more carefully when they are destructive, and to enlarge our resources for conducting and changing relationships without resort to violence. It is reflections on a changing world that prompt the claim that we need a new relational paradigm for the study and practice of politics.

NOTES

1. For elaboration, see Harold H. Saunders, *Politics Is about Relationship: Blueprint for the Citizens' Century* (New York: Palgrave Macmillan, 2005), Chapter Two, "A Proper World View, Appropriate for Its Time."
2. This section draws heavily from Harold H. Saunders, *Politics Is about Relationship*, 8.
3. Euro-Atlantic Security Initiative (EASI), *Historical Reconciliation and Protracted Conflicts* (Moscow, Brussels, and Washington, DC: Carnegie Endowment for International Peace, 2012), 5.

10 Delivering Digital Public Diplomacy

Information Technologies and the Changing Business of Diplomacy

Charles Causey and Philip N. Howard

INTRODUCTION

Digital media have come to mediate global power in interesting ways. International news agencies now rely upon content generated by citizen journalists or captured by mobile phone users as events unfold in distant streets.[1] Social media, while providing new ways for diplomats and their staff to reach new audiences on a global scale, also challenges the ways that diplomatic work is conducted. As these new media have expanded vertical channels of communication, they have similarly broadened horizontal channels of communication between networked individuals. The decentralized nature of these new participatory and communicative networks means that public diplomacy now requires productive engagement with individuals within these networks. Yet, how to do so successfully remains an unresolved puzzle. The U.S. Department of State has pointed to the role of social media in increasing openness in government. Alec Ross, the Senior Adviser for Innovation to Secretary of State Hillary Clinton, contends that "[a] lot of the 21st-century dynamics are less about . . . traditional liberal-conservative ideological lines. Today it is—at least in the spaces we engage in—Is it open or is it closed?"[2] In addition to navigating the intricacies of traditional statecraft, governments are finding it necessary to develop new information management strategies in light of these new media—the impact of which is highly contingent and often spontaneous. The costs of monitoring events in near real time have dropped significantly in an age of ubiquitous and instantaneous information sharing. At the same time, the call for open government and increased information sharing may be more outward facing than inward, as we saw when the more traditional behind-the-scenes work of diplomats was laid bare when Julian Assange's WikiLeaks organization released thousands of classified U.S. diplomatic cables on its website in 2010.

Moving toward an open model of public diplomacy in which diplomats engage more directly with citizens within and without their borders also presents a collective action problem vis-à-vis the actions of other sovereign states. Deviating from traditional forms of diplomacy, where diplomats act strategically as agents of their states to further a relatively clearly defined foreign policy, is risky if other states do not choose a similar path. Yet creatively using social media can also make one country's diplomats more effective than another's.

Are diplomatic efforts to increase their online and social media presences genuine efforts to engage in a new form of public diplomacy? Or are these efforts merely traditional statecraft wrapped in a new online packaging? Maintaining a unified message and image has proven to be difficult, as diplomatic offices seek to find a balance between official and less formal diplomatic action. As seen in the discussion below of Libyan and Syrian activist social media campaigns, authenticity seems to play a role in how digital diplomacy is perceived by insiders and outsiders. Struggling with this balance of authenticity while attempting to present a unified diplomatic message is complicating the practice of public diplomacy. Adopting a diplomatic posture that favors greater openness and engagement with nontraditional actors can backfire if statements are at odds with actions or seem manufactured. Contradictions can damage diplomatic credibility in the eyes of potential networked collaborators. Yet, the messy realities of statecraft increase the likelihood that an open and authentic posture will be undermined at some point. While commitments to engaging in networked public diplomacy may be more attractive in the long term, the short-term costs and benefits of traditional statecraft can win the day. The cultural norm for diplomats is to be conservative and guarded with information; tradition-bound officials often resist accepting the new digital realities.[3]

Each of the above questions poses a unique opportunity for scholars to elucidate the ways that social media are reshaping international relations. Following the call by the political scientist Henry Farrell, identifying the causal mechanisms by which and under what conditions social media affects diplomacy in the twenty-first century is the next step in developing testable hypotheses.[4] Clearly, the impact of social media on diplomatic behavior is variable. Rather than focusing on the impact of social media qua social media, it may benefit researchers to expand existing international communication theory to incorporate these new media.

Although these same arguments have long been made with respect to the mass media, digital and social media have increased participatory capacity, by orders of magnitude.[5] Entry costs to engaging with new media are not zero, and a significant digital divide remains, but costs continue to fall and access to these media continue to rise. Whereas gatekeepers, news routines, and high start-up costs characterize traditional media, social media circumvent these processes and allow those without previous access to engage in political discourse and disseminate information—both horizontally and vertically. The digital media landscape shifts rapidly as new tools, apps, and outlets for information sharing appear. These shifts provide diplomats with new ways to reach audiences and collect information, and for nonstate actors to take part in diplomatic agenda setting previously unavailable to them on such a widespread scale. While it is tempting to point to this explosion in participatory capacity as a game-changer in public diplomacy, it does not guarantee its actualization or efficacy. Governments, diplomats, and social networks interact in a complex process embedded within an existing and complicated framework of actors and institutions that remain relevant. In this chapter, we discuss the role of massive information revelation via WikiLeaks. We then detail two international crises that highlight how the influx of new information via digital media is shaping decisions surrounding military interventions—first in Libya, where digital media appeared to have played a role in the establishment of a No-Fly Zone, and then in Syria, where both opposition fighters, exiled activists, and the Assad regime are waging battles in the streets and on the internet to control the narrative. Throughout, we contend that the increased participatory capacity afforded by social media presents both opportunities for new communication between citizens and states as well as challenges to the practice of statecraft.

WIKILEAKS, BAD TWEETS, AND GLOBAL
DIPLOMATIC PRACTICE

In November 2010, WikiLeaks released approximately a quarter-million internal American diplomatic cables sent between 1966 and 2010 through its websites and partnerships with major Western media outlets like the *Guardian* and the *New York Times*. Major data leakages, including the WikiLeaks content, not only provide a look into the timbre of diplomatic correspondence, but also demonstrate the importance of digital media in maintaining diplomatic conversations. Underscoring how sensitive the Obama administration considered this information, it has pursued a bevy of legal charges against the alleged leaker, U.S. Army Private Bradley Manning, including charging him under the Espionage Act. Simultaneously, the State Department aggressively denounced the release of the documents, contending that they would strain diplomatic relations with strategic allies and have a chilling effect on diplomats who may be unwilling to disclose their thoughts on sensitive matters, for fear of appearing in the press.

As Nicholas Cull points out, leaking state secrets is an age-old phenomenon and not unique to digital media or the internet. Trotsky, for example, released the details of the czar's secret treaties, while advocating for a model of open diplomacy.[6] Although the text of many of the cables appeared in the *Guardian*, the *New York Times*, and other online sources, the State Department cautioned current and potential employees that viewing the cables without the proper security clearance constituted a violation of security policy. This reaction suggests emphasizing that pre-internet practices may be ill equipped to deal with the explosion of freely available information.[7] Moreover, the sweeping changes to journalism, foreign relations, and government secrecy predicted by some have failed to materialize, with former Secretary of Defense Robert Gates calling their impact "limited."[8]

Although some have pointed to the role of WikiLeaks in the mass uprisings of the "Arab Spring," few scholarly investigations of this claim have been conducted to date. While U.S. officials protested vociferously that the leaks constituted a grave attack against U.S. interests, analysts at Human Rights Watch argued that the release of the cables ultimately proved beneficial for American interests. The cables publicly revealed information about other states that would be impossible for diplomats to reveal via traditional public diplomacy. U.S. diplomats, for example, were constrained from speaking publicly about former Tunisian leader Ben Ali's increasing disconnect with the Tunisian people, or about Saudi support for an attack on Iran to cripple its nuclear capacities.[9]

Exposing the diplomatic backstage to a wider audience is not the only way in which digital media have complicated statecraft. Whereas the publication of diplomatic cables was a security breach that diplomatic services could not be blamed for, there have been several high-profile gaffes from tweeting diplomats. With six weeks remaining in the Bush administration, Deputy Assistant Secretary of State for Public Diplomacy Colleen Graffy tweeted about the inconvenience of having left her gym bag at home during a mission to Iceland during a Middle East crisis.[10] Similarly, the aforementioned Alec Ross and his State Department colleague Jared Cohen tweeted about a visit to Starbucks while on a visit to pre-conflict Syria.[11] These incidents highlight the tension between authenticity and a unified diplomatic message. A more conversational style on social media can be interpreted as insincere or out-of-touch when crises emerge. Diplomats are faced with expectations about openness and authenticity, but also with competing expectations of gravitas.

As a result of WikiLeaks, and related scandals, many foreign ministries re-evaluated their information security practices. More important, a conservative culture of information management became even more conservative. Agencies that had no formal policies on social media use drafted them quickly. Agencies with existing policies tightened their restrictions and began enforcement. Some foreign ministries in the West contemplated developing their own social media platforms as a way of playing the game but setting the rules, though these applications achieved limited success.[12] As foreign ministries find themselves struggling to balance information management policies with effective strategies for reaching audiences, these same audiences are presented with new ways of contributing to foreign policy discussions. Unfortunately for diplomats, the solution is not unilateral or obvious; adapting public diplomacy to the digital age also requires shifting expectations on the part of the public. Traditional media can vilify actions that are welcomed by social media users. Reacting to missteps by hewing toward a traditionally conservative stance is unlikely to produce a successful strategy for engaging with networked publics, however.

THE ARAB SPRING AND ITS DIPLOMATIC
RESPONSE TO PUBLIC PRESSURE

The Arab Spring has had several consequences for digital public diplomacy. Scholars of science and technology studies may debate the proper way of describing the causal role of digital media in the Arab Spring. But regardless of one's epistemic position on the role of information technologies in social change, it is difficult to tell the story of the Arab Spring without some acknowledgment of how the inspiring stories of civil resistance cascaded from country to country through digital narratives. Not only were social movements across North Africa and the Middle East inspired by digital stories of successful challenges to authoritarianism, but the counterinsurgency strategies of ruling elites also had digital aspects. Social media provided opportunities for previously silent actors to participate in shaping the narrative of the uprisings. Relationships between Egyptian activists and European activists affiliated with the Centre for Applied Non Violent Actions and Strategies (CANVAS), who came of political age ousting Slobodan Milosevic, were made possible through the use of social media.[13] Diasporas around the world had regular supplies of news and information; digital media networks allowed them to maintain often-direct contact with the friends and family who were facing tear gas and bullets at home. A simple observation is that governments, especially those under attack, quickly lost the ability to manage their "crisis communications." The governments of Tunisia, Egypt, and many other countries in the region were used to controlling domestic media, constraining international news agencies, discrediting diaspora critics, and resisting multilateral action against them. These techniques did not work so well against personal, digital testimonials about corruption and abuse so easily distributed online.

First, it is clear that governments of all kinds have now developed online crisis management strategies that involve putting their own propaganda online as quickly as possible in times of crisis. Importantly, the increased participatory capacity of social media does not apply solely to pro-democracy activists. Governments also employ agents to rapidly and widely disseminate propaganda; the Syrian government has been especially adept at this. Second, a number of governments—usually the most authoritarian ones—have built internet "kill switches" and censorship strategies that, in times of crisis, can be used to prevent citizens from talking across borders. Moreover, as discussed by Amelia Arsenault in this volume, Western corporations heralding from the same countries that urge greater openness are the prime builders of the technologies underpinning these strategies. However, stifling online speech may have unintended consequences for mobilization. As Navid Hassanpour argues, internet and mobile disruptions may draw previously uninvolved citizens into the streets.[14] And, as Philip Howard, Sheetal Agarwal, and Muzammil Hussain find, democratic states are more likely to interfere with internet operations, even if authoritarian regimes are more likely to shut down communications.[15]

The two strategies of propaganda and censorship may not be the most surprising: it seems reasonable that a government would want to put its political spin on events into the public domain as quickly as possible; disabling internet access in times of crisis means that foreign governments and multilateral agencies have less information to use in crafting a reasonable intervention. It also prevents international actors from dealing directly with domestic actors other than the government. While digital media provide new avenues of communication for state and nonstate actors, it is often the regime that ultimately controls the capacity to do so; both despots and democrats recognize that social media substantially increase participatory capacity.

While the Arab Spring may have demonstrated how dictators can be caught off-guard by tech-savvy democratic activists, it may also demonstrate how the rise of new governments is a digitally mediated process. Governments in exile have long asserted their own legitimacy through media. But where the fall of a regime can be marked by the collapse of digital communications, the rise of a new or challenger regime government can be marked by its new digital presence. Indeed, Libya's Transitional Authority established its homepage before its provisional ministers had even arrived in country. Syria's diaspora openly negotiated online over which of its members might form a credible government-in-exile. The international news media—and foreign governments—rely heavily on the online pronouncements and social media feeds of new political leaders and new parties for information about what is going on during political interregnum. And while the military is still firmly in control of Egypt's political transition, its decisions about public policy and electoral rules are made online through Facebook and other digital media. However, the increased online visibility of governments-in-exile does not necessarily equate to power on the ground; interviews with Syrian rebels have called into question the impact of external discussions on the domestic anti-Assad movement. Identifying relevant actors with whom to engage is a fundamental challenge for networked public diplomacy.

LIBYA, SYRIA, AND THE DECISION TO INTERVENE

The participatory capacity of new digital media provides a new method of communication between publics and states, running in the opposite direction, with nonstate actors trying to engage directly with states. In both Libya and Syria, activists and opposition fighters have taken to Facebook, YouTube, and other forms of social media to appeal directly to the United States, European Union, and United Nations for international intervention. The Syrian National Council maintains an active presence across numerous forms of social media in both Arabic and English. Protests are streamed live on the web, including a protest at Aleppo University staged while United Nations observers were visiting the site.[16]

Discerning the impact of digital and social media on the West's decision to intervene in Libya is not straightforward, as the majority of popular and scholarly work on the topic, as well as the broader Arab uprisings, focuses on the role of new media on the uprisings themselves.[17] Juan Cole, among others, contends that the majority of Libyan social media activity occurred outside of Libya itself.[18] Yet, this is precisely what would be expected, first with the so-called CNN effect and, perhaps more aptly given recent events, an "Al Jazeera" effect, with which activists are able to transmit their message to interested individuals abroad, who then magnify the message to garner support for the cause.[19] Analysis of Twitter data produced during the uprisings supports this; while the authors did not find that new media contributed to collective action, they did find that new media was important in spreading information from within conflicts to foreign media, both traditional and not.[20] Monitoring social media for incoming information in addition to using these media as a platform will be a necessary component of the diplomatic toolbox.

Given that the debate over the existence or magnitude of the effect of the media on foreign policy decision-making has filled numerous journal pages, it is no surprise that a similar debate over the role of social media is beginning anew. However, the playing field has changed; while states have always had to contend with the media to varying degrees, the rise of social media has increased the number of potential interfering actors by orders of magnitude. Citizen journalists have an opportunity to provide real-time, on-the-ground information from conflict zones, although, they are not subject to the same journalistic norms as are traditional media. The vast increase in the volume of available media can present a fractured and unfiltered narrative, making it difficult for any actor to ensure that target audiences view their media. While many have pointed to the role of social media in the Arab Spring, it has been argued that the true impact of these media came when satellite networks such as Al Jazeera combined user-submitted footage and updates into a coherent narrative. Increased participation in social media is accompanied by an increased noise-to-signal ratio and suggests that governments will need to develop filtering strategies for listening to constituencies and developing credible channels of communication.

The belief that exposure of unseemly regime activities to a global audience will be enough to spark outside intervention is hardly new; each time communication technology has increased the velocity of news, the claim has been made that it will be a force for increasing peace and exposing dictators. As former U.S. Secretary of State George Shultz famously claimed in *Foreign Affairs*, "[totalitarian societies] will never be able entirely to block the tide of technological advance."[21] Increased mobile and internet penetration have opened new channels of communication between citizens and the outside world, but it is clear that exposure of regime actions is not sufficient to energize the international community for intervention.

So why has social media seemingly bolstered support for international intervention in Libya and not in Syria? One substantive difference rests on the capacity for incumbent regimes to control and manipulate the flow of information in and out of the country. The Gaddafi regime excelled at traditional forms of censorship and information blockade, essentially creating an informational black hole in the country. The Assad regime has engaged in similar forms of internet censorship, although proxies are fairly common. However, when Libyans and their supporters began to broadcast details of protests and regime responses via social media, the Gaddafi regime was ill equipped to mount a defense. Gaddafi himself offered (ham-handed at times) narratives of events in the country that were in direct contradiction with the events unfolding before the world's eyes. The Assad regime, on the other hand, has shown a markedly better ability to counter activists' social media activities, providing videos of violence purported to be committed by the opposition and using regime-controlled media outlets to assert that Al Jazeera staged the opposition footage in mock-up cities in Qatar.[22] Further, the Assad regime has a greater base of technologically savvy supporters—both in and outside of Syria—who are willing to take to the internet and combat pro-opposition narratives. In addition to allegedly arming its military with Iranian weapons, Assad has made monitoring and tracking of the opposition via social media part of his counterinsurgency strategy.[23]

The differing intervention outcomes underscore familiar debates surrounding the impact of the internet on political behavior. In both cases, activists have used social media to raise awareness, coordinate protest events, and document violence by the Gaddafi and Assad regimes, respectively. However, the quick formation of a multilateral coalition to intervene in Libya, justified using the United Nations' "Responsibility to Protect" doctrine, stands in stark comparison to the ongoing conflict in Syria, where international intervention has, to date, been ruled out as an option. While videos of regime atrocities emerging from Libya prompted an international outcry, the number of deaths of civilians and both opposition and loyalist fighters in Syria long ago surpassed many estimates of those in Libya.

A number of factors diminished the likelihood of quick, direct intervention in Syria: the Assad regime's close alliance with Iran and Hezbollah, the shared border with Israel, Assad's ability to calibrate his degree of repression to the limits of international tolerance followed by dead-on-arrival ceasefires, and the cooling of global enthusiasm for involvement in the region since the heady days of late 2010 and early 2011. Given that Syria has a much higher degree of internet penetration than Libya, it would be reasonable to expect that social media would be used by a larger number of activists and reach a broader audience than in Libya.[24] The fact that international intervention has, to date, been anemic in Syria argues against the ability for digital media to overcome traditional geopolitical constraints.

The absence of intervention in Syria underscores the need to work through counterfactuals—would the international community have intervened in Libya as quickly, or at all, had activists not been able to broadcast their struggle to the world? Consider an episode that demonstrates the complexity of this question. Senator John McCain, in a cable revealed by WikiLeaks, appeared previously to advocate for aid to Gaddafi in the form of military hardware; he later became one of the more outspoken proponents of intervention in Libya.[25] This proposes another interesting counterfactual—would McCain have advocated so strongly for an intervention had WikiLeaks not brought attention to his early stance on Gaddafi?

SOFT POWER, DIGITALLY MEDIATED

Today, there are two broad approaches to the study of diplomats and diplomacy. One body of research treats diplomats as important personalities involved in the game-theoretic strategies of states. With nation-states as the primary unit of analysis and the most sensibly discrete actor in an international system, diplomats do the work of transmitting preferences and collecting intelligence. Their choice of language in official communiqués, their involvement in the domestic issues of other states, and occasionally their mistakes, have consequences for the strategic interaction between governments. Another body of research investigates the effectiveness of public diplomacy, which involves the range of cultural and economic exchanges between countries that can help governments achieve foreign policy goals. In contrast with the blunt instruments of diplomatic posturing, economic sanctions, or military action, public diplomacy relies on student exchanges, cultural programming, and shared business opportunities to build the strong ties between people that can make for alliances between countries.

Several governments, particularly in the West, are using digital media to do the work of convincing rather than coercing allies and opponents alike. President Obama, whose 2008 presidential campaign set new benchmarks for the use of digital media in electoral politics, has taken to YouTube yearly since 2009 to directly address the Iranian people on Nowruz, the Iranian New Year. The wives of two European ambassadors to the United Nations similarly uploaded a video plea to Asma Assad, the Syrian president's wife, to push for her husband's exit. The United States, following in the tradition of Radio Free Europe and the Voice of America, operates Al Hurra, an Arabic-language satellite news network to counter a putative anti-U.S. bias in the mainstream Arab press, although this effort is widely perceived to have fallen flat.[26] The previously distinct lines that demarcated official state action are becoming blurred, with significant implications for how soft power is projected.

DIGITAL PUBLIC DIPLOMACY IN THE FUTURE

In theory, a significant amount of soft power—the ability to convince rather than coerce others to act with shared goals—could accrue to the diplomats who use social media effectively. Shared knowledge and information integration can help foreign policy experts define and solve problems shared with other actors in the international system. New information technologies have helped coordinate development programs, policy interventions, and services to citizens abroad.[27] Several challenges, however, remain. Diplomats must navigate multiple information networks. Foreign service personnel simultaneously serve as nodes in:

(1) *Intraorganizational networks* where information sharing can take place across different bureaucratic levels of a sovereign government's foreign service, with some governments looking to establish Wiki-style information repositories;

(2) *Interorganizational networks* where information sharing can take place with other government units that might serve a sovereign government but be operating in concert internationally;

(3) *Extraorganizational networks* where information sharing can take place with peer diplomats working for the governments of other sovereign states;

(4) *Public networks* where information sharing can take place with elected officials, journalists, and interested citizens at home or abroad.

↳ *elites*

So for digital media to really serve a diplomatic community and the interests of a diplomat's political masters, what would a good digital media strategy look like? Cull makes sensible recommendations on relevance, cooperation with country representatives tweeting from the same perspective on the same issue, being aware of who the audience is, and being realistic about the possible impact of each message. Of course, diplomats are receiving as well as transmitting information. Most important may be learning how to listen through digital media, not just produce content. It is more important, Cull argues, for diplomats to at least appear to be listening to opinion leaders through social media, than to be worried about building their own big base of readers and followers.[28] To be effective in networked public diplomacy, practitioners need to strike a balance between broadcast and reception, and to establish effective procedures for information collation and filtering; this requires being flexible and willing to depart from established practices.

As Philip Seib has argued, one of the lessons of both of the international crises in Syria and Libya is that the pace of events increases along with the rate of information flow. Policymakers must fine-tune their operating procedures to improve their ability to move quickly but still wisely, and to anticipate the shifting degrees of importance of issues and relevance of particular media tools.[29]

easier said than done

CONCLUSION

In *Renaissance Diplomacy*, Garrett Mattingly argued that the collapse of Christendom left behind a political world of territorially discrete, politically self-serving nation-states.[30] This new kind of state required a professional class of arbiters, a group of strategic thinkers with the nation-state's goals at heart, the ability to move unhindered across international borders, and the authority to speak for sovereigns. Until this work, little scholarly consideration was given to the formation of diplomatic institutions and practices. In the twenty-first century, governments, often to their chagrin, are faced with the reality that information now joins diplomats in moving freely across borders. Diplomats are now situated in global networks that include extra-institutional political actors with access to information and the means of its dissemination. Navigating these networks and productively engaging with new global publics is the twenty-first-century challenge for public diplomacy.

NOTES

1. Philip Seib, *The Al Jazeera Effect: How the New Global Media Are Reshaping World Politics* (Dulles, VA: Potomac Books, 2008).
2. Jesse Lichtenstein, "Digital Diplomacy," *New York Times*, July 16, 2010, accessed May 31, 2012, http://www.nytimes.com/2010/07/18/magazine/18web2–0-t.html
3. Wilson Dizard, *Digital Diplomacy: U.S. Foreign Policy in the Information Age* (Westport, CT: Praeger Paperback, 2001).
4. Henry Farrell, "The Consequences of the Internet for Politics," *Annual Review of Political Science* 15(1), (2012): 35–52.
5. Maxwell E. McCombs and Donald L Shaw, "The Evolution of Agenda-Setting Research: Twenty-Five Years in the Marketplace of Ideas," *Journal of Communication* 43(2), (1993): 58–67; Maxwell E. McCombs and Donald L. Shaw, "The Agenda-Setting Function of Mass Media," *Public Opinion Quarterly* 36(2), (1972): 176–87.
6. Nicholas J. Cull, "WikiLeaks, Public Diplomacy 2.0 and the State of Digital Public Diplomacy," *Place Branding and Public Diplomacy* 7(1), (2011): 1–8.
7. Christopher Hood, "From FOI World to WikiLeaks World: A New Chapter in the Transparency Story?" *Governance* 24(4), (2011): 635–38; Eric Lipton, "Don't Look, Don't Read: Government Warns Its Workers Away from WikiLeaks Documents," *New York Times*, December 4, 2010, accessed May 28, 2012, http://www.nytimes.com/2010/12/05/world/05restrict.html
8. National Public Radio, "Gates: Limited Damage from WikiLeaks Documents," *NPR*, October 15, 2010, accessed May 28, 2012, http://www.npr.org/templates/story/story.php?storyId=130600687
9. Tom Malinowski, "Whispering at Autocrats," *Foreign Policy*, January 25, 2011, accessed May 28, 2012, http://www.foreignpolicy.com/articles/2011/01/25/whispering_at_autocrats
10. Al Kamen, "Live from Iceland, or Possibly Greenland, It's the DipNote Tweet Show!" *Washington Post*, December 10, 2008, accessed June 1, 2012, http://www.washingtonpost.com/wp-dyn/content/article/2008/12/09/AR2008120902774.html
11. Lichtenstein, "Digital Diplomacy."
12. Christopher Bronk and Tiffany Smith, "Diplopedia Imagined: Building State's Diplomacy Wiki," *Proceedings of the 2010 International Symposium on Collaborative Technologies and Systems* (2010): 593–602, accessed September 25, 2012, http://www.bakerinstitute.org/publications/TSPP-pub-BronkSmithDiplopediaDraft-051810.pdf
13. Tina Rosenberg, "Revolution U," *Foreign Policy*, February 16, 2011, accessed May 30, 2012, http://www.foreignpolicy.com/articles/2011/02/16/revolution_u

14. Navid Hassanpour, "Media Disruption Exacerbates Revolutionary Unrest: Evidence from Mubarak's Natural Experiment," paper prepared for the Annual Meeting of the American Political Science Association, Seattle, Washington, (2011), accessed May 1, 2012. http://papers.ssrn.com/sol3/papers.cfm?abstract_id=1903351
15. Philip N. Howard, Sheetal D. Agarwal, and Muzammil M. Hussain, "The Dictators' Digital Dilemma: When Do States Disconnect Their Digital Networks?" *Center for Technology Innovation at Brookings' Issues in Technology Innovation* 13 (2011): 35–52, http://www.brookings.edu/~/media/research/files/papers/2011/10/dictators%20digital%20network/10_dictators_digital_network
16. Jillian Dunham, "Syrian TV Station Accuses Al Jazeera of Fabricating Uprising," *New York Times: The Lede Blog*, September 14, 2011, accessed May 28, 2012, http://thelede.blogs.nytimes.com/2011/09/14/syrian-tv-station-accuses-al-jazeera-of-fabricating-uprising/
17. Philip N. Howard and Muzammil M. Hussain, "The Role of Digital Media," *Journal of Democracy* 22(3), (2011): 35–48; Marc Lynch "After Egypt: The Limits and Promise of Online Challenges to the Authoritarian Arab State," *Perspectives on Politics* 9 (2011): 301–10; Nivien Saleh, "Egypt's Digital Activism and the Dictator's Dilemma: An Evaluation," *Telecommunications Policy* 36(6), (2012): 476–83.
18. Juan Cole, "TV, Twitter, Facebook and the Libyan Revolution," *Informed Comment*, July 24, 2011, accessed May 28, 2012, http://www.juancole.com/2011/08/tv-twitter-facebook-and-the-libyan-revolution.html
19. Philip Seib, *Real-Time Diplomacy: Politics and Power in the Social Media Era* (New York: Palgrave Macmillan, 2012); Piers Robinson, *The CNN Effect: The Myth of News Media, Foreign Policy and Intervention* (London: Routledge, 2002).
20. Sean Aday et al., "Blogs and Bullets II: New Media and Conflict after the Arab Spring," *PeaceWorks*, United States Institute of Peace (July 2012), accessed September 8, 2012, http://www.usip.org/publications/blogs-and-bullets-ii-new-media-and-conflict-after-the-arab-spring
21. George P. Shultz, "Shaping American Foreign Policy: New Realities and New Ways of Thinking," *Foreign Affairs* 63(4), (1985): 716.
22. Elisabeth Bumiller, "U.S. Syria Intervention Would Be Risky, Pentagon Officials Say," *New York Times*, March 11, 2012, accessed May 26, 2012, http://www.nytimes.com/2012/03/12/world/middleeast/us-syria-intervention-would-be-risky-pentagon-officials-say.html
23. Bumiller, "U.S. Syria Intervention Would Be Risky."
24. Racha Mourtada and Fadi Salem, "Arab Social Media Report: Civil Movements: The Impact of Facebook and Twitter," Dubai School of Government, Report 1 (2), May 2011, accessed May 15, 2012, http://www.ArabSocialMediaReport.com
25. Philip N. Howard, Aiden Duffy, Deen Freelon, Muzammil M. Hussain, Will Mari, and Marwa Mazaid, "Opening Closed Regimes: What Was the Role of Social Media during the Arab Spring?" Project on Information Technology & Political Islam (2011), http://www.scribd.com/doc/66443833/Opening-Closed-Regimes-What-Was-the-Role-of-Social-Media-During-the-Arab-Spring; Lynch, "After Egypt: The Limits and Promise of Online Challenges"; Saleh, "Egypt's Digital Activism."
26. Monroe E. Price, "End of Television and Foreign Policy," *The ANNALS of the American Academy of Political and Social Science* 625(1), (2009): 196–204.
27. Sharon S. Dawes, Anthony M. Cresswell, and Theresa A. Pardo, "From 'Need to Know' to 'Need to Share': Tangled Problems, Information Boundaries,

and the Building of Public Sector Knowledge Networks," *Public Administration Review* 69(3), (2009): 392–402.

28. Nicholas Cull, "WikiLeaks, Public Diplomacy 2.0 and the State of Digital Public Diplomacy," *Place Branding and Public Diplomacy* 7(1), (2011): 1–8.

29. Seib, *Real-Time Diplomacy*.

30. Garrett Mattingly, *Renaissance Diplomacy* (New York: Cosimo, 2010).

11 The "Virtual Last Three Feet"

Understanding Relationship Perspectives in Network-Based Public Diplomacy

Hyunjin Seo

INTRODUCTION

Networked digital technologies, including the internet, have significantly altered the ways people create and share information and connect with others. For example, recent reports showed that increasing numbers of people in the United States and other countries are turning to the web to keep in touch with friends and acquaintances.[1]

These new types of transnational and decentralized social networks, fueled by the increasing availability and affordability of digital devices, have influenced the conduct of public diplomacy.[2] Governments have begun utilizing social media to interact with international publics as part of their public diplomacy efforts. For example, the U.S. Department of State actively uses Facebook and Twitter to engage citizens around the world, as well as to get out its messages. Other countries, including the United Kingdom, Norway, and Sweden, have expanded their public diplomacy efforts into the digital sphere.[3]

Building and maintaining meaningful connections or relationships with people around the world is at the heart of digital media–based public diplomacy efforts. Former head of U.S. Information Agency Edward R. Murrow once said personal contact at the "last three feet" is crucial to enhance mutual understanding and forge networks with global publics. While face-to-face interactions are ideal, social media may provide opportunities for public diplomacy actors to initiate and facilitate connections with global publics at the "virtual last three feet," especially when security conditions prohibit meaningful offline engagements.

In this chapter, I discuss what types of relationships should be emphasized and how those relationships can be nurtured and enhanced through digital media–based public diplomacy. Understanding the relationship perspectives of international publics that a country aims to engage is one of the first steps to answer the question. I first examine theoretical arguments related to public diplomacy in the networked information age, and then introduce original empirical research on the public's perspectives of relationships in the context of public diplomacy. Conclusions from this study provide clues to governmental and nongovernmental organizations working in the area of public diplomacy as to what types of networks might be facilitated to maintain and strengthen relationships with global publics.

PUBLIC DIPLOMACY IN THE NETWORKED INFORMATION AGE

Social media have become an essential part of public diplomacy. Social media sites such as Facebook and Twitter help users to maintain or build social relationships around similar identities or goals.[4] For example, under Secretary of State Hillary Clinton, the U.S. Department of State launched the 21st Century Statecraft initiative, defined as "the complementing of traditional foreign policy tools with newly innovated and adapted instruments of statecraft that fully leverage the networks, technologies, and demographics of our interconnected world."[5] Under this initiative, the U.S. Department of State has incorporated new digital technologies into its formal training programs and U.S. diplomats are encouraged to use Twitter or Facebook to directly engage publics in their host country.[6] Further, as part of efforts to encourage global dialogue on democracy, in 2009 and 2010, the U.S. Department of State sponsored the Democracy Video Challenge, a worldwide competition of short videos defining democracy. The delivery platform was YouTube, and all updates regarding the competition were posted to Twitter and Facebook. In yet another example, the U.S. embassy in Seoul has maintained an online community called Café USA since 2004 as a means of directly interacting with the younger generation in South Korea, a substantial proportion of which hold anti-U.S. sentiments.[7]

These new public diplomacy programs utilizing digital networks are in contrast to traditional public diplomacy initiatives that focused on elites such as journalists, businessmen, scholars, and artists to distribute information overseas and promote national image abroad. That is, these new initiatives offer an opportunity for a shift from the *informational framework* to the *relational framework* in engaging ordinary citizens in other countries.[8] As R. S. Zaharna has pointed out, public diplomacy in the past focused mainly on information transfer, often with the goals of persuasion and control. In contrast, the relational framework is geared toward building relationships and nurturing "social structures" for advancing objectives. Commitment and mutual trust are important aspects of the relational framework that aim to "find commonalities and mutual interests between publics and then ways to link those publics via some form of direct interpersonal communication."[9] New digital technologies may facilitate the shift from the informational to relational framework.

Further, as more countries become democratic, the importance of communicating and connecting with mass publics becomes greater, since these publics can constrain elites. It is not only the development of digital networking and communication but also changing political realities that are pushing for "new" public diplomacy techniques. Both factors are, for now, reinforcing each other.

My argument here is not that these digital media–based initiatives can replace person-to-person exchange programs, but rather that they offer alternative ways of both deepening and broadening relationships with international publics. Person-to-person exchange programs such as the Fulbright Program and International Visitor Leadership Program have played and will continue to play an important role in public diplomacy by enhancing mutual understanding.[10] In this networked information age, however, an important link in international communication has emerged at the "*virtual last three feet.*"

"VIRTUAL LAST THREE FEET"

People in disparate parts of the world collaborate to produce content on wikis and share their opinions with widely distributed internet users through social media such as Facebook, YouTube, and Twitter. These new types of transnational and decentralized social networks are expected to continue to grow, as suggested by recent global survey reports.[11]

This, in turn, offers important opportunities for countries to build relationships with international publics at the "virtual last three feet." I argue that to best utilize these opportunities both *online social relations* and *online information use* should be considered, as they often work interdependently rather than independently. I use the term *online social relations* to refer to the degree and intensity of social networks built and maintained online. At an individual level, the nodes of a social network consist of people—friends, families, and others. At a macro level, it includes groups or organizations as well. For example, the U.S. Department of State may not only connect with South Koreans through social networking sites but also facilitate online exchanges and possibly friendships between the U.S. and South Korean college students by providing an online forum for the two sides. Previous research indicated that offline social networks play a significant role in forming one's attitudes toward other countries.[12] Whether this might hold for online social relations is an important topic to study.

Providing or sharing information is also an important part of building relationships, and thus public diplomacy actors are encouraged to present useful information in an engaging and interactive manner. While traditional mass media continue to influence people's perceptions of other countries, diverse online communication tools such as social media have also become important channels for obtaining information about various aspects of our personal and social life, including events happening in other countries. Individuals may form perceptions of other countries through simply seeking information about the countries as well as through their online interactions with people from those countries.

In considering initiatives for strengthening online social relations and information use, public diplomacy actors should understand the level of technology adoption and patterns of technology use of their target international publics. Without proper understandings of where and how those publics spend time online, one cannot come up with effective and relevant strategies.[13] Another important aspect is to understand aspects related to relationship building and management, to which I now turn.

RELATIONSHIP DIMENSIONS

Scholars have suggested different definitions and dimensions of relationships. For example, Glen Broom, Shawna Casey, and James Ritchey argued that relationships consist of "patterns of linkages through which the parties in relationships pursue and service their independent needs."[14] T. Dean Thomlison suggested that a relationship is "a set of expectations two parties have for each other's behavior based on their interaction patterns."[15] W. Timothy Coombs offers a similar perspective, defining relationships as interdependence between two or more people with long-lasting connections and mutual exchanges.[16]

Important dimensions of relationships include access, assurances, networking, openness, positivity, trust, and commitment.[17] *Access* refers to sharing information and providing opportunities to build and maintain relationships. *Assurances* are demonstrations of commitment to building and maintaining relationships. *Networking* is having common individuals or groups through which all parties can build and maintain connections. *Openness* is a sincere willingness to communicate thoughts, feelings, concerns, and problems as well as parties' satisfaction and dissatisfaction with each other. *Positivity* means that both sides enjoy their relationships and are happy about them. *Trust* is based upon each party's belief that the other party has integrity and is dependable. And *commitment* is related to how much parties involved view their relationship as worth maintaining and developing.

As social media have become an integral component of many organizations' communication with publics, studies have begun to examine how different relationship dimensions are supported in digital media settings. In their study of Fortune 500 websites, Eyun-Jung Ki and Linda C. Hon found that openness and access are the most commonly used relationship cultivation strategies of the organizations' websites.[18] Tom Kelleher and Barbara M. Miller's study shows that conversational human voice and communicating relational commitment led to more positive relationship outcomes.[19]

These aspects have important implications for relationship-based public diplomacy and are taken into account in the empirical research introduced later in this chapter. As nongovernmental organizations and private individuals have direct access to transnational communication links, governments can no longer claim an exclusive ability to influence public opinion in other countries. Therefore, it has become ever more important that governments share information and become more open and transparent. This is what Barry Fulton terms the change from "megaphone diplomacy" to "network diplomacy."[20] It has become increasingly important to learn to understand and engage alternative views and opinions, rather than speaking over them, as was the case in megaphone diplomacy.

CULTURAL CONSIDERATIONS

Culture is an important factor to consider in building relationships with international publics. Studies have shown that cultural differences influence relationship formation and development as well as how messages are formed and interpreted.[21] For a successful public diplomacy program, cultural conditions of the country where the program is implemented should be taken into account. This is not an easy task. It is challenging to adapt activities to different cultures while preserving distinct core values. Heath epitomizes this challenge in international communication, saying the most compelling issue is "whether a global organization can meet or exceed the expectations of a Babel of voices and cultures without losing its identity by trying to be everything to all markets and publics."[22]

Some theoretical frameworks in international and intercultural communication offer guidance. Here I focus mainly on literature on international public relations, as both public relations and public diplomacy emphasize building *mutually beneficial relationships* with its key stakeholders to achieve an environment that helps the country or organization achieve its goals.[23]

Greg Leichty and Ede Warner suggested a *cultural topoi* perspective, which focuses on cultural premises about the social world and human relationships in different societies.[24] A *topos* refers to commonly used lines of argument that can be adjusted to a variety of subjects and audiences. The scholars identify five types of cultural premises: fatalism, egalitarianism, hierarchy, autonomous individualism, and competitive individualism. According to the fatalist cultural bias, both nature and human nature are "capricious and unpredictable," and everything is decided by fate.[25] Pervasive social distrust and suspicion prevents members of society from welcoming appeals for cooperative social action. In comparison, the egalitarian cultural bias regards human nature as good but argues it is "distorted by social institutions that perpetuate inequality."[26] Therefore, maximizing equality is egalitarians' main objective. A society with the hierarchical cultural bias puts a significant emphasis on disciplines to cultivate world order and those who challenge hierarchical values are punished. On the opposite side of the hierarchical cultural bias is autonomous individual culture. Autonomous individualists seek to abstain from all coercive relationships and to promote equality in their efforts to preserve the norm of reciprocity. Lastly, the competitive–individualist cultural bias suggests that human nature is self-seeking but competition can channel it in a positive way.

Other approaches that can help public diplomacy actors to understand cultural conditions of a country include cultural dimensions theory by Geert Hofstede[27] and contextual research.[28] Hofstede's theory explains how a society's culture influences the values of its members and suggests how those values then constrain behavior via four dimensions: power distance, uncertainty avoidance, individualism–collectivism, and masculinity–femininity. The power distance dimension is related to the extent to which individuals accept differences in power. The uncertainty avoidance dimension is about how members of a society react to uncertain or ambiguous events. The individualism–collectivism dimension relates to the extent to which individuals are integrated into groups. The masculinity–femininity describes different degrees of emphasis on achievements versus relationships by men and women. In comparison, the contextual approach recognizes that political, social, economic, cultural, and technological aspects are so closely intertwined that it is difficult to have a balanced understanding of a society without considering the interactions of these multiple aspects.

These cultural considerations may help public diplomacy actors better conceptualize how relationships are understood in a particular society. As an example, let's consider South Korea. Hierarchy and collectivism are still prominent in South Korea as a consequence of Confucianism. Confucianism puts relationships at the center of a person's existence, and a person's identity is constituted by the duties and responsibilities one has to others. Seen from this perspective, an overriding social objective becomes maintaining a harmonious balance based upon each person understanding, accepting, and fulfilling roles in the set of relationships which, taken together, constitute the social order. Public diplomacy actors should consider such aspects when they engage South Korean publics. Culture varies; it is important to bear this in mind and to not rigidly apply a one-size-fits-all public diplomacy perspective.

Cultural variability together with different dimensions of relationships are important for understanding the differing perspectives or assumptions international publics may hold. The issue of relationships in public diplomacy has largely been studied from the perspectives of public diplomacy actors. However, it is important to examine how the publics engaged through social media–based public diplomacy programs actually view relationships. The following empirical research was designed to specifically investigate the topic.

U.S. NETWORKED PUBLIC DIPLOMACY IN SOUTH KOREA: A CASE STUDY

While more and more scholars have emphasized relationship building and management in public diplomacy, there has been little empirical research on this topic. In this section, I introduce a research study[29] designed to shed light on several specific aspects of relationships publics emphasize in considering countries other than their own. In doing so, I examine Café USA, run by the U.S. embassy in Seoul.

Café USA was launched by the U.S. embassy in Seoul in 2004 to forge interactive communication between the U.S. government and South Koreans and quickly became a leading example of networked public diplomacy. This Café USA online community is part of the embassy's efforts to better relate to South Koreans, especially young South Koreans, by listening to what they have to say, as well as discussing U.S. positions. Engaging South Koreans online is important especially as South Korea is one of the world's most wired countries.[30] In announcing the launch of Café USA, then-U.S. ambassador to South Korea Christopher Hill said:

> As we live in a high-tech era, the Embassy must find new ways to reach out to people. I look forward to reading the views of the Korean public by reading the posts on Café USA and sharing my thoughts on Korea–U.S. relations with the Korean people. I know it is important for us to listen to Korean viewpoints, and I hope people will find Café USA a useful forum to express their views on Korean-American relations.[31]

Café USA, hosted on South Korean servers, offers interactive features such as multiple chat groups and a space for South Koreans to ask questions of the ambassador and other embassy staff.[32] Most of the content is provided both in Korean and English. As of August 2012, Café USA had about 11,000 registered online members.

Studying what aspects of relationships Café USA members emphasize will help us better understand public diplomacy in the networked age. This study examined (a) South Koreans' perspectives on their relationships with the United States, and (b) how Café USA members' perspectives on relationships with the United States might differ from South Korean groups who were not members of Café USA. I suspected there might be a difference because there is considerable variety in South Koreans' perspectives on the United States, given both the significance of the United States for many aspects of Korean society and the controversy surrounding Korea–U.S. relations. South Korea and the United States have maintained a robust, if sometimes tumultuous, political and military alliance dating back to the end of World War II. The two countries also maintain strong economic relations and recently signed a bilateral free trade agreement.

It was important to have participants with varied experiences with the United States, so I contacted three specific groups of people for the study: (a) South Korean members of Café USA; (b) South Korean Fulbright scholars; and (c) South Korean journalists covering South Korea's Foreign Ministry. In the end, there were sixty participants total, twenty in each group.

Since the focus of this research is on types of reasoning rather than attributes of individual respondents, I used Q methodology[33] to identify South

Koreans' perspectives on relationships with the United States. I developed a sample of thirty-three statements drawn from materials generated by focus groups of South Koreans and previous studies on relationships. I then asked participants in the three groups to order the statements on a continuum ranging from *most disagree* to *most agree*.

Perspectives on Relationship

Through my research, I identified three types of relationship perspectives South Koreans have with the United States: *sincerity based*, *outcome based*, and *access based*. Trust and sincerity were considered essential to the sincerity-based group, in terms of their relationships with the United States. People from this group were most likely to agree with such statements as "to make people like me feel respected" and "to treat people like me fairly and justly." This group was less concerned about the United States being successful or providing opportunities. In the open-ended responses, they emphasized the importance of trust and mutual respect for their relationships with the United States, and Café USA members were the most prominent group loaded on this factor.

The outcome-based group emphasized results and providing opportunities as important aspects for their relationships with the United States. The highly ranked statements for this group include "to provide various opportunities to people like me," "to be successful at the things it tries to do," and "to have the ability to accomplish what it says it will do." In their open-ended responses, those belonging to this group emphasized as important that the United States be efficient in dealing with issues related to South Koreans. Fulbright scholars were the most prominent group associated with this perspective.

The access-based group emphasized information sharing. The statements that represent their views include "to keep people like me informed of U.S. policies on a regular basis" and "to share enough information with people like me about its governance." Not surprisingly, journalists tended to fall into this group.

Cultural contexts may help understand the findings. The sincerity group may represent a more traditional Korean Confucian ontology that puts relationships at the center of a person's existence. From Confucian perspectives, maintaining the harmony of the society is paramount, and it is, therefore, important that individuals understand, accept, and fulfill their roles as defined by their relationships with others.[34] The sincerity group's concern with relations is exemplified by their interpretation of several defining moments of U.S.–South Korea alliance. For example, people belonging to this group often expressed dissatisfaction with how the United States handled the death of two teenage South Korean girls hit and killed by a U.S. armored vehicle in 2002. At that time, many Koreans called for sincere apology from the U.S. government and felt the United States failed to provide one. The U.S. position at that time was that they were handling the situation based on the existing Status of Forces Agreement (SOFA) and other bilateral agreements.

In contrast, the outcome-based group may represent Aristotelian ontology.[35] This group stresses formal processes and regulations and is less concerned with sincerity. This group is likely to take *quid pro quo* approaches and remain satisfied with the United States, as long as it is efficient and transparent in dealing with issues related to them—evidenced, for example, by speedy issuance of visas. Indeed, being efficient and successful were the aspects emphasized by those who belong to the outcome-based group in their relationships with the United States.

Relational Commitment and Networked Public Diplomacy

The most important finding here is that, compared with the other groups, the sincerity-based group representing Café USA members put more emphasis on U.S. commitment to relations with South Koreans. This is significant, in that previous research showed communicating relational commitment is important for an organization to forge positive relationships with its publics engaged online.[36] The main objective of the U.S. embassy in Seoul in operating Café USA is to enhance mutual understanding and build trust.[37] The embassy's continued efforts of engaging them through this relationship-based online community may help the two sides improve mutual understanding, without necessarily ensuring policy agreement.

While the purpose of this research was not to generalize the findings, I believe the results of this research have implications beyond the United States and South Korea. Most of all, public diplomacy officials hoping to engage global publics through social media–based programs will need to understand ways of effectively communicating their commitment to relationships with those publics. In laying out online strategies, they should consider country- and culture-specific factors that may affect how they view relationships. There still exists the misconception that all public diplomacy is propaganda. Careful considerations of those factors may help convey the message that online engagement efforts are aimed at sincere, two-way dialogue with global publics rather than one-sided dissemination of positive ideas and opinions of the country.

The trends outlined in this article suggest several areas for future research. First, comparative studies are needed that explore how citizens in different countries and in different cultures respond to and engage with public diplomacy social media campaigns. Second, research is needed into how the characteristics of the country that initiates PD programs via social media influence outcomes. Finally, researchers should also consider exploring how these trends operate in countries at differing levels of internet and mobile penetration.

CONCLUSION

The ubiquity of interactive networked communication technologies has provided public diplomacy actors with important tools with which to build and maintain relationships with global publics. In this chapter, I discussed how social media–based public diplomacy initiatives provide alternative ways of facilitating and strengthening relationships with ordinary citizens in other countries.

Publics vary regarding how they understand relationships, and this variability has significant implications for the ways in which public diplomacy campaigns build and maintain relationships with those publics. For example, my empirical research suggests that communicating sincere commitment to relationships is more important to publics engaged through social media–based public diplomacy programs than those who are not. Effective use of social media enables relationships to be at the core of network-based public diplomacy.

Public diplomacy actors should understand how information production and dissemination has become decentralized and how this has affected publics' expectations in online social relations and information use. Most of all, these understandings must be augmented with a contextual and cultural awareness of target publics' relationship perspectives with regard to countries other than their own.

Incorporating these factors is not an easy task. I believe that is why we need a closer collaboration between public diplomacy practitioners and scholars. With more increased and institutional discussions and exchanges, the two sides will benefit from each other in addressing real challenges facing public diplomacy in the networked information age.

As Slaughter put it,[38] "connectedness" has become "the measure of power" in international affairs, and, thus, it is essential to understand how different types of connections are initiated, developed, maintained, and strengthened in this networked information age. Public diplomacy initiatives should include strategies designed to build relationships with global publics, rather than simply delivering information to them. In doing so, public diplomacy practitioners must understand that people are differentiated not only based on demographics but also on their understandings of relationships.

NOTES

1. Amanda Lenhart, Kristen Purcell, Aaron Smith, and Kathryn Zickuhr, *Social Media & Mobile Internet Use among Teens and Young Adults* (Washington, DC: Pew Research Center, 2010); Nielsen, "State of the Media: The Social Media Report Q3 2011," http://blog.nielsen.com/nielsenwire/social/; Pew Research Center, "Global Digital Communication: Texting, Social Networking Popular Worldwide," December 20, 2011.

2. Philip Seib, *Real-Time Diplomacy: Politics and Power in the Social Media Era* (Palgrave Macmillan, 2012); Hyunjin Seo and Stuart J. Thorson, "Evaluating Social Networking in Public Diplomacy," in *Politics, Democracy and E-Government: Participation and Service Delivery*, ed. Christopher G. Reddick (New York: IGI Global Publishing, 2010).
3. Foreign and Commonwealth Office, *Engagement: Public Diplomacy in a Globalized World* (London: Foreign and Commonwealth Office, 2008); Spiegel Online, "Cyber Diplomacy: Sweden Opens Virtual Embassy in Second Life," January 30, 2007.
4. Danah Boyd and Nicole Ellison, "Social Network Sites: Definition, History, and Scholarship," *Journal of Computer-Mediated Communication* 13 (2007): 210–230.
5. U.S. Department of State, "21st Century Statecraft," accessed July 17, 2012, http://www.state.gov/statecraft/overview/index.htm
6. Michele Kelemen, "Twitter Diplomacy: State Department 2.0," February 21, 2010, http://www.npr.org/blogs/alltechconsidered/2012/02/21/147207004/twitter-diplomacy-state-department-2-0
7. Sunhyuk Kim and Wonhyuk Lim, "How to Deal with South Korea," *The Washington Quarterly* 30 (2007): 71–82.
8. R.S. Zaharna, "Mapping Out a Spectrum of Public Diplomacy," in *Routledge Handbook of Public Diplomacy*, ed. Nancy Snow and Philip M. Taylor (New York: Routledge, 2009); R.S. Zaharna, *Battles to Bridges: U.S. Strategic Communication and Public Diplomacy after 9/11* (Basingstoke: Palgrave MacMillan, 2010).
9. Zaharna, "Mapping out a Spectrum of Public Diplomacy," 91.
10. Giles Scott-Smith, "Exchange Programs and Public Diplomacy," in *Routledge Handbook of Public Diplomacy*, ed. Snow and Taylor (New York: Routledge, 2009).
11. Lenhart et al., "Social Media & Mobile Internet Use"; Nielsen, "State of the Media"; Pew Research Center, "Global Digital Communication."
12. Sora Park, "The Impact of Media Use and Cultural Exposure on the Mutual Perception of Koreans and Japanese," *Asian Journal of Communication* 15 (2005): 173–87.
13. Charlene Li and Josh Bernoff, *Groundswell: Winning in a World Transformed by Social Technologies* (Boston: Harvard Business Press, 2008).
14. Glen M. Broom, Shawna Casey, and James Ritchey, "Toward a Concept and Theory of Organization-Public Relationships," *Journal of Public Relations Research* 9 (1997): 95.
15. T. Dean Thomlison, "An Interpersonal Primer with Implications for Public Relations," in *Public Relations as Relationship Management: A Relational Approach to the Study and Practice of Public Relations*, ed. John A. Ledingham and Stephen D. Bruning (Mahwah, NJ: Lawrence Erlbaum, 2000), 178.
16. W. Timothy Coombs, "Interpersonal Communication and Public Relations," in *Handbook of Public Relations*, ed. Robert L. Heath (Thousand Oaks, CA: Sage, 2004).
17. Daniel J. Canary and Laura Stafford, "Relational Maintenance Strategies and Equity in Marriage," *Communication Monographs* 3 (1992): 243–67; Larissa A. Grunig, James E. Grunig, and David M. Dozier, *Excellent Public Relations and Effective Organizations: A Study of Communication Management in Three Countries* (Mahwah, NJ: Lawrence Erlbaum, 2002); John A. Ledingham and Stephen D. Bruning, "Relationship Management in Public Relations: Dimensions of an Organization-Public Relationship," *Public Relations Review* 24 (1998): 55–65; John A. Ledingham and Stephen D.

Bruning, "A Longitudinal Study of Organization-Public Relationship Dimensions: Defining the Role of Communication in the Practice of Relationship Management," in *Public Relations as Relationship Management: A Relational Approach to the Study and Practice of Public Relations*, ed. John A. Ledingham and Stephen D. Bruning (Mahwah, NJ: Lawrence Erlbaum, 2000).

18. Eyun-Jung Ki and Linda C. Hon, "Relationship Maintenance Strategies on Fortune 500 Company Websites," *Journal of Communication Management* 10 (2006): 27–43.

19. Tom Kelleher and Barbara M. Miller, "Organizational Blogs and the Human Voice: Relational Strategies and Relational Outcomes," *Journal of Computer-Mediated Communication* 11 (2006): 395–414.

20. Barry Fulton, "Net Diplomacy I: Beyond Foreign Ministries" (Washington, DC: U.S. Institute of Peace, 2002).

21. Ling Chen, "Communication in Intercultural Relationships," in *Handbook of International and Intercultural Communication*, ed. William B. Gudykunst and Bella Mody (Thousand Oaks, CA: Sage, 2004); Maureen Taylor, "International Public Relations: Opportunities and Challenges for the 21st Century," in *Handbook of Public Relations*, ed. Heath.

22. Robert L. Heath, "Globalization—The Frontier of Multinationalism and Cultural Diversity," in *Handbook of Public Relations*, 625.

23. Scott M. Cutlip, Allen H. Center, and Glen M. Broom, *Effective Public Relations* (Englewood Cliffs, NJ: Prentice Hall, 1994); Kathy R. Fitzpatrick, *Future of U.S. Public Diplomacy: An Uncertain Fate* (Leiden: Martinus Nijhoff, 2010).

24. Greg Leichty and Ede Warner, "Cultural Topoi: Implications for Public Relations," in *Handbook of Public Relations*, ed. Heath.

25. Ibid., 65.

26. Ibid.

27. Geert Hofstede, *Culture's Consequences: International Differences in Work-Related Values* (Newburk Park, CA: Sage, 1984).

28. Ray E. Hiebert, "Global Public Relations in a Post-Communist World: A New Model," *Public Relations Review* 18 (1992): 117–26; Taylor, "International Public Relations."

29. Hyunjin Seo and Dennis F. Kinsey, "Incorporating Relationship Perspectives into Public Diplomacy," *Public Relations Review* (in press).

30. Korea Internet & Security Agency & Korea Communications Commission, "2009 Survey of South Koreans' Internet Use" (Seoul, South Korea: KISA, 2009).

31. U.S. Embassy in Seoul, "U.S. Embassy Launches Café USA," accessed March 10, 2008, http://seoul.usembassy.gov/caf_usa.html

32. Seo and Thorson, "Evaluating Social Networking."

33. Q methodology allows for systematic investigation of human subjectivity demonstrating perspectives, opinions, beliefs, attitudes, sentiments, etc. Q methodology combines the qualitative study of patterns of thought with statistical applications of traditional quantitative research. A benefit of Q methodology is that it does not require large numbers of participants since the sampling unit is the statement rather than the individual respondent. An online Q-sort program was used in this research to more efficiently reach target respondents who were living in different parts of South Korea.

34. Raymond Cohen, *Negotiating across Cultures: Communication Obstacles in International Diplomacy* (Washington, DC: United States Institute of Peace Press, 1991); Richard E. Nisbett, *The Geography of Thought* (New York: Free Press, 2003).

35. Nisbett, *Geography of Thought*.
36. Kelleher and Miller, "Organizational Blogs."
37. Seo and Thorson, "Evaluating Social Networking."
38. Anne-Marie Slaughter, "America's Edge: Power in the Networked Century," *Foreign Affairs* 88 (2009): 94–113.

Part III

Networks & Collaboration
The Connective Mindshift

12 Network Purpose, Network Design
Dimensions of Network and Collaborative Public Diplomacy

R. S. Zaharna

INTRODUCTION

One of the fallacies of "network public diplomacy" is that there is one "network." As organizational structures, networks vary greatly. When we speak of a "network" initiative, we need to ask: what type of "network" is it? Does it resemble a terrorist network composed of loosely held-together individuals working in cells, rarely communicating together? Or is it a tightly knit, dense network, whose members interact frequently, offering support and engaging in frequent dialogue, as might be seen in a women's empowerment network? Does the structure align with the purpose?

Beyond network structure, there are the communication dynamics. Human networks in public diplomacy are not inanimate grids, but dynamic organisms that can grow and thrive—or wither and die. Culture is an inherent feature of human communication and, by extension, of public diplomacy. Culture can distort perceptions and produce misunderstandings, or provide novel perspectives and synergistic insights.[1]

These internal communication or relational dynamics help distinguish networks from collaborative public diplomacy initiatives. I have deliberately separated the two in the title to underscore networks as a *structure* and collaboration as a *process*. Public diplomacy initiatives using social media tools such as Facebook or Twitter make it fairly easy to create a network structure. Not surprisingly, there has been a surge of network initiatives. Collaborative initiatives in public diplomacy are far less common.[2] Collaboration means individuals are not only connecting and sharing information, but through the process of their interactions are generating knowledge, innovation, and synergistic results.

In recent years, two examples of effective network-based collaborative initiatives stand out. The first example is the often-cited political initiative of the International Campaign to Ban Landmines (ICBL). ICBL began with a handful of NGOs and grew into global network of more than 1,000 NGOs located in sixty countries. Working collaboratively, the

ICBL successfully promoted the passage of an international treaty to ban landmines in less than two years and won the 1997 Nobel Peace Prize. Another initiative that has captured global attention, though as a cultural rather than a network-based collaborative initiative, is the Chinese government-sponsored Confucius Institute (CI). Unlike most cultural institutes that are based on "stand alone" modules, the Confucius Institute initiative utilizes synergistic relational strategies built upon a layered global network. Not coincidentally, the number of Confucius Institutes has grown exponentially from one in 2004 to more than 350 in 2010. More significantly, the collaborative activities and pooled experience among the institutes around the globe have greatly advanced innovative methods for teaching Chinese, a language once shunned for its perceived difficulty.

On the surface, these two initiatives, one by a nonstate actor and the other by a state actor, are quite different. Peering below the surface, what both share is an alignment of design with purpose. What makes an initiative effective depends on the alignment between public diplomacy goals and the network initiative's structure and communication/relational dynamics. Understanding this alignment is critical.

In this chapter, I draw upon insights from the ICBL and China's CI initiatives to construct a roadmap for identifying and analyzing dimensions of effective network and collaborative initiatives in public diplomacy. The analysis begins with a broad network overview of different elements that are common to public diplomacy (PD) initiatives. The next layer of the analysis focuses on network structure and network effects. The third layer of analysis probes the relational dynamics or network synergy. The final layer, network strategy, examines the information dynamics of the network. Both network synergy and strategy contain the potential to transform a collection of network ties into a dynamic, sustainable collaborative initiative. The chapter concludes with "networks of purpose" to illustrate the alignment of different network structures and communication dynamics to different public diplomacy goals.

IDENTIFYING ELEMENTS OF A NETWORK OVERVIEW

Our roadmap for identifying and analyzing a network initiative in public diplomacy begins by gaining an overview or orientation of the overall network. The overview consists of the key characteristics common to network-based initiatives, such as sponsor participants, purpose, time frame, and communication mode.

By way of illustration, we can draw on examples from more extensive analysis of the ICBL and China's Confucius Institutes initiatives.[3] The ICBL began with the merger of five Western and one Asian NGOs in October 1992.[4] From the beginning, the group had shared leadership. A steering committee developed a broad global strategy and then let the NGOs decide on local tactics. By 1996, more than 1,000 NGOS from across Asia, Africa, and Latin America had joined the ICBL. In addition to regional diversity, the NGOs brought a diversity of perspectives from different sectors: human rights, children's rights, development issues, refugee issues, and medical and humanitarian relief. The ICBL's relationship-building strategies included external coalition building by the nonstate actors to gain the support of nation-states. Securing the support of Canada was a major turning point for the ICBL in November 1995. The Canadian Foreign Minister Lloyd Axworthy headed a group of "like-minded" small and medium-size nations and initiated what was called the "Ottawa process." In contrast to other conventional arms treaties that took a decade or more, the ICBL treaty moved through the Ottawa process in an astounding eighteen months.[5]

China's National Office for Teaching Chinese as a Foreign Language or Hanban (an abbreviation of Hanyu Bangonshi) launched the Confucius Institute in 2004. Rather than establishing independent cultural institutes, the Hanban created partnerships between a prominent Chinese university and a prestigious foreign academic institute that would house the Confucius Institute. Both the foreign host university and the Chinese university are linked back to the Hanban. This partnering established immediate and concrete bonds and provided a platform for direct interpersonal communication and sustained, long-term relationship building. Each institute is expected to complement its teaching activities with cultural activities for the students and the local community, and to link with other institutes. The Hanban facilitates this global linking of institutes by hosting an annual conference in Beijing and through its interactive web portal, Confucius Institute Online. The online and offline venues facilitate information sharing between the institutes about the different approaches to teaching Chinese, as well as complementary cultural activities.

Sponsors, Partners, and Stakeholders

A first step in analyzing a network is identifying its key participants. Traditional state-centric public diplomacy would assume a state sponsor. Newer conceptions of public diplomacy that now include nonstate actors highlight the fact that nonstate actors can also sponsor or initiate network initiatives. Policy-oriented network initiatives oftentimes have a shared partnership between state and nonstate actors to achieve political goals. Rather than targeting passive audiences or publics, sponsors seek to identify, attract, and retain active network members or strategic stakeholders.[6]

Identifying sponsorship is important for several reasons. Knowing the sponsor provides insight into the network purpose and prospects. Sometimes the network may mirror the sponsor's characteristic attributes or values. Direct and indirect sponsorship matters in public diplomacy because of the implications for trust, credibility, and accountability. Direct sponsorship lends itself to greater visibility and accountability. Although indirect sponsorship, especially by states, may provide short-term advantages, such as gaining entry and building credibility with potential stakeholders, in the long term it may undermine the viability of the initiative.[7]

Purpose

Public diplomacy initiatives often have multiple and sometimes conflicting purposes. These may include the sponsor's specific political and communication goals as well as the often unarticulated needs of the stakeholders. A careful analysis should identify as many dimensions as possible, particularly the sponsor's and key stakeholders' underlying goals. Broadly speaking, network initiatives span from politically to nonpolitically oriented goals. Nonpolitical network initiatives may engage stakeholders on issues such as science, medicine, education, or the environment and seek goals such as mutual understanding, relationship building, or collaborative exchanges. Naturally, sponsors may have strong, underlying political motivations for these apolitical initiatives. In contrast, policy-oriented networks have an explicitly articulated and advanced political goal, such as policy advocacy, policy formation, or agenda setting. Politically oriented initiatives often entail greater levels of engagement and trust, because stakeholders often assume higher levels of risk than in nonpolitical initiatives.

Aligned with these broad strategic objectives are tactical communication goals that can range from creating awareness (e.g., raising public consciousness about a political or social issue), informing (e.g., circulating information on education, culture, science, or policy), influencing (e.g., shaping attitudes and behavioral preferences, cultivating shared norms or values), advocacy (e.g., calls to action around a policy agenda), collaboration (e.g., working together toward a shared outcome), or innovation (e.g., knowledge generation or problem solving).

The stakeholder goals are equally important as those of the network sponsor. Stakeholders may consider the network purpose to be task orientation (i.e., the network is dedicated to achieving a specific task they support), social orientation (i.e., the network fulfills their need for belonging and social affinity), or identity orientation (i.e., the network fulfills their need for identity expression and self-actualization). The ICBL's political agenda gave it a strong task orientation, and it contained an identity orientation for activists. The China's CI initiative has a strong social orientation, as well as an identity orientation for students of Chinese heritage. Networks that fulfill stakeholder needs are likely to be more robust and sustainable than those that revolve solely around the sponsor's goals.

Time Frame

Duration is not normally stressed in network studies. Time considerations, however, are important for public diplomacy initiatives. An initiative may be conceived as a long-term venture but die prematurely due to political or financial reasons. A series of such failed initiatives may erode the credibility of a network sponsor. Gauging a network's time horizon may indicate a vision for the relational dynamic. Open-ended initiatives with a long-term horizon imply commitment and may bolster stakeholder trust and reciprocal commitment. Network initiatives focused on a specific task, especially emergent networks, may be able to accommodate greater stakeholder diversity if the time frame is finite.

Communication Mode

Another critical dimension of any network is the primary communication mode or ways that the members in a network exchange information or interact with each other. Everett Rogers raised the importance of communication modes in his pioneering work on the diffusion of innovations, which theorizes how new ideas spread among people.[8]

The network's preferred communication mode can illuminate the dynamics of stakeholder relations. Different modes of communication offer different advantages. Technologically mediated communication is typically the fastest and most efficient way to spread the most information to the greatest number of people. Interpersonal (face-to-face) communication, on the other hand, is generally regarded as more persuasive because it provides the full sensory experience individuals look for when assessing such factors as trust, credibility, and satisfaction.

For policy makers, communication mode relates to the communication purpose of a network initiative. Mediated communication may be ideal for generating awareness throughout a large network. Interpersonal communication may be better if the goal is changing attitudes and behavior. A transnational network that relies primarily on mediated communication might enhance collaboration by augmenting virtual connectivity with opportunities for face-to-face interaction, such as annual conferences or exchange visits. Adding multiple communication modes as well as media platforms for stakeholders can increase the variety of engagement, which research suggests can help promote trust.[9] Table 12.1 provides an overview of the critical elements for developing a network overview.

Table 12.1   Elements of Network Overview

Dimensions	Variations	ICBL	China CI
Conception	Emerging/planned	Emergent	Planned, managed
Sponsorship	• State/nonstate • Shared partnership • Direct/indirect	Nonstate Shared Direct	State State sponsor, Institutes partner Direct
Purpose	• Policy/non-policy orientation • Stakeholder need: task, social, identity	Policy Task oriented	Non-policy Social oriented

Time frame	• Temporary, open-ended
	• Short-term, long-term
		Temporary,
		    short-term
			Open-ended,
			    long-term vision

Communication objective	• Generate awareness
	• Inform
	• Influence
	• Advocacy
	• Innovation
		Policy advocacy
		Consciousness
		    raising, call
		    to action,
		    problem
		    solving
			Cultural promotion
			
			Cultivate shared
			    norms, innovate

Communication mode	• Interpersonal/mediated • Single/multiple modes • Personal/impersonal • Participatory/passive	Initial interpersonal, move to mediated (fax machines), conferences (interpersonal)	Interpersonal (direct between partner institutes), CI Online move to Web 2.0, conferences— interpersonal

NETWORK STRUCTURE: WHOLE-NETWORK LEVEL

Within the PD literature, networks have been contrasted with hierarchies in such a way that there appears to be such thing as one "network" public diplomacy. In fact, there are many different types of networks. Different network structures or typologies produce different network effects. Understanding network structures allows practitioners to align networks to communication and public diplomacy goals, and vice versa.

Recent literature reviews find that the majority of social network analysis (SNA) and network studies focus on the individual level by mapping the "ego-centric" network of an individual node (actor or ego) and the evolution of its pattern of ties (relations).[10] In terms of evaluating an overall network initiative, however, knowing the position or power of any *one* individual member inside a network is not as helpful as knowing the strength of the network overall. How robust is the network? How efficient is the information flow? How diverse are the network members? To explore these types of questions, we need a "whole-network" level of analysis.[11] Several scholars have noted that studies at the level of the whole network are "rare," including in the field of international relations.[12] There are several whole-network measures that can inform the design and execution of PD initiatives.

Density: Cohesion and Openness

Within network analysis, *density* refers to the proportion of actors connected to each other.[13] The greater the number of links between the members in a network, the greater the network density. Several observations by scholars about network density are important for analyzing and designing networks with specific public diplomacy goals. Rowley drew attention to the relationship between density, communication, and shared norms.[14] Members in denser networks communicate with greater frequency and ease. This leads to the development of shared behaviors and expectations, and to the diffusion and reinforcement of norms across the network.[15] Members in a highly dense network also imitate behaviors as a way of gaining access to or legitimacy within a network.[16]

Both dense and open network structures have advantages and disadvantages. Denser networks are more robust because more members are connected to one another. Members of denser networks are also less likely to separate into cliques or groups, which makes them less vulnerable to external manipulation, which inhibits network fragmentation. On the other hand, dense networks can become too closed and vulnerable to the mistakes of groupthink. Sparser networks also exhibit less redundancy, and can be comparatively more efficient than the dense network.

For public diplomacy policy makers and analysis, density addresses questions such as: How cohesive are the members in the network? Is it a tightly woven network? Assessing the desired density also relates back to purpose of the network initiative. The dense interweaving of the Confucius Institute network appears ideal given the goal of developing and reinforcing shared cultural norms. The relatively open network of the ICBL may have been key for introducing diverse perspectives for problem solving and policy advocacy in the political arena.

Network Size and Tie Strength: Quantity—Quality

Ali Fisher and I once reflected on the question, which is better: network reach or network density? Is it better to have a big network that spans the globe, or a small, but tightly knit, network? Research into measures of the quantity and quality of network ties sheds light on this question.[17] In terms of quantity a large network may be particularly successful at creating awareness.[18] The greater the number, the larger and more expansive the network, and, hence, the wider the potential diffusion of information. Large, highly visible networks may convey to those outside the network that a public diplomacy initiative is particularly strong. The rapid growth or expansion of a network size may also provide a useful measuring stick for soft power appeal.

The quality of ties (i.e., tie strength) between network members is also critical. Many people may belong to a large network, but their connections may be weak. Network members with strong ties, such as close friends and family, interact on a regular basis. Their associations are commonly characterized by trust, commitment, and longevity. Those connected by weak ties—such as acquaintances or friends of friends—communicate less frequently. Intuitively, a smaller number of relations within a network suggests stronger ties, while a larger number suggests weaker ties.[19]

Both weak and strong ties have their advantages and disadvantages. Hansen suggests that weak ties are less costly to maintain.[20] Weak ties can serve as bridges or boundary spanners between groups. Granovetter argues that weak ties provide access to non-redundant rich information, hence the phrase, "the strength of weak ties."[21] Weak ties may be the source of novel information, but strong ties more effective in enhancing knowledge transfer and learning, especially complex information.[22] Strong ties are also important for social support and reinforcing norms.[23] There is still debate over whether strong on weak ties lead to greater innovation.[24]

For policy makers and analysis, the question is: What kinds of ties suit the purposes of the network? For a PD initiative that requires coordination of efforts and frequent communication, a smaller network with strong ties may be important. A PD initiative focused on youth empowerment may go either way: strong ties to facilitate social support and reinforcement of new behaviors, or large quality of weak ties for visibility (strength in numbers). For PD initiatives, the cohesion of the network whole is essential. Clusters of strong ties within a large network, for example, may fragment or destabilize the network whole. This brings us back to the importance of centralization, network bridges, and the role of a network weaver in a PD initiative.

Centralization: Stability—Flexibility

Centralization measures the degree to which one or a few actors act as central or focal points in the network. Network structures range along a continuum from centralized to decentralized.[25] In a highly centralized network, members are connected to one or a few actors. China's CI is highly centralized; all of the institutes worldwide are linked to the Hanban as well as to the portal, Confucius Online. The ICBL, with its defused and shared leadership, reflects a decentralized structure.

Both ends of the centralization spectrum offer advantages and disadvantages. When a single hub serves as the information gatekeeper, the network may be inefficient and vulnerable.[26] However, a central entity responsible for maintaining the stability, growth, and diversity of the network whole can be essential for its long-term viability. Robust networks have what Valdis Krebs and June Holley call a "network weaver" who facilitates relations among members.[27] Keith Provan and his colleagues in their discussion of network governance and effectiveness noted,

> Unlike dyadic relationships [partners], which are managed by the organizations themselves, and unlike serendipitous networks, which have no formal governance structures at all, the activities of whole, goal-directed networks must generally be managed and governed if they are to be effective.[28]

For policy makers and analysis, centralization focuses on who, if anyone, is in control of the network. And, relatedly, how much control or centralization is desired? Provan and Milward demonstrated that centralization facilitates network integration and coordination, which are particularly important features for diverse networks.[29] Margarita Mayo and Juan Carlos Pastor highlighted the link between centralization and network diversity in enhancing network performance and social cohesion. Greater centralization may help reduce uncertainty conflicts, because certain members are assigned bridging and facilitator roles.[30] The optimal degree of centralization depends on the purpose of the initiative. Centralization may be beneficial when focused on simple tasks, but less effective for complex tasks.[31] As mentioned before, China's CI initiative is highly centralized, which may be ideal, given the need to integrate and coordinate the diversity of all its associated students around the globe.

Diversity: Coordination—Innovation

As we will see in the next section, diversity is a critical for network synergy. *Homogeneity* refers to how similar the network members are. *Composition* refers to the proportion of network members who share particular characteristics. In networks, diversity poses both advantages and disadvantages.[32] Diversity increases communication and coordination problems. The network may face problems of member integration and retention. Diverse teams can spend either "too much time engaging in conflicts and clearing up misunderstandings or too little time interacting with those different from themselves."[33] Homogeneous networks may be more stable and run more smoothly and efficiently. The positive side of the "different" in diversity is "variety." Scott Page, who has written extensively on diversity, argues that multiple perspectives are particularly valuable for unlocking new ways of thinking about protracted or complex problems.[34] Table 12.2 provides an overview of the dimensions of whole network for analyzing initiatives with examples from ICBL and China's CI initiative.

Table 12.2   Elements of Network Structure

Dimensions	Critical Questions	ICBL	China CI
Density	• How cohesive is the network? Dense/sparse, open/closed	Initially dense, becomes more open, sparse	High-density, closed network design
Size / Ties	• Quality of ties: How strong are the relations within the network?	Fairly rapid growth —global	Rapid growth, regional, span to global
Centralization	• How is the network governed? Centralized/ decentralized	Decentralized	Centralized
Diversity	• How diverse is the composition of stakeholders or members within the network?	Initially Western NGOs, NGOs diversify, add state actors, diversify state actors	Early CI institutes in Asia, expand to Western Europe and U.S., then to Africa and South America

NETWORK SYNERGY: RELATIONAL DYNAMICS

Network synergy focuses on the relational dynamics that transform a network structure of links between nodes into a collaborative process of relationship building and knowledge generation between people. It is the network synergy that makes the difference between networks that thrive and those that wither away. To explore the dimension of network synergy, we can examine three inter-related relational processes: internal relationship building, external coalition building, and incorporating diversity. The presence or absence of these relational dynamics helps condition network effectiveness and the potential for collaboration.

Internal Relations: Bonding and Team Building

Internal relationship building has implications for overall network productivity, coherence, and sustainability. There are two prominent types of internal relationship building: bonding and team building. Oftentimes, the problem in network development is retention rather than recruitment.

Much of the literature assumes that shared or mutual interests are a prerequisite for relationship building. However, this assumption may be rooted in Western concepts of individualism and based on the transactional view of relationships. Asian research reveals a relational dynamic that begins with bonding tactics and then proceeds to the cultivation of shared interests.[35] Bonding is important for maintaining network membership and sustaining the vitality of the overall network.

A second dimension of internal relational process focuses on transforming a group of individuals into a team. Whereas a group relies on the combined contributions of separate individual members working independently, a unified team draws upon a synergistic exchange among the members to multiply their combined impact.[36] When network members work together as a team, they create a self-perpetuating type of energy, or synergy, that grows exponentially. Task-oriented activities help create a sense of achievement. Social-oriented activities help create a sense of community. Positive interpersonal experiences also can serve to validate and strengthen individual personal commitment to a team effort.

Internal relationship building is a prominent feature in China's CI initiative and is reflected in the strategic pairing of "teaching activities" (or, task cohesion) with "cultural activities" (or, social cohesion) mandated for all institutes.[37] An institute's teaching activities provide the initial bonding process through task cohesion as students share the task of trying to learn a new language. The cultural activities are in essence opportunities for building social cohesion. Participating in dragon boat racing, Chinese New Year festivities, or online competitive challenges provide emotional rewards for pursuing language study (maintaining the bonds, measuring achievements) and help build team spirit as well as sense of community.

External Coalition Building

While internal relationship building helps transform individual network members into a team, external relationship building helps boosts the network's reach, resources, impact, and legitimacy. Often, external coalition building is prompted by recognizing limitations or the need for a particular resource, be it additional financial funds or a specialized expertise. External relationship building is also a vital source of diversity. According to Krebs and Holley, uniting with others who share a similar goal but who bring new and different perspectives creates the ideal environment for an effective network: "Similarity helps the communication and building of trust, while diversity presents new ideas and perspectives."[38] Plus, as Krebs and Holley add, "to get transformative ideas, you often have to go outside of your group."[39]

Mark Pachucki and Ronald Breiger introduced the idea of "cultural holes," which represent differences or gaps in meanings, practices, or discourse in social structures.[40] A network bridge, often a person on the periphery of a network, serves as a conduit for information and resources and can facilitate external relationship building on behalf of the network. In public diplomacy initiatives, this would mean identifying or even cultivating persons to serve as network bridges to facilitate the external relationship-building process. External relationship building can also occur through specifically designed events that facilitate interaction across boundaries.[41]

We see external relationship building in both the ICBL and Confucius Institute networks. The nonstate ICBL engaged in external bridging through coalition building with like-minded organizations and countries. In China's CI initiative, each institute is encouraged to build external relations locally with the community and globally with other Confucius Institutes. Hanban facilitates connections among the institutes through its interactive portal "Confucius Institute Online" and offline through its annual conference in Beijing.

Incorporating Diversity

A third relational process and critical source of synergy emerges through the combination of internal and external relationship building is the synergy of incorporating diversity. External and internal relationship building represent *exposure* to diversity. How a network initiative responds to differences is critical. Diversity can be the greatest source of friction—but also the greatest source of transformative synergy.[42] Without an ability to absorb and integrate diversity, the network can ossify, succumb to the perils of groupthink, or fall prey to a more robust and innovative network organism. Networks that incorporate and use diversity as a source of synergy are able to create knowledge, solve problems, and innovate. These are the networks that ultimately survive and thrive. Absorbing and integrating diversity is at the heart of collaboration, the network has gone beyond exposure, beyond addition, and actively seeking integration of knowledge, experiences, and perspectives.

For policy makers, a network initiative that fails to demonstrate these relational processes may collapse as a dynamic organism. Without internal bonding, the network may become a nebulous, undefined group of individuals working independently or even at cross-purposes with each other. Without external relationship building, the network may not be able to sustain its internal vitality by the influx of new resources, material and otherwise. Failure to incorporate diversity represents an inability to adapt and the network becomes static, rigid, and ultimately vulnerable to breaking, decaying, or fragmenting.

A sponsor may be able to sustain the network but it will most likely require substantial investment of resources to essentially do what a dynamic network organism should be able to do on its own. Conversely, when a network initiative demonstrates these relational processes or relational synergy, the initiative has the potential to grow and sustain itself over time. Not

Table 12.3 Elements of Network Synergy

Dimensions	Critical Questions	ICBL	China CI
Internal relationship building	• Is the network engaged in internal relationship building?	Strong focus on building trust, social capital	Strategic pairing of teaching activities and cultural activities
External relationship building	• Is the network expanding external connections?	Yes, move from NGO (nonstate) to state actors	Global expansion of institutes
Incorporation of diversity	• Is the network diversifying?	Yes, local–global	Yes, centralized coordination, appointment of cultural bridges

only will the network initiative demonstrate stability and vitality, relational synergy may enable the network to excel beyond a sponsor's investments and expectations.

For both the ICBL and China's CI initiative, network synergy is one of the most notable features. Both grew at a rapid rate by absorbing a culturally diverse global membership and achieved notable success in problem solving and innovation. Table 12.3 provides a summary of the dimensions of network synergy for the ICBL and China's CI initiative.

NETWORK STRATEGY: INFORMATION DYNAMICS

A final dimension in designing and analyzing networks is the network strategy. Whereas network synergy focuses on the relational dynamics, network strategy focuses on the information dynamics. Information is the lifeblood of networks. For stakeholders, network strategy is the invitation to join and the reason to stay connected to a network. Network strategy is defined by its generative capacity to transform information into a value-added commodity for generating knowledge or problem solving. This value added aspect is what transforms network structures into a collaborative process. Network strategy encompasses how the network circulates and uses information among members to define perceptions of credibility, tap into member identities through the co-creation of narratives, and foster knowledge creation and problem solving.

Credibility flows from the relational, dynamic feature of information within the network strategy. Credibility is not the property of any one communicator, nor is it embedded in messages as facts or objectivity. In today's information saturated environment, even seemingly obvious "facts" are vulnerable to selective attention and perception. In a network strategy, relational affinity more than neutral facts determine perceptions of credibility. Because information gains value through its circulation, the most circulated information can become the most credible.

The dynamic, relational quality of information in a network strategy is similarly evident in the distinction between message and narrative. Unlike media-driven initiatives that are based on messages predefined or framed by a sponsor, "messaging" in networks is a co-creative, participatory process. No one source independently crafts or controls the message. The sequence is important.

Rather than beginning the process by designing a message independent of an audience, network communication focuses first on creating the structure and relational dynamics for effective communication among network members, and *then* members collaborate to co-create a storyline. More important than creating a "winning story" (message content) is building strong relationships (message exchange). By focusing first on message exchange, and then on co-creating message content, global network initiatives are able to retain message currency as they cross national and cultural borders. Information thus evolves from simple messages to a master narrative for the network whole.

Network narratives are important for developing a shared identity that gives existing members a sense of belonging and purpose and help to recruit new or potential members. Network analysis literature highlights two basic types of network narratives. Task-based narratives forefront the mission or goal of the network in which members can participate. The ICBL's narrative was a commitment to ban the use of landmines. A social-based narrative stresses the appeal of belonging or associating with like others. China's CI on the surface may appear to coalesce around a task-based narrative, the learning of the Chinese language. However, for network members, their participation in the cultural activities adds a social-based narrative to the CI initiative.

While often overlooked, a third type, identity-based narratives, is a critical mechanism for attracting and retaining network members. Both task-based and social-based narratives leverage member identity. However, identity-based narratives specifically highlight and reinforce a sense of being (rather than belonging or doing) that is often centered around a trait with which people identify, such as gender, ethnicity, or religion. Examples include women's empowerment and diaspora network initiatives.

It is important to point out that narratives, unlike messages, are dynamic and co-created by network members. The most successful networks commonly create narratives that capture task-based, social-based, and to some degree identity-based features. The inclusion of all three types of cohesion cues allows network members to tap aspects of the larger narrative that resonate most strongly. In the ICBL, in addition to the task-based narrative,

Table 12.4   Elements of Network Strategy

Dimensions	Critical Questions	ICBL	China CI
Credibility	• Using information to gain credibility internally and externally?	Nonstate actors join with state actors	Internal credibility language expertise, working external
Narrative	• Task-based—appeal to achieving specific goal • Social-based—appeal to creating bonds, shared norms and values, sense of belonging • Identity-based—resonates with ethnicity, personal definition, or experience	• Task—goal to ratify treaty • Identity—activist, landmine victims	• Task—language learning • Social—belonging, shared norms • Identity—ethnicity (for some), shared "student" experience
Generative	Value-added information, Knowledge creation, problem solving	Problem solving, knowledge generation on policy advocacy	Developed innovative teaching methods

there is also the social-based narrative that would appeal to activists, or the identity-based appeal of those who may have suffered the consequences of landmines.

A final critical aspect of a successful network strategy is when it combines with network synergy to transform information as a value-neutral commodity into a value-added commodity. Again both the ICBL and Confucius Institute illustrate the dynamic, generative capacity of network strategy. The ICBL network strategy produced new ways of viewing the problem of landmines (knowledge generation) and developed strategies for overcoming past hurdles (problem solving). Several of the Confucius Institutes speak of developing new methods for teaching Chinese and the annual conferences highlight pedagogical innovation.

Table 12.4 provides a summary of the dimensions of network strategy with examples from the ICBL and China's CI initiative.

CONCLUSION: NETWORKS OF PURPOSE

As one can see, the network structure, synergy, and strategy of the ICBL and China's CI are very different. However, based on their design and dynamics, they appear aptly suited and effective in meeting the purpose of the initiative. Based on the dimensions of network communication outlined in this chapter, it is possible to envision matching network design and network purposes vis-à-vis public diplomacy. *Networks of awareness* are dedicated to disseminating information. Ideally, they may be large, sparse, and open, use social media, and coalesce around a virally driven narrative. *Networks of influence* aim to change attitudes or behaviors. They may seek greater density, rely on interpersonal communication modes, and be organized around an identity-based narrative. *Networks of exchange* aim to facilitate the exchange of information and resources. These may be sparse, open networks that incorporate diversity to maximize network synergy. *Networks of empowerment* focus on creating personal or institutional capacity. This type of network may be more sustainable over the longer term if they maintain slow growth focused on building strong network ties of social and material support. *Networks of cooperation* are necessarily focused on coordination and division of labor or resources in order to achieve a cooperative goal. Such networks may strive for structures that facilitate exchange such as sparse networks; or if trust is a concern, they may focus on building strong ties and network density in order to achieve network synergy. *Networks of collaboration* strive to generate value-added information. They may initially focus on network structure, and then focus on relational dynamics of network synergy, before being able to reap the rewards of network strategy.

Each of these different networks of purpose may vary in their network structure, network synergy, and network strategy. Exploring and documenting these differences represent a future challenge in network public diplomacy research and theory.

Network public diplomacy is not universally effective, or even a substitute for other communication approaches. Ideally, a comprehensive public diplomacy grand strategy will encompass a wide breadth of strategic initiatives to advance a state's national interests and fulfill its global responsibilities. However, network initiatives can be instrumental in building bridges, particularly when they are well considered and designed for specific, limited purposes.

Knowing the purpose and desired goal of launching or engaging in a network initiative is important, for several reasons. First, it recognizes the diversity of networks. The tendency has been to speak about networks in generic terms. Networks vary greatly. Their network structure as well as relational and information dynamics are inextricably connected to their purpose and goals. Second, it acknowledges the limitations of the different types of networks. A women's empowerment "network" may be initiated in order to diffuse information and create awareness. These are limited, identifiable, and objective goals. Third, it helps set realistic benchmarks that can be used to measure progress or the effectiveness of various initiatives.

In public diplomacy, what makes a network initiative effective is not so much the structure or even technology, but rather the genesis and vision of a purposeful design. The majority of network studies have focused on egocentric or emergent networks,[43] which appear to serendipitously grow and develop on their own. However, as several scholars have noted, purposeful or goal-oriented networks are often designed and managed.[44] The scholars cautioned that one cannot design and "implement" a network in the same way as one would a communication campaign. That may be so. However, if one is aware of the implications of different communication and relational dynamics along with network effects of different network structures, then it is possible to monitor and foster more effective network and collaborative initiatives. Or, as Ali Fisher suggests, to "increase the odds."[45]

NOTES

1. R. S. Zaharna, *The Cultural Awakening in Public Diplomacy* (Los Angeles: USC Center for Public Diplomacy Perspectives, 2012).
2. Geoffrey Cowan and Amelia Arsenault, "From Monologue to Dialogue to Collaboration: The Three Layers of Public Diplomacy," *The ANNALS of the American Academy of Political and Social Science* 616 (2008): 10–30; and Ali Fisher, *Collaborative Public Diplomacy* (New York: Palgrave, 2012).
3. For ICBL, see R. S. Zaharna, "The Soft Power Differential," in *Battles to Bridges: U.S. Public Diplomacy after 9/11* (Baskingstoke: Palgrave, 2010); and R. S. Zaharna, "Analyzing China's Confucius Institutes as a Network Public Diplomacy Initiative," International Studies Association, San Diego, CA, April 1–4, 2012.
4. See "Campaign History," ICBL official site, www.icbl.org
5. Julian Davis, "The Campaign to Ban Landmines: Public Diplomacy, Middle Power Leaders and an Unconventional Negotiation Process," *Journal of Humanitarian Assistance*, posted July 6, 2004, http://jha.ac/articles/a134.htm
6. R. S. Zaharna, "The Public Diplomacy Challenges of Strategic Stakeholder Engagement," in *Trials of Engagement*, eds. Ali Fisher and Scott Lucas (Leiden: Martinus Nijhoff, 2011), 201–30.
7. Michael Pfau, M.H. Haigh, J. Sims, and S. Wigley, "The Influence of Corporate Front-Group Stealth Campaigns," *Communication Research* 34 (2007): 73–99.
8. Everett Rogers, *Diffusion of Innovations* (New York: Free Press, 2003).
9. British Council, *Trust Pays*, London, July 2012, ttp://www.britishcouncil.org/trustresearch2012.pdf
10. Candace Jones, William Hesterly, and Stephen Borgatti, "A General Theory of Network Governance: Exchange Conditions and Social Mechanisms," *Academy of Management Review* 22 (1997): 911–45.
11. For review, see Keith Provan, Amy Fish, and Joerg Sydow, "Interorganizational Networks at the Network Level: A Review of the Empirical Literature on Whole Networks," *Journal of Management* 33 (2007): 479–516.
12. Emilie M. Hafner-Burton, Miles Kahler, and Alexander H. Montgomery, "Network Analysis for International Relations," *International Organization* 63 (2009): 559–92.
13. Linton Freeman, "Centrality in Social Networks: Conceptual Clarification," *Social Networks* 1 (1979): 215–39.
14. Timothy J. Rowley, "Moving beyond Dyadic Ties: A Network Theory of Stakeholder Influences," *Academy of Management Review* 22 (1997): 887–910.

15. J. W. Meyer and B. Rowan, "Institutional Organizations: Formal Structures as Myth and Ceremony," *American Journal of Sociology* 80 (1977): 340–63.
16. J. Galaskiewicz and S. Wasserman, "Mimetic Processes within an Interorganizational Field: An Empirical Test," *Administrative Science Quarterly* 34 (1989): 454–79.
17. As Ali and I debated, Amelia raised the question of tie strength.
18. Michael Suk-Young Chwe, "Structure and Strategy in Collective Action," *American Journal of Sociology* 105 (July 1999): 128–56.
19. Peter M. Blau, "Parameters of Social Structure," *American Sociological Review* 39 (1974): 615–35.
20. M. T. Hansen, "The Search-Transfer Problem: The Role of Weak Ties in Sharing Knowledge across Organization Subunits," *Administrative Science Quarterly* 44 (1999): 82–111.
21. M. S. Granovetter, "The Strength of Weak Ties," *American Journal of Sociology* 78 (1973): 1360–80.
22. Corey Phelps, Ralph Heidl, and Anu Wadhwa, "Knowledge, Networks and Knowledge Networks: A Review and Research Agenda," *Journal of Management* 38 (July 2012): 1115–66.
23. James Coleman, "Social Capital in the Creation of Human Capital," *American Journal of Sociology* 94 (1988): 95–121; Blau, "Parameters of Social Structure."
24. Walter W. Powell and Stine Grodal, "Networks of Innovators," in *Innovation*, eds. Jan Fagerberg, David C. Mowery, and Richard R. Nelson (New York: Oxford University Press, 2004), 56–85.
25. Freeman, "Centrality in Social Networks."
26. Valdis Krebs and June Holley, *Building Smart Communities through Network Weaving* [White paper] (2002). Retrieved from Orgnet.com, http://www.orgnet.com/BuildingNetworks.pdf
27. Ibid.
28. Provan et al., "Interorganizational Networks at the Network Level," 507.
29. Keith Provan and H. Milward, "A Preliminary Theory of Network Effectiveness: A Comparative study of Four Community Mental Health Systems," *Administrative Science Quarterly* 40 (1995): 1–33.
30. Margarita Mayo and Juan Carlos Pastor, "Networks and Effectiveness in Work Teams: The Impact of Diversity," *IE Working Paper* C08–107-I, Instituto de Empresa, Madrid, February 9, 2005.
31. Ibid., 8.
32. Miller McPherson, Lynn Smith-Lovin, and James Cook, "Birds of a Feather: Homophily in Social Networks," *Annual Review of Sociology* 27 (2001): 415–44.
33. Mayo and Pastor, "Networks and Effectiveness in Work Teams."
34. Scott Page, *The Difference: How the Power of Diversity Creates Better Groups, Firms, Schools and Societies* (Princeton, NJ: Princeton University Press, 2008).
35. Oliver Yau, Jenny Lee, Raymond Chow, Leo Sin, and Alan Tse, "Relationship Marketing the Chinese Way," *Business Horizons* 43 (2000): 16.
36. J. R. Katzenbach and D. K. Smith, *The Wisdom of Teams: Creating the High-Performance Organization* (Boston: Harvard Business School Press, 1993), 88.
37. For individual institute reports, see http://english.hanban.org/node_10971.htm
38. Krebs and Holley, "Building Sustainable Communities through Network Building."
39. Ibid.

40. Mark A. Pachucki1 and Ronald L. Breiger, "Cultural Holes: Beyond Relationality in Social Networks and Culture," *Annual Review of Sociology* 36 (2010): 205–24.
41. Sun-Ki Chai and Mooweon Rhee, "Confucian Capitalism and the Paradox of Closure and Structural Holes in East Asian Firms," *Management and Organization Review* 6, 1 (2009): 5–29.
42. Page, *Differences*.
43. Jones et al., "A General Theory of Network Governance," 911–45.
44. Provan et al., "Interorganizational Networks at the Network Level."
45. Fisher, *Collaborative Public Diplomacy* (New York, NY: Palgrave, 2013).

13 Networks of Freedom, Networks of Control

Internet Policy as a Platform for and an Impediment to Relational Public Diplomacy

Amelia Arsenault

INTRODUCTION

At the time of writing, approximately 1 billion internet users participate in the vast global network of social media networks and are responsible for approximately 1 billion Facebook posts and 190 million tweets per day.[1] These myriad social media users are connected across cultures and across territorial boundaries in a complex web of associations with close friends, acquaintances, and family members and nonprofit, business, and government organizations. Facebook users alone are connected through more than 100 billion "friendships:"[2] but these social media platforms are only the tip of the iceberg. An infinitely more vast and complex web of individuals connect daily via the 6 billion registered mobile phone and 2.3 billion internet subscriptions worldwide.[3] Given that, on average, the number of iPhones sold (377,900) per day now rivals the number of babies born (377,900), these trends in connectivity are only likely to increase.[4] The sheer size and scope of internet and mobile networks dwarf any traditional one-way mass communication outlets and far outpace any and all interpersonal communication efforts. Not surprisingly then, the proliferation of internet and mobile networks has facilitated a corresponding preoccupation among diplomats and academics as to how to leverage these electronic networks for "networked public diplomacy." They increasingly view social networks as the primary conduits between governments and foreign publics, and between foreign publics and domestic publics, and actively seek to build networks of fans, followers, and friends.

Concurrent to the "social media craze" in public diplomacy, states around the world are increasingly moving to lock down and control these electronic networks, through combinations of formal and informal legal and policy controls and trade agreements. This chapter is principally concerned with the implications of these simultaneous activities for the longevity and the efficacy of electronically networked public diplomacy. In *The Future of Power*, Joseph Nye distinguishes between two simultaneous and often

competing conceptions of power: power as measured by control over resources, and power as measured by behavioral outcomes, or what he terms
"relational power." His central point is that power over resources does not
necessarily lead to influence and vice versa, but that states need both kinds
of power to succeed.[5] Anne Marie Slaughter adds to Nye's dichotomy a
third conception of power, that of "collaborative power . . . the power of
many to do together what no one can do alone."[6]

This chapter argues that attempts to utilize electronic networks in service
of relational public diplomacy (i.e., relational power) must take into account
all three of these conceptions of power. In other words, attempts to exert
relational power (as measured by behavioral outcomes) *through* connective technologies are inextricably linked to state attempts to exert resource
power *over* those same technologies. The solutions to the tensions caused
by these often-contradictory activities likely lies in collaboration among and
between governments, internet users, and the many businesses that produce
the infrastructure through which electronically networked public diplomacy
takes place.

The chapter proceeds in three interrelated sections. First, it examines the
different dimensions of contemporary thinking about the connective promise of electronic networks for public diplomacy. Second, it explores how the
ability to realize this promise is influenced by efforts to control the resources
that make up the global network of internet and mobile networks. Third, it
highlights the major problems that internet policy brings to utilizing internet-based social networks as a public diplomacy tool, and outlines how solutions are contingent on collaboration between internet users, governments,
and internet businesses, or what Slaughter calls "collaborative power."

THE CONNECTIVE PROMISE OF NEW TECHNOLOGIES

Diplomats and public diplomacy practitioners have embraced the potential
of electronic networks to foster dialogue, collaboration, and relationship
building on two levels. First, public diplomacy practitioners have begun experimenting with how to forge meaningful connections with foreign publics
through what has been termed "public diplomacy 2.0." Second, Western
countries have made internet freedom a central tenet of their diplomatic
agenda, arguing that human rights like freedom of assembly and freedom of
expression and intellectual property should be universally protected online.
While interrelated, these two groups of activities take a slightly different
view of the internet and are often compartmentalized in different bureaus
and initiatives. Public diplomacy 2.0 efforts use the internet as a tool to
build engagement and relationships, while internet freedom activities are
more focused on codifying a particular conception of the internet as a *virtual space* rather than simply a *technological tool*. However, as this section

will explore, both bodies of activity represent efforts to capitalize on and enhance the power of the internet to expand transnational connectivity and sharing in service of cross-cultural understanding and positive social change.

Public Diplomacy 2.0

Countries around the world are shifting public diplomacy resources from programs that *present messages* to those that attempt to utilize social networks and internet and mobile technologies to *form relationships* with foreign publics. In *Battles to Bridges*, R. S. Zaharna highlights the challenges and opportunities raised by new players using internet technologies. This usage has shifted the focus from "message content" and "public diplomacy as a product" to "message exchange" and "public diplomacy as a process."[7] In April 2011, the U.S. State Department archived its America.gov website, an ambitious digital information portal launched in 2008. Instead, it redirected its digital resources toward a "more proactive" web strategy based on engagement. As Deputy Assistant Secretary for International Information Programs, Duncan MacInnes explained, "the new paradigm . . . is people don't visit you, you have to go to them."[8] Similarly, in October 2010, Korean Foreign Minister Kim Sung-Hwan announced a paradigm shift to "total and complex diplomacy," which engages both diplomats and the private sector in "digital network diplomacy . . . to enhance mutual understanding and our [Korea's] national image."[9] Embrace of the benefits of the internet and social media for public diplomacy has become so widespread it is often treated as axiomatic.

If officials see the promise of the internet, Web 2.0, and social networks for public diplomacy, academics and pundits have been optimistic but more cautious.[10] There have been several investigations into how different governments (mainly Western ones) are using the internet as a platform for engagement.[11] This includes Seo's excellent investigation into how the U.S. government is using social media for public diplomacy in South Korea (published in this same volume). Kristen Lord, in another example, suggested that the U.S. government—through strategic partnerships with the private sector—should "co-develop social networking sites."[12]

Major questions, however, surround these early efforts in the use of social networks for public diplomatic outreach: To what extent do government uses of new media really reflect something new and networked? In other words, does the use of social networking technologies equal the building of relational networks? While governments and, to a certain extent, academics have embraced the potential of the internet and mobile technologies as critical tools for networked public diplomacy, we must remember that these technologies are still relatively new. YouTube, Facebook, and Twitter moved to global prominence in 2005, 2008, and 2009, respectively.

Governments are struggling with how to use these media with varying degrees of success. Social networks have facilitated complex networks of connection that entail complicated social etiquettes. The old rules may no longer apply, but the new rules of engagement lack consensus. Social networking technologies hold the promise of creating meaningful connectivity. However, for many users, they still serve as little more than a unidirectional information provision system. For example, more than 200 million of the total 1.12 billion Facebook account holders make no contributions at all, and less than a fifth of Twitter users post any text at all.[13] Combinations of legal and cultural mores influence how comfortable users are with the autonomous mass self-communication inherent in social media networks. Emerging powers such as Argentina, Brazil, and India, for example, have the highest penetration of social network usage and the highest usage frequency and intensity; while in countries such as Ukraine, Jordan, and Egypt, social network usage is comparatively low.[14] The diversity of connectivity and engagement patterns does not negate the importance of relationally focused online outreach activities, but suggests that public diplomacy practitioners' efforts to forge relationships online are heavily context dependent. Not surprisingly, diplomats, both formally and informally linked to public diplomacy efforts, are paying greater attention to the conditions that shape that context of message exchange. These contextual determinants include normative standards of etiquette and culture as well as more practical issues like internet penetration and the laws and policies governing the usage of new technologies.

Internet Freedom Agenda

Particularly since the thwarted 2009 Green Revolution in Iran, nicknamed the "Twitter Revolution," calls for "internet freedom" have been on the rise. Governments are beginning to take notice of the importance of how and why information exchanges on the internet are taking place. U.S. Secretary of State Hillary Clinton delivered perhaps the most visible acknowledgments of the importance of information exchange in two high-profile policy speeches delivered in January 2010 and February 2011 that inculcated the "freedom to connect" and the "freedom to virtual assembly" as cornerstones of "21st-century statecraft."[15] Freedom to connect refers to the ability of individuals and societies to connect to the global network of communication networks without interference. The freedom to virtual assembly involves the extension of the right to association, declared a human right the 1948 Universal Declaration of Human Rights, to the internet space; individuals should have the right to meet and cooperate in virtual online spaces, free from intimidation or censorship.

Actions by other governments followed. In December 2011, the European Commission outlined a "no disconnect strategy," premised on developing circumvention tools, educating activists, monitoring censorship, and building cooperative networks of stakeholders interested in increasing access to information. Discussions about internet freedom are not limited to the West, but were championed in regional stakeholder meetings, such as the Asia Pacific Regional Internet Governance Forum, the Central Africa Internet Governance Forum, the East Africa Internet Governance Forum, the West Africa Internet Governance Forum, the European Dialogue on Internet Governance, and the Latin America and Caribbean Internet Governance Forum.[16]

Public diplomacy practitioners have begun to take a more visible role in supporting these efforts to establish and advocate for individual rights on the internet. The U.S. State Department, for example, is working to build "consensus around international norms of state behavior in cyberspace." Central to these norms is the idea mentioned earlier that we should think about the internet as a virtual space, rather than simply as a tool. Under this conception, the internet is not simply a *tool* for communication, but rather is a *virtual space* where people can gather to communicate with one another. The distinction between tool (which can be privately owned) and virtual space (which implies participation by others) is critical to understanding the tension between efforts (often made by the same government) to both control and liberate the internet.

The conception of the internet as a space is undergirded by two policy priorities: (1) promoting the idea that the internet is a public space open to all regardless of geography or state; and (2) championing the idea of a "single" internet, while resisting any attempts by states, such as Iran, Russia, and China, to create sectioned-off national internets.[17] It is in these two priorities that we see the critical role of internet policy, or attempts to exercise "resource power" or control over the internet. As the next section will argue, these actions that leverage the relational power of the internet are conditioned by parallel efforts to control the internet through the exertion of resource power.

RESOURCE POWER: THE CRITICAL ROLE OF INTERNET POLICY

When thinking about the relational potential of electronically networked technologies for public diplomacy, we must remember the dual role of communication networks. On the one hand, networks are the conduits through which different public diplomacy actors attempt to achieve particular goals, whether they are information sharing, relationship building, collaboration, or strategic foreign policy promotion. On the other hand, the electronic networks that form these communication conduits are objects of power struggles. Countries, companies, and the private sector at times collaborate, and at other times compete, to control the form and content of these networks. As John Arquilla and David Ronfeldt noted in 1993, "information is becoming a strategic resource that may prove as valuable and influential in the post-industrial era as capital and labor have been in the industrial age."[18] Information communication technologies are not just platforms or applications, but are scarce and valuable resources over which different groups compete for access and control.[19] By controlling these resources, they also control likely exposure to informational resources and participation in online community and sharing. Some nation-states are motivated to control these resources out of regime insecurity, and want to clamp down on "unfriendly" chatter, while others are more concerned with the economic implications of piracy and interconnection rates, or insecurity wrought by identity theft and hacking.

"Information policy," as Sandra Braman observed, "is among the most ancient forms of governance."[20] Efforts to control the mechanisms of communication are not new, nor likely to end soon, if ever. Current efforts by states to assert resource power (i.e., attempts to exert control) over the internet are diverse, often interrelated, and surround three major areas: (1) censorship and blocking, (2) economics and trade, and (3) privacy and security. All of these exhibitions of resource power over informational systems have critical implications for electronically networked public diplomacy.

Censorship and Blocking: "Failed to Open Page"

State policies of internet filtering and censorship provide one of the most obvious examples of attempts to control the strategic resources of information. The normative, legal, and cultural characteristics of the country or community of interest are, thus, critical. Governments have multiple ways of controlling the conditions of access to the internet, including: blocking specific keyword searches, limiting internet traffic, blocking particular web addresses, and inspecting and blocking e-mail traffic according to content.

China, for example, maintains strict domestic internet controls, blocking access to major social media sites such as Twitter, Flicker, WordPress, and YouTube, and considers the discourses taking place within those sites as a threat to national sovereignty and domestic harmony. The nation has deployed a wide range of policies for the censorship and surveillance with sophisticated techniques, including filtering devices such as "Blue Shield" and "Huadun" that store user identification information, domain-name controls requiring real-name verification, and law enforcement for individuals regarded political dissidents.[21] Iran restricts download and upload speeds, which makes utilizing social media or accessing objectionable media inconvenient, if not at times impossible.

Table 13.1 outlines the forty-two countries involved in internet filtering, as identified by data collected by the OpenNet Initiative between 2008 and November 2011. As outlined in Table 13.1, political content refers to the blocking of websites that express negative views about the government. Social content includes material related to sexuality, gambling, and illegal drugs and alcohol, as well as to other topics that may be socially sensitive or perceived as offensive. Conflict and security refers to content related to armed conflicts, border disputes, separatist movements, and militant groups.

Table 13.1 Internet Filtering around the World

Level of censorship	Political content	Social content	Conflict content	Internet tools
Selective	Azerbaijan, Belarus, Georgia, Indonesia, India, Jordan, Kyrgyzstan, Kuwait, Kazakhstan, Libya, Moldova, Mauritania, Oman, Pakistan, Qatar, Russia Sudan, Thailand, Tajikistan, Turkey	Armenia, Azerbaijan, Belarus, Colombia, Ethiopia, India, Italy, Kyrgyzstan, South Korea Kazakhstan, Morocco, Pakistan, Russia, Singapore, Syria, Thailand Turkmenistan, Tunisia, Turkey, Uzbekistan, Venezuela, Vietnam	United Arab Emirates Armenia Bahrain Belarus Ethiopia Georgia, India Kuwait Morocco Mexico Qatar Saudi Arabia Syria Turkmenistan Uzbekistan Vietnam Yemen	Armenia, Belarus, Ethiopia, Indonesia, India, Morocco, Pakistan, Thailand, Turkmenistan, Tunisia, Turkey, Uzbekistan
Substantial	UAE, Armenia, Ethiopia, Saudi Arabia, Yemen	China, Indonesia Burma, Gaza/ West Bank, Sudan	Iran, Burma, Pakistan	Bahrain, China, Burma, Oman, Sudan, Vietnam
Pervasive	Bahrain, China, Iran, Burma, Syria, Turkmenistan Uzbekistan, Vietnam	UAE, Bahrain Iran, Kuwait, Oman, Qatar, Saudi Arabia, Yemen	China, South Korea	UAE, Iran, Kuwait, Qatar, Saudi Arabia, Syria, Yemen

Source: OpenNet Initiative "Summarized Global Internet Filtering Data" (November 8, 2011), http://opennet.net/research/data

The final category, internet tools, includes websites that provide e-mail, internet hosting, search, translation, social networking, telephone service, and circumvention methods.

Each of these categories of censorship impacts internet-based public diplomacy activities. This includes the transmission of traditional one-way communications via the internet, as well as more participatory efforts. The BBC, for example, streams content in twenty-eight languages via the internet, but has found that an increasing number of these localized language services are delivered into countries that implement some form of internet censorship.[22] Censors have also intermittently blocked the U.S. consulate in Shanghai's blog, which has 80,000 followers and has been lauded for its interactions with Chinese citizens.[23]

Domestic internet policies have significant implications for the implementation of relational diplomatic strategies and practice with social networking tools. The level of censorship and technological restrictions influence both the quantity and quality of communication networks among government entities and constituents. At the same time, even countries advocating internet freedom and cultural diversity continue to play a major role in the deployment of filtering software and policy regimes that propagate these censorship activities.

Economics and Trade: Right to Connect and Purchase

In practice, the internet freedom agenda joins a long history of what has been called "iPod liberalism," as practiced by the West. This term, first coined in 2005 by Stratfor Global Intelligence Consulting, refers to "the idea that anyone who listens to rock 'n' roll on an iPod, writes blogs, and knows what it means to Twitter must be an enthusiastic supporter of Western liberalism."[24] Like an iPod, the idealized communications environment in this conception depends on technical specifications, connectivity, content, and consumerism. It is for this reason that espousing the relational potential of the internet can often times seem disingenuous when juxtaposed against government efforts to exploit its commercial opportunities.

Historically, U.S. championing of open communication networks has been justified according to financial rather than cultural or relational reasons. For example, the Clinton-era "Connecting the Globe Initiative" was launched during the height of the U.S. push for developing countries to accept the telecommunications policies outlined in the World Trade Organization General Agreement on Trade and Services (GATs) agreement. As then FCC Chairman William Kennard described in his foreword,

> In a very real sense, we . . . are architects—designing and building a dynamic international community. We too are fundamentally involved in bringing people together, connecting communities with one another. Together we can continue to draft the blueprint for this grand, *global*

economy [my emphasis] where individuals, communities and nations can all participate.[25]

We see similar economic and commercial themes permeating the internet freedom messaging strategies. Speaking to a Saudi Arabian audience, BBG Board member Michael Meehan explained, the U.S. "Broadcasting Board of Governors promotes Internet freedom because the unhampered flow of information is a prerequisite for democratic and economic development."[26] The American Strategy for Cyberspace places equal weight on the utility of electronic networks for commerce as it does for freedom of expression and freedom of virtual assembly.

The United States has encouraged countries to adopt multilateral agreements it deems particularly desirable (e.g., GATs) and/or reject those it finds undesirable (e.g., the proposal for a New World Information and Communication Order put forward in UNESCO during the 1970s). It has also encouraged states to enact domestic reforms designed to develop and expand national information environments so that those states might better participate in a host of multilateral and bilateral economic agreements, thereby increasing economic and trade opportunities. Given the size of the communications sector, it is not surprising that economic superpowers such as the United States take an active role in promoting favorable policies. Globally, internet service providers generate approximately $196.5 billion and telecommunications services providers approximately $1,219.7 billion in annual revenue.[27] A 2012 U.S. Commerce Department report estimates that that intellectual property-intensive industries support at least 40 million jobs and contribute more than $5 trillion dollars to, or 34.8 percent of, the U.S. gross domestic product.[28]

Protecting the vast internet economy, however, does not always easily align with the internet freedom agenda. Over the last decade and a half, multiple pieces of legislation, such as the Anti-Counterfeiting Trade Agreement, have been negotiated. These agreements, which are designed to inhibit copyright infringement and software and content piracy, have empowered internet service providers to filter content deemed to be in violation of those treaties. The provisions allow businesses and governments to request that internet service providers facilitate the removal of pirated or infringing material, or shut off the internet accounts of infringing users. Opponents argue that these measures undermine privacy on the internet and threaten to create a system where states and businesses can track and punish users under the auspices of copyright.

Crime and Security

The prevalence of criminal activities like phishing, e-mail scams, identity theft, and general information insecurity has prompted governments and multilateral organizations around the world to pass legislation. Treaties and agreements formulated over such issues as cybercrime and security can further empower governments to take action against dissident groups. In 2012, the Philippines, ranked sixth in the world for internet freedom, passed the Cybercrime Prevention Act, which included broad restrictions on internet libel, prompting concern that the state might use these expanded provisions to attack dissenting organizations. The 2010 Hungarian Media Law created a national censorship authority with the ability to take down content and censure journalists according to largely undefined criteria such as the protection of public order or the right to receive "accurate" public affairs information.[29]

Countries are also reasserting sovereignty over the net by criminalizing undesirable speech, employing professionals (sometimes in the thousands) to influence online conversations in ways that favor the government, engaging in offline intimidation, and increasing surveillance.[30] Rather than filtering and blocking, the *2012 Freedom on the Net Report* concluded that "restrictions on internet freedom . . . have continued to grow, though the methods of control are slowly evolving and becoming less visible." In India, the government has censored particular Twitter feeds and websites out of concern for "communal issues and rioting" in the Assam province of northeast India. It also enacted a broad-reaching Facebook campaign "in the interest of Facebook fans" that Facebook activity could "ignite a riot, or lead you into danger."[31]

National security interests often trump internet freedom concerns. At the time of writing, the United States was still attempting to prosecute Julian Assange, the founder of the controversial information-sharing web service that featured leaked government and corporate documents. In her 2011 Internet Freedom Speech, Hillary Clinton maintained that "WikiLeaks does not challenge our commitment to internet freedom." However, skepticism about the genuineness of the American commitment to internet freedom abounded.[32]

As will be further elaborated in the following section, the simultaneous promotion of the open trade of internet technologies for economic gain, and an open internet that elevates connectivity and sharing, do not easily co-exist.

COMPLEXITIES OF COLLABORATION

Countries are vying for resource power over the internet and mobile networks, and are experimenting with leveraging relational power through these same networks, espousing values of dialogue, collaboration, sharing, and virtual community. Brian Hocking has argued that the network model of public diplomacy "recognizes the importance of policy networks in managing increasingly complex policy environments through the promotion of communication, dialogue and trust."[33] Hocking was referring to the fact that these policy networks represent critical source of social capital that ultimately serves public diplomacy outcomes. He goes on to argue, "in the network image, the focus is on the identification of policy objectives in specific areas and of 'stakeholders' who possess interests and expertise related to them."[34] As this section will stress, Hocking's arguments are particularly relevant to the diverse stakeholder networks invested in shaping the material, practical, and legal conditions through which social networks operate. These stakeholders are critical to the successes and failures of networked public diplomacy. While there are numerous possible examples, the following sections outline two particularly germane communities: technology companies and advocacy networks.

Role of Technology Corporations

As a 2011 UNESCO report concluded, "Freedom of expression is not an inevitable outcome of technological innovation. It can be diminished or reinforced by the design of technologies, policies, and practices—sometimes far removed from freedom of expression."[35] There are no clear boundary lines demarcating states that promote internet freedom, and those that advocate internet censorship and control. The two are often one and the same. Table 13.2 captures this tension.

The United States, which champions the "right to connect," is also home to the main purveyors of internet filtering software. The Great Chinese Internet Firewall is built from blocks by Western technology corporations. Users seeking out the Voice of America website, for example, are commonly redirected to more suitable websites through a process known as DNS hijacking.

There are no easy solutions for nations wanting to limit the sale of these products to foreign governments for censorship, because there are many legitimate uses for the technology. McAfee's SmartFilter, for example, is ostensibly designed for corporations wanting to "reduce legal liability, increase employee productivity, and preserve bandwidth for productive work."[36] The product is also used by governments to provide country-level internet filtering. According to McAfee, the company "has no control over, or visibility into how, an organization implements its own filtering policy." Websense has a policy that "government-mandated censorship projects will not be engaged," and that they only sell to businesses and nonprofits operating in countries with censorship policies. However, the use of Websense technology has been documented in such countries as Yemen and China.[37]

In response to formal and informal pressures, however, business networks have begun to promote responsible technology distribution. Despite earlier criticisms of adapting to state demands, companies like Google, Microsoft, and Websense, for example, have joined collective action groups like the Global Network Initiative. Google and Twitter now maintain searchable databases of government requests to censor information. While these steps

Table 13.2 Major Internet Filtering Technologies by Country of Origin and Use

Filtering technology	Country of origin	Countries used in
Blue Coat Systems	United States	Iraq, Syria
NetSweeper	Canada	India, UAE, Qatar and Yemen
Smart Filter (owned by McAffee)	United States	Saudi Arabia, the United Arab Emirates, Kuwait, Bahrain, Oman, and Tunisia
WebSense	United States	China, Yemen

likely represent an effort to stave off legal interventions, they suggest that corporations can serve as important partners in reform movements relevant to public diplomacy activities on the internet. One of the critical points about these internet transparency and reform movements is that they subject all governments to equal scrutiny, which some practitioners may consider risky because they highlight the roles of both sending and receiving states. However, if network public diplomacy is about expanding associations, the internet freedom agenda and by extension public diplomacy 2.0 are ultimately improved by this transparency.

Internet? Activist Networks

International nongovernmental networks such as the Open Rights Group, the Index on Censorship, Article 19, and the Internet Freedom Coalition have been instrumental in highlighting the importance of internet technologies for freedom of expression as well as cross-cultural dialogue and understanding. These organizations represent potential collaborators and potential watchdogs of governments involved in internet engagement and internet freedom activities. Indeed, the U.S. State Department has provided major funds for internet activists through the Digital Defenders Partnership, as has the EU through its No Disconnect Strategy. At the same time, liaising with these activist networks has several potential dangers for diplomats and public diplomacy practitioners.

Governments still exert control over the conditions through which people can and do connect to online platforms. We are witnessing cycles of engagement and governmental response that suggest that online strategies need to be considered and practiced with extreme care. Successful demonstrations of the power of the internet to connect citizens and states around the world excite many, and alarm those who do not approve of the terms of engagement. Considerable debate remains about the relative role of networked public diplomacy, social media, and citizen activism in the 2009

Green Revolution in Iran, and in the still-evolving political changes surrounding the Arab Spring revolutions in the Middle East in North Africa. For networked public diplomacy, this debate is secondary. Perhaps the most lasting legacy of these events has been to entrench conceptions that the internet and accompanying mobile technologies have important implications for state power. The more that foreign actors attempt to leverage those technologies to solidify network associations, the more likely we will continue to see governments asserting control over electronic resources.

With a few notable exceptions, electronically networked public diplomacy takes place in highly visible forums. Strategic attempts to leverage electronic networks often color these visible public diplomacy 2.0 efforts. In 2012, for example, the U.S. Department of State's Office of Syrian Opposition Support and the U.K.'s Foreign Office began funding activist network hubs through the provision of training and communications technologies. This networked approach to international relations has important implications for public diplomacy in the region, as well as more globally for those concerned with the implications of foreign actors promoting regime change

On the one hand, it may encourage the diffusion of information that supports democracy and reform. On the other hand, it makes relational public diplomacy on the web a riskier enterprise. It is often difficult to tell whether activities are motivated by a desire to forging meaningful connections with stakeholders, or more strategic foreign policy goals. As a consequence, even the most banal online engagement activities may provoke government fears of electronic colonialism. The most obvious means of protecting electronic sovereignty comes in the form of reasserting territoriality over the internet. Countries from Iran, to Russia, to Burma have begun plans for autonomous or semi-autonomous "national internet" systems. In December 2012, government representatives from around the world will meet in Dubai for the World Conference on International Telecommunications (WCIT) to discuss whether the controls dictating telecommunications should be extended to the internet, a proposition that has ignited activist networks fearful of increased government intrusion into the internet.

There are, of course, inherent problems in either tailoring initiatives based on fear of state reprisals or in general. The United States and other Western nations have been accused of using the internet freedom agenda as a strategic foreign policy tool because they have been inconsistent in how and where they promote internet rights. Cairo-based Middle East analyst Issandr El Amrani, for example, explains, "It's a big idea that comes at relatively low cost. And while the administration has been helpful in Syria, we haven't seen Clinton or Obama push aggressively for internet freedom in China. We haven't seen any real efforts to ban the export of software to let governments spy on citizens."[38]

Several governments have been involved in funding anticensorship software that lets these activist networks circumvent state controls. However, "liberation technology" is not a panacea. First, sites allowing users to circumvent internet filtering, such as http://gardennetworks.com and http://peacefire.org, are commonly blocked in countries like Morocco and China.[39] Second, there have been serious cases of failed software. In perhaps the most high-profile example, a U.S. programmer, Austin Heap, with support of the U.S. State Department, released a circumvention tool called Haystack. The project was abruptly canceled after fatal flaws in its design came to light, potentially revealing information about its users to Iranian state monitors.

NETWORKS OF FREEDOM, CONTROL, AND COLLABORATION

There are no easy solutions to the problems outlined in this chapter. The tension between electronic resource allocation and capitalizing on the relationship-building potential of the internet will likely remain a constant component of relational public diplomacy. The network approach to public diplomacy stresses that the building blocks of networks are the associations that link individuals. The conditions through which meaningful associations are formed online are heavily interlinked with formal and informal internet policies. Relational public diplomacy using connective technologies should be about much more than counting the number of tweets, Facebook friendship requests sent and accepted, or likes of particular comments. It is about working in collaboration with stakeholders to find the optimal balance between information rights and information sovereignty.

In my work with Geoffrey Cowan, we advocated looking at the available tools open to public diplomacy practitioners in terms of three layers: monologue, or one-way communication; dialogue, or two-way communication; and collaboration, the common working on a common goal.[40] Shaun Riordan has similarly called for a new paradigm of "dialogue-based public diplomacy," and in this volume Ali Fisher calls for a "collaborative model of public diplomacy."[41] The central argument here is that these same principles of dialogue and collaboration that inform current thinking about ideal practices for relational and networked public diplomacy should also inform our thinking about the intersection between public diplomacy, activating networked forms of associations, and internet policy.

Western governments cannot champion the connective promise of networking technologies without paying close attention to the critical role of diplomacy and international policy makers in conditioning the terms through which network linkages are formed. In short, social media and internet technologies hold great promise for providing platforms through which relational public diplomacy can be practiced. Resolving the tensions between state efforts to shape the material conditions of the internet (i.e., the weighing of resource power) and state efforts to use the internet as a tool to achieve network public diplomacy demands a more collaborative and relational approach. Evoking a variation on the classic Edward R. Murrow quote, public diplomacy needs to be ingrained into the larger questions of how these technologies are governed and shaped as well as used during times of crisis or as a tool for relationship building.

NOTES

1. International Telecommunications Union, *Trends in Telecommunications Reform 2012: Smart Regulation for a Broadband World* (Geneva: ITU, 2012), 5.
2. Facebook, "Form S-1 Registration Statement," submitted to the United States Securities and Exchanges Commission, Washington, DC, February 1, 2012, accessed October 1, 2012, http://www.sec.gov/Archives/edgar/data/1326801/000119312512034517/d287954ds1.htm#toc287954_10
3. International Telecommunications Union, *Key Statistical Highlights: ITU Data Release* (Geneva: ITU, June 2012).
4. "There Are Now More iPhones Sold Than Babies Born in the World Every Day," *The Next Web*, January 25, 2012, accessed March 15, 2012, http://thenextweb.com/apple/2012/01/25/there-are-now-more-iphones-sold-than-babies-born-in-the-world-every-day/
5. Joseph S. Nye, *The Future of Power* (New York: Public Affairs, 2011), 10–11.
6. Anne-Marie Slaughter, "A New Theory for the Foreign Policy Frontier: Collaborative Power," *The Atlantic*, November 30, 2011.
7. R. S. Zaharna, *Battles to Bridges: U.S. Strategic Communication and Public Diplomacy after 9/11* (New York: Palgrave Macmillan, 2010), 88, 170.
8. Alica M. Cohn, "State Department Shifts Digital Resources to Social Media," *Hillicon Valley: The Hill's Technology Blog*, April 24, 2011, http://thehill.com/blogs/hillicon-valley/technology/157501-state-dept-shifts-digital-resources-to-social-media
9. Foreign Minister Kim Sung-hwan, *36th Inaugural Address* (October 8, 2010) Korean Ministry of Foreign Affairs and Trade.
10. See for example, Evan Potter, "Web 2.0 and the New Public Diplomacy: Impact and Opportunities," in *Engagement: Public Diplomacy in a Globalised World*, eds. Jolyon Welsh and Daniel Fearn (London: Foreign Commonwealth Office, 2008); Lina Khatib, William Dutton, and Michael Thelwall, "Public Diplomacy 2.0: A Case Study of the US Digital Outreach Team," *The Middle East Journal*, 66 (2012): 453–72.
11. Amelia Arsenault, "Public Diplomacy 2.0," in *Toward a New Public Diplomacy: Redirecting U.S. Foreign Policy*, ed. Philip Seib (Boston: Palgrave, 2009), 135–53.
12. Kristin M. Lord, *Engaging the Private Sector for the Public Good: The Power of Network Diplomacy*, Policy Briefing (Washington, DC: Center for a New American Security, 2012).
13. *Social Platforms Report Q2* (Essex: GlobalWebIndex, September 2012).
14. Steven Van Belleghem, Dieter Thijs, and Tom De Ruyck, "Social Media around the World," *InSites Consulting* (September 25, 2012), accessed September 25, 2012, http://blog.insites.eu/2012/09/25/social-media-around-the-world-2012/
15. Hillary Rodham Clinton, "Remarks on Internet Freedom," The Newseum, Washington, DC, January 21, 2010, accessed on February 1, 2010, http://www.state.gov/secretary/rm/2010/01/135519.htm; Hillary Rodham Clinton, "Internet Rights and Wrongs: Choices & Challenges in a Networked World,"

George Washington University, Washington, DC, February 15, 2011, accessed on March 1, 2011, http://www.state.gov/secretary/rm/2011/02/156619.htm

16. Shanthi Kalathil, "Internet Freedom: A Background Paper," prepared for the Aspen Institute International Digital Economy Accords (IDEA) Project.

17. Clinton (2010); see also Roy Revie, "The Tangled Web of Internet Freedom, A Reaction to the 2012 Milton Wolf Seminar," (Philadelphia, Center for Global Communication Studies, 2012), http://global.asc.upenn.edu/fileLibrary/PDFs/RevieMWS.pdf

18. John Arquilla and David Ronfeldt, "Cyberwar Is Coming!" *Comparative Strategy* 12(2) (1993): 141–65.

19. For more on the idea of ICTs as a resource, see Ernest J. Wilson, *The Information Revolution and Developing Countries* (Cambridge, MA: MIT Press, 2004).

20. Sandra Braman, *Change of State: Information, Policy, and Power* (Boston: MIT Press, 2006), 1.

21. Rebecca MacKinnon, "China's 'Networked Authoritarianism,'" *Journal of Democracy* 22(2) (2011): 32–46.

22. Karl Kathuria, *Casting a Wider Net: Lessons Learned in Delivering BBC Content on the Censored Internet* (Toronto: Canada Centre for Global Security Studies and Citizen Lab at Munk School of Global Affairs, University of Toronto, 2011).

23. Didi Tang, "U.S. Social Media Account in China Disappears," *Boston.com*, July 13, 2012, accessed September 15, 2012, http://www.boston.com/business/technology/articles/2012/07/13/us_social_media_account_in_china_disappears/

24. George Friedman, "Western Misconceptions Meet Iranian Reality," *Stratfor Global Intelligence*, June 15, 2009, accessed June 30, 2012, http://www.stratfor.com/weekly/20090615_western_misconceptions_meet_iranian_reality

25. William Kennard, *Connecting the Globe: A Regulator's Guide to Building a Global Information Community* (Washington, DC: Federal Communications Commission, 1999), i.

26. Broadcasting Board of Governors, "Internet Freedom, Innovation Top BBG's Agenda at Conference in Saudi Arabia," Press Release, accessed October 1, 2012, http://www.bbg.gov/press-release/internet-freedom-innovation-top-bbgs-agenda-at-conference-in-saudi-arabia/

27. *IBISWorld Industry Report I5121-GL: Global Internet Service Providers* (Melbourne: IBISWorld, May 2011).

28. *Intellectual Property and the U.S. Economy: Industries in Focus* (Washington, DC: U.S. Department of Commerce, April 2012).

29. Hungarian Parliament, "Act CIV of 2010 on the Freedom of the Press and the Fundamental Rules on Media Content" (March 2011).

30. *Freedom on the Net 2012* (Washington, DC: Freedom House, 2012).

31. "Here's That Creepy Indian Facebook PSA Campaign You Never Asked For," *Business Insider*, August 23, 2012, accessed August 25, 2012, http://www.businessinsider.com/heres-that-creepy-indian-facebook-psa-campaign-you-never-asked-for-2012-8

32. See for example, Glen Greenwald, "Hillary Clinton and Internet Freedom," *Salon.com*, December 9, 2011. http://www.salon.com/2011/12/09/hillary_clinton_and_internet_freedom/

33. Brian Hocking, "Reconfiguring Public Diplomacy: From Competition to Collaboration," in *Engagement: Public Diplomacy in a Globalised World*, eds. Joylon Welsh and Daniel Fearn (London: Foreign Commonwealth Office, 2008), 64.

34. Ibid., 66.

35. William Dutton, Anna Dopatka, Ginette Law, and Victoria Nash, *Freedom of Connection—Freedom of Expression: The Changing Legal and Regulatory Ecology Shaping the Internet* (Paris: UNESCO, 2011).

36. McAfee, "Smartfilter 2013 Product Description," accessed September 1, 2012, http://www.mcafee.com/us/products/smartfilter.aspx

37. Helmi Noman and Jillian C. York, "West Censoring East: The Use of Western Technologies by Middle East Censors, 2010–2011," *OpenNet Initiative Bulletin*, March 2011.

38. Quoted in, "Inside Washington's High Risk Mission to Beat Web Censors," *The Guardian*, April 15, 2012, accessed May 30, 2012, http://www.guardian.co.uk/technology/2012/apr/15/commotion-wireless-new-america-foundation

39. Global Internet Filtering Map, Last updated November 1, 2011, (Cambridge, Toronto, & Ottawa: Open Net Initiative, 2012), http://map.opennet.net

40. Geoffrey Cowan and Amelia Arsenault, "From Monologue to Dialogue to Collaboration: The Three Layers of Public Diplomacy," *The ANNALS of the American Academy of Political and Social Science*, 616 (2008): 10–30.

41. Shaun Riordan, *Dialogue-based Public Diplomacy: A New Foreign Policy Paradigm?* No. 95 (The Hague: Netherlands Institute of International Relations Clingendael, 2004).

14 Standing on the Shoulders of Giants
Building Blocks for a Collaborative Approach to Public Diplomacy

Ali Fisher

INTRODUCTION

We live in an interconnected world; the connections within this "network society" enable but also constrain our actions.[1] The dynamics of the multi-dimensional environment require strategies that can be conducted around numerous hubs, can navigate multiple flows of information, and can engage with the interests pursued by a wide range of communities. The building blocks of a collaborative approach focus on ways to include the multiple dimensions, hubs, and flows of information that combine to form complex operational environments. Public diplomacy in a globalized world embraces networking and collaboration with diverse actors as a fundamental necessity in devising novel solutions to complex problems. No single actor has the answer; it must be generated collaboratively. Public diplomacy is an attempt to change the odds of specific outcomes occurring.

In developing an open, collaborative approach to public diplomacy, practitioners and scholars have the opportunity to draw on the experience of others in shifting from hierarchical to collaborative approaches. For example, in 1984, the GNU project set out to develop a free "open-source" operating system. A decade later, in 1997, the Debian Social Contract outlined the concepts which would govern the free exchange of ideas among computer scientists committed to the production of free software. These ideas were captured in the 1999 book *Open Sources: Voices from the Revolution*.[2] The subsequent *Open Sources 2.0: The Continuing Evolution* in 2005 continued charting the complex challenges and incredible opportunities for the free exchange of information.[3]

These voices from the open-source revolution, however, do not speak only to a narrow community of hackers and digital innovators. As important as the computer code was, the real insight was creating a means through which individual actions could collaborate to produce something meaningful.

While the development of a computer operating system may not seem relevant to public diplomacy, the fundamental underlying purpose of these initiatives was to influence behavior in a way that allowed communities to coordinate and collaborate. The open-source methodology has much to offer public diplomacy. There are many examples in which groups of dedicated individuals with little, if any, financial resources have shown themselves capable of influencing the way communities behave—often achieving greater success than many better-funded public diplomacy initiatives. For example, the "Occupy" movement has triggered protests in 150 communities across the United States and in more than 1,500 cities worldwide.[4] In addition, the loose affiliation of hackers known as *Anonymous* has also drawn numerous supporters, copycats, and collaborators.

Understanding factors behind the success of small-group collaborative action has become increasingly important in recent years, due to the emphasis on efficiency and impact. Nobel Prize winner Elinor Ostrom has highlighted a "paradox that individually rational strategies lead to collectively irrational outcomes."[5] Groups in collaborative initiatives often behave in the manner that provides an optimum outcome for the actors *collectively*; this requires a different mindset from that which might produce the optimum result for those seeking to compete *individually*.

Often, public diplomacy assumes an external authority must bring about change within an "audience"; this significantly underestimates the agency and power of citizens within target communities. The challenge for future public diplomats is how to translate the desire for greater impact into action within this complex social environment. Whether the shift to a more nuanced networked and collaborative approach is articulated in Russian "multi-vector" or American "multidimensional" terms, the development of collaborative approaches will consider three elements of complex environments:

- First, unilateral attempts to redefine a relationship through focus on polishing often backfire; everyone in the relationship must be involved, to increase the odds of success.
- Second, public diplomacy must focus on the most likely means to influence *behavior*, not just on improving messages and perception.[6]
- Third, in complex environments, collaboration and connection will be key elements driving innovation.[7]

Building on these core concepts of Open Source Public Diplomacy, this chapter draws on empirical research from a range of disciplines—including behavioral economics, psychology, network analysis, and neuroscience—to identify the building blocks of collaborative approaches to public diplomacy. The first section discusses the first building block, the relationships and information pathways through which information flows. This recognizes the way relationships influence the type of information that reaches communities and the way they respond. The second section identifies the role of focal or coordination points in creating the potential to aggregate opinion and action. The third section uses research into network analysis and innovation to consider the role social structures can have on the sharing and development of ideas. The final section focuses on the actions likely to encourage collaborative behavior, identified through research into psychology and behavioral economics.

RELATIONSHIPS AND INFORMATION PATHWAYS

The first building block in outlining a collaborative approach rests on understanding the relationships or different pathways through which information flows. Relationships can empower an individual, such as access to information on employment opportunities or warnings to flee from an imminent natural disaster. However, relationships may also constrain the information available to an individual. Equally, relationships and interpersonal communication influences the way information flows through a community.[8] Thus, the opportunities for a collaborative approach vary, depending on different pathways through which information flows within and between communities.[9]

A useful model for public diplomacy for understanding the importance of pathways comes from the study of crisis communication. Crisis communication research has identified three pathways in which information flows during a crisis situation. The first pathway is the communications within the public affected by a crisis. This first level pathway would most likely consist of peer-to-peer exchanges, direct relationships among the interactants, with information content having a value of immediacy or relevancy for each individual as well as the collective. A second pathway exists between members of the public who are affected by the crisis and those outside it. This level would consist of concerned family members or citizens, and would facilitate exchange of information between those with insider and outsider perspectives. A final pathway exists between the official public information officer function and members of the affected public. The institution disseminates what it considers the most immediate and relevant information. This dissemination focuses on instructions for the affected public, information for a wider audience of indirectly affected communities, and updates for unaffected citizens, often intended to keep people away from a crisis area.

These pathways provide to public diplomacy a helpful means to understand the different dynamics of the communication environment. The first two pathways contain forms of exchange that may offer the greatest potential for insight into collaborative action. Truly meaningful engagement comes from collaborative approaches and genuinely networked responses to a particular situation. The third pathway of information dissemination is similar to many of the individual, unilateral assertive public diplomacy strategies. This institution–public communication, the linear transmission of public information in a crisis, is the pathway perhaps most familiar and recognized within traditional or assertive public diplomacy.

The increasingly relational approach to public diplomacy mirrors a view of crisis communication that "the old, linear model for information dissemination of authorities-to-public relations-to-media is outmoded."[10] While traditional media can be a valuable and timely source of information, international broadcasters—social, familial, and community networks, alongside new media—provide alternatives.[11] As Leysia Palen and Sophia B. Liu state, "People are natural information seekers, and will seek information from multiple sources, relying primarily on their own social networks— friends and family—to validate and interpret information coming from formal sources." These networks also allow communities "to calculate their own response measures."[12] A collaborative approach considers the role of active networks sharing and interpreting content and avoids the mindset of transmitting messages through a single pathway to passive audiences.

The research into responses to crisis has identified the creation of improvised groups that can work on immediate challenges, including evacuation, treating the injured, or rescuing individual from collapsed buildings.[13] These improvised groups may only exist as "ephemeral organisations," but they play an important role for the short time during which communities connect through them.[14]

A practical demonstration of these networks was identified during the SARS epidemic in China. P. Law and Y. Peng showed that during the SARS epidemic, Chinese state news was the primary source of information. However, individuals validated official information through the use of cell phones and, particularly, text messages. According to their research, confirmation was sought via family and social relationships, which connected information seekers with individuals living in areas featured in the state-approved news.[15] Social validation makes it imperative that strategy is developed considering community alongside a focus on the individual.

Understanding how an interaction fits with other relationships becomes particularly important when one considers that communities within a society may adopt different responses to the same scenario. There are numerous documented studies showing how communities living in the same city respond differently to the warnings, a phenomenon exemplified in the varied responses during Hurricane Katrina.[16] While the distinctions may be less clear in some public diplomacy context than deciding whether or not to evacuate, this body of research emphasizes the importance of community and connection in the response to information. For public diplomacy, these insights emphasize the need to envision and engage with different communities in different ways. Given the power of existing relationships, these will have to be taken into account in the development of collaborative public diplomacy strategy.

While the collaborative approaches identified in the study of communication during crisis provide useful insights for public diplomacy, contemporary public diplomacy does not operate only in crisis. There are many communication environments that contain numerous information pathways, and in which communities turn to improvised or ephemeral organizations. Additionally, because future public diplomacy strategy will increasingly rely on collaboration, there is a growing imperative to adopt the behaviors appropriate to the different information pathways. This will require organizations to focus on helping communities achieve what they seek to do, rather than trying to tell them what they should do. This mindset can be framed as part of a Nash Equilibrium, in which an actor looks beyond using others as a conduit to spread his ideas exclusively. Collaborative public diplomacy focuses on working with others, accepting and working with *their* ideas in combination with your own.[17] The focus is on finding good answers to complex situations by trading in the bazaar, rather than asserting that one side has the answer, which will be delivered *ex cathedra*.[18]

The research on information pathways highlights that collaborative strategists, rather than viewing publics through the lens of the passive concept of "target audience," can adopt strategies based on understanding, facilitating, or supporting the networks of interaction between active members of a community. This is because nonlinear information pathways emphasize communication between participants, recognizing a reliance on the knowledge and behavior of others within the community.

The challenge for strategists will be to integrate the linear and hierarchical tendencies of many public diplomacy organizations into an environment where collaboration and improvisation are more appropriate.[19] In addition to the understanding of information pathways, the transition to collaborative strategies will rely on the remaining building blocks, the behaviors likely to facilitate collaboration, the factors that influence innovation, and the role of focal or coordination points around which opinion and behavior can be aggregated.

COORDINATION AND AGGREGATION

The second building block of a collaborative approach moves the focus away from individuals and their relationships, to identify key coordination points where communities interact. This provides a public diplomat with the potential to engage within the environment preferred by that community. It also provides the potential to understand a community through aggregating interactions or opinion. In some cases, a diplomat may even be able to facilitate greater impact through supporting the desire of the community to aggregate the impact of their individual actions.

Societies and communities are the aggregated result of dynamic individual interactions, where relationships are renegotiated and reinforced or undermined and decrease in intensity. Drawing on research from ecology, a flock or swarm provides a practical model to conceive of the communication between communities of interest or networks sharing content through social media. "The aggregate motion of a flock of birds, a herd of land animals, or a school of fish is a beautiful and familiar part of the natural world."[20] As Craig Reynolds describes a flock:

> It is made up of discrete birds yet overall motion seems fluid; it is simple in concept yet is so visually complex, it seems randomly arrayed and yet is magnificently synchronized.[21]

The collective behavior typified by a flock or swarm has proven resilient across numerous environments.[22] In addition to ecology, swarm intelligence has become increasingly the focus of advanced robotics and communication between autonomous underwater vehicles.[23]

Conceptualizing interaction as engaging with a swarm is important to collaborative public diplomacy strategy. Such conceptualization emphasizes the need to identify the overall structure of interaction within a community, as well as being sensitive to the impact of individual relationships. Being able to envision the larger structural dimension and individual-level dynamic allows public diplomacy to engage at the focal points where communities already seek and share information.

A greater understanding of these "focal points" is borrowed from the field of economics and the phenomenon known as "Schelling points." Nobel Prize-winning economist Thomas Schelling advance research into micromotives and macrobehavior by identifying the focal points around which communities swarm. He "explores the relation between the behaviour characteristics of the individuals who comprise some social *aggregate*, and the characteristics of the *aggregate*." To demonstrate this approach, Schelling outlines how individuals choose to sit in an auditorium to introduce the idea that individuals adopt *"contingent behaviour."*[24] He argues that the behavior of individuals and their "goals or purposes or objectives related directly to other people and *their* behaviour, or constrained by an environment that consists of other people who are pursuing their goals or their purposes or their objectives."[25]

Schelling points provide a model from which collaborative public diplomacy can draw. In public diplomacy, engaging with a community about a specific behavior may not be the most effective approach, because the behavior may be contingent on circumstances and on behaviors beyond the community's control. Assertive and linear communication strategies that deliver attractive narratives or messages may merely add to the volume of information, rather than address the circumstantial causes behind the behavior. In collaborative strategies, the drivers of change associated with change are key factors, as influence flows along numerous pathways within the complex architecture of multi-hub, multidirectional networks, of which the reason a community adopts a behavior and the drivers of change may be key parts. In addition, the community must be able to contribute to the framing of any engagement, creating answers in their own terms—rather than within the frame of reference created by public diplomat or researcher.

Research based on network analysis has demonstrated the ability to aggregate individual interactions and identify focal points identified during a social movement. An illustrative example is the protest movement following the 2009 Iranian election.[26] The research provides two key insights. The first is the ability to understand opinion and behavior by being able to aggregate individual expressions or actions within a particular community. The second is to facilitate collaboration with communities of activists to support the aggregation of their individual actions. Taken together, these observations applied to collaborative public diplomacy emphasize that the focus of professional public diplomacy will increasingly fall on the aggregated connections and activity across society.

In addition to aggregating individual experience, collaborative public diplomacy can draw inspiration from tools such as *Ushahidi*, which means testimony in Swahili. *Ushahidi* was initially developed as a platform to crowd-source information sent via mobile phones and map reports of violence in Kenya after the post-election fallout in 2008.[27] *Ushahidi* has since developed into a platform used in other crises and initiatives around the world to allow individuals access to information and to aggregate their efforts. Another example of an innovative collaborative tool is *FrontlineSMS*. For NGOs, the ability to aggregate opinion and coordinate action is often a challenge, due to the difficulty or cost of communication. *FrontlineSMS*, created by Ken Banks, founder of kiwanja.net, is free open-source software designed to enable "users to send and receive text messages with groups of people through mobile phones."[28] *FrontlineSMS* is currently in use across Africa, Asia, Europe, and Latin America.[29]

These tools are facilitative, in the sense that the aim is not to tell people what to do, but to enable users to communicate with others to achieve their goals. Insight and inspiration can also be drawn from the method through which many of these devices were developed. Projects including *Swiftriver* have been built using *GitHub*, which claims to be "the most important open source community in the world today." *GitHub* focuses "on lowering the barriers of collaboration" and currently allows over a million developers to collaborate on more than 3 million repositories (projects). To unlock the potential of a collaborative approach, a public diplomat can draw on the *GitHub* tagline: "We make it easier to collaborate with others and share your projects with the universe."[30]

The above examples show that facilitating connection is a powerful alternative to asserting specific messages in complex operational environments. Yet, despite the success of these initiatives, governments often struggle to envisage how these approaches can be applied. Initial steps taken by foreign ministries, including Canada and Sweden, were identified in "Music for the Jilted Generation."[31] More recently, the Australian government attempted an in-depth study on ways to integrate the open-source and web 2.0 methodologies into state activity. During the study, an event known as GovHack was held over the weekend in Canberra. According to the report, "over 100 people came from around the country and worked throughout the weekend—many not stopping for sleep—to build online tools to show what Government 2.0 could be like." One outcome from GovHack, held in collaboration with Mashupaustralia, was "its-buggered-mate," a mashup that allowed an individual to "Tell your local council what is buggered in your neighbourhood. Find your location on the map, then scribble on it, and leave notes about what is wrong."[32] A similar version exists in the UK: Fixmystreet.com. These examples highlight the power of engaging around coordination points and facilitating the realization of goals by local communities. They demonstrate the potential application and impact of collaborative approaches across international development, health communication, and information sharing in a crisis.

From the perspective of collaborative public diplomacy, the role of each of these initiatives is to facilitate interaction at a focal point for connection and action. The strategy focuses on identifying focal points, whether common desires or locations, that already exist within a society. It identifies ways of collaborating with communities who already want to take action and aggregate that impact. This may be thought of as identifying the points in a bazaar where trading around a particular issue takes place, and then finding the best way to facilitate the greatest benefit for the participants. Rather than focusing on how attractive a message can be and asserting how others should be trading, trading emerges organically from the dynamic of the collective.

INTER-ORGANIZATIONAL INNOVATION

Having identified the likely information pathways and the benefit derived from collaborating around focal points where individuals cluster to communicate or aggregate behavior, the third building block of collaborative public diplomacy fuses individual relationships and societal focal points to create innovation. The potential contribution made by individuals or organizations with different positions or roles within a network can be understood through research into the source/s and diffusion of innovation.

Network position has previously been recognized in public diplomacy as having the potential to influence the speed of idea diffusion.[33] The modeling run by Thomas Valente and Rebecca Davis highlighted the significant difference in adoption speeds between scenarios where the early adopters were positioned in central parts of the network, and those where the early adopters were on the periphery.[34] They concluded that when first adopters are those on the margins, the rate of diffusion is slowest, because "the innovation must percolate through the network before it reaches opinion leaders who are in the position to set the agenda for change."[35] This argument is supported by Barbara Wejnert, who argued that the predictive power of an individual actor's status on adoption of an innovation varies positively with the prominence of the actor's position in a network.[36]

While other factors, including structural equivalence of individual and collective actors, also influence diffusion, the targeting of well-connected individuals may appear to be the way to rapidly spread information through a network. However, this assertion creates a problem for public diplomacy. As noted earlier, it is not opinion leaders who tend to be early adopters, but instead "marginals . . . who first adopt an innovation."[37]

The relationship between innovation and network position is equally important in collaborative approaches to public diplomacy. Collaboration may be required to produce innovation, prior to diffusion. Earlier work on information and innovation in sociology has highlighted that social interactions are exchanges that are embedded in social relationships. Furthermore, research has shown that hierarchical approaches to communication can rapidly transform voluntary exchange into top-down, forced coercion.[38] As scholarship on the nature of exchange and innovation expanded, closure and structural holes have become key concepts in examining the development of social capital within (or between) organizations.[39]

Ronald Burt, who expanded on the importance of "bridges" proposed by Mark Granovetter, has suggested that structural holes are the source of value added, but network closure can be essential to realizing the value buried in the holes.[40] Explaining the concept of social capital, Burt conceived of society "as a market in which people exchange all variety of goods and ideas in pursuit of their interests." Within this environment Burt argues,

> people who do better are somehow better connected to certain people, or certain groups are connected to certain others, trusting certain others, obligated to support certain others, dependent on exchange with certain others. Holding a certain position in the structure of these exchanges can be an asset in its own right. That asset is social capital.[41]

The argument presented by Burt creates a building block for a collaborative theory of public diplomacy, as it emphasizes the role of connection in achieving goals within a bazaar-style interaction. Collaborative public diplomats find ways to bridge structural holes between those who have information and those who need information. By creating this bridge, public diplomats can help spur innovation, while developing social capital. An example of facilitating connections comes from the area of development. Reuben Abraham demonstrated how the creation of new information pathways through mobile phone communication among local stakeholders can help to improve the fishing industry in India.[42]

The importance of bridging structural holes, however, has a caveat that should not be overlooked. The bridging position varies depending on the task in hand, as structural holes that exist in one instance cannot be assumed to be in a similar position when that community faces a different

challenge.[43] Equally, as Sun-Ki Chai and Mooweon Rhee have demonstrated, structural holes are less important in some cultures than in others.[44]
Researchers identified a cultural contingency of social capital in Chinese
high-tech firms, and highlight the importance of strong direct ties in job
seeking in China.[45] These findings from the East Asian context contrast with
the strength of weak ties proposition presented by Granovetter, who based
his studies on Western communities.

In terms of collaborative public diplomacy strategy, these examples highlight the value of different roles and positions within a network and the way
in which local culture can lead to further variation. Identifying a network
position through which to facilitate connection can yield both social capital
and influence for a sponsor engaged in collaborative public diplomacy. Similarly, if these cultural differences are considered and respected, collaborative
public diplomacy has the potential to achieve impact through the facilitation of connection and innovation.

COLLABORATIVE BEHAVIORS

The final building block of a collaborative approach to public diplomacy
consists of the specific factors that are likely to encourage collaborative behaviors. Whether seeking to build or destabilize networks, the success of this
approach will be influenced by certain factors, which effect the adoption of
collaborative or cooperative *behaviors*.[46] Larry Wall, writing about the development of the Perl programming language in *Open Sources: Voices from
the Revolution*, emphasized that the virtues of community were "diligence,
patience, and humility."[47] While certainly helpful, the fields of psychology
and behavioral economics suggest additional factors that can influence collaborative behaviors.

Autonomy

The first determining factor of collaborative approach is autonomy, or
individual agency. The decision and ability to engage in collaboration is
based on choice rather than on coercion. Autonomy is considered one
of the key factors in successful behavior change. Empirical research on
human motivation showed that autonomous motivation stemming from
personal desire yields more effective performance and greater longer-term
persistence in adopting behaviors than do external motivating factors,
such as rewards, punishment, or social pressure.[48] Thus, collaborative
public diplomacy would focus on facilitating the autonomous form of
motivation rather than seeking to define and pressure others to act a certain way.

Autonomy is not only a factor in motivation. Those engaged in public
diplomacy must recognize the agency of every actor and their respective

potential to engage in action. They are not passive audiences, but are active participants within their own communities. Respecting the autonomy of others allows communities to opt in to a network rather than resent being co-opted or publicly included without consultation. In effect, operating in a network society is closer to an autonomous peer-to-peer environment rather than an objectified audience upon which power is exerted.

Inclusion

A second influencing factor in collaborative public diplomacy is inclusion. Inclusion is the corollary need of autonomy that individuals have in collective or collaborative ventures. This factor primarily focuses on the sense of inclusion or belonging felt by participants in the larger group. Evidence of inclusion may include active, reciprocal participation in decision making, task sharing, and social activities among the participants.

Inclusion is particularly important when seeking collective rather than individual return from a resource system. Experiments have demonstrated that people who recognize each other as belonging to the same group tend to be more generous to group members than to "outsiders."[49] Applying this insight to public diplomacy, the collective return stems from the identification of shared goals around which participants can collaborate. The importance of inclusion and its association with in-group generosity is also underscored by the flipside, namely the phenomenon of "free riding" often found in collective ventures. Those who do not feel included may choose to "free-ride," to benefit from investment by others without having to incur the same (or any) cost.[50]

Given that individuals can do nothing and still receive benefit, any organization pursuing an assertive approach rather than seeking genuine collaboration is likely to encourage "free-riding." Those not included may also adopt their own initiatives; in an interconnected world, it is difficult to exclude a specific group from having the potential to influence others. Ensuring a sense of inclusion within collaborative public diplomacy has the potential to increase the odds of successful initiatives.

Involvement

Involvement entails genuine and direct input into a collective process rather than having a pre-defined role within a pre-existing structure foisted upon an actor in the name of cooperation. Involvement is not a question of saying "do you wanna be in my gang?" In collaborative approaches to public diplomacy, individuals or groups are genuinely involved in the strategy, implementation, and benefits from an initiative. Genuine involvement generates a sense of ownership, which allows a project to draw on the more powerful autonomous motivation and resulting stronger adherence to group norms and shared group goals.

Encouraging cooperation and collaboration rather than free-riding is more than making a show of listening; communities must feel they are involved and are genuinely heard.[51] Ensuring individuals have a recognized stake, or sense of ownership in the process, helps reduce the propensity to free-ride and makes them more likely to commit to the common cause—even at personal cost.

In addition, genuine involvement entails recognition of competence, a key element in long-term behavior change.[52] Furthermore, in a study of water rights, it was concluded that shared ownership can be more efficient than land ownership and "farmer owned systems that devise boundary and allocation rules to fit their local circumstances are more likely to perform better than government-owned systems relying on a limited set of rules."[53] In cases like these, involvement of local communities pays greater dividend than attempting to usher the community into a predetermined cathedral-like program. This provides not only the potential for a sense of inclusion within the process but allows strategists to draw on local knowledge and understanding in developing a public diplomacy initiative.

Knowledge

Knowledge is a fourth, and multifaceted, factor influencing collaborative public diplomacy. Building on the previous discussion of aggregating information, knowledge has three roles in collaborative approaches to public diplomacy. First, knowledge of the connections, needs, and resources of the community can facilitate collaboration. Facilitating these connections is based on local knowledge of the network and known as network weaving.[54] Second, knowing you are connected, or feeling a sense of relatedness, is a key part of intrinsic motivation in fostering sustainable behavior change.[55] Third, local knowledge is be vital to the sustainability of collective systems. Studies have shown that approaches imposed from outside and which lacked a level of local insight have at times led to devastating consequences for those involved.[56] Local knowledge can help an organization to avoid crowding out initiatives that were already having a positive impact, as was documented in attempts to encourage citizenship.[57] Placing great value on local knowledge and facilitating information sharing within collaborative public diplomacy has the potential to greatly empower practitioners, build adherence, and develop locally appropriate responses to common challenges.

Fairness

A fifth factor influencing collaborative behavior is fairness. While the potential to access information has numerous advantages, it can also create challenges around concepts of fairness, legitimacy, and trust. In public diplomacy terms, this is not a question of fair versus unfair societies, but rather different interpretations of what being treated fairly actually entails.

Fairness may be an understudied aspect in public diplomacy, given the implication of emerging research. Transcultural neuroimaging studies have demonstrated that "one's cultural background can influence the neural activity that underlies both high- and low-level cognitive functions."[58] This difference in thought patterns at a neurological level echoes experimental evidence of diverse cultural interpretations of fairness shown through the strategies adopted in trust games.[59]

The relationship between actions and fairness in the eyes of the communities with which public diplomacy programs engage is a key concern for those strategists seeking to develop sustainable collaboration. If collaborative public diplomacy is to engage local communities, those communities must be involved in a system they consider fair and over which they feel ownership.

Punishment

Reinforcing the importance of perceptions of fairness, strategists also need to consider the possibility that a community will choose to punish an individual for the individual's actions if it is perceived the individual acted unfairly. This is because individuals will incur cost to themselves to punish other individuals seen to transgress the collective understanding, or shared norms, of fairness. In other words, "punishment almost invariably is costly to the punisher, while the benefits from punishment are diffusely distributed over the members."[60] As a transgression of fairness may be a result of cultural interpretation, the danger of punishment becomes increasingly important to consider and re-emphasizes the need for inclusion and involvement of local communities within collaborative approaches to public diplomacy.

Forms of punishment are not all the same; some may deliberately undermine or challenge an initiative, while other individuals may display displeasure simply by no longer actively contributing to the goal. Most importantly, a public diplomacy organization cannot assume that an individual will accept treatment that individual perceives to be unfair just because the initiative was intended to benefit them or their community. Politicians saying, "We do good things and people still do not like us," miss the point. Once people perceive they are being treated unfairly, they will exact punishment, even though "punishment almost invariably is costly to the punisher."[61]

Negative Impact

However well intentioned, initiatives can have a negative impact on the very communities they were intended to support, particularly if the factors listed above have not been sufficiently considered.[62] For example, in Taiwan, the government attempted to gain support of the farmers by funding the local farming associations. The result, however, was the collapse of the local associations, because the government funds crowded out community activity.[63] This is not an isolated case; "the disastrous effects of nationalizing formerly communal forests have been well documented," and these mistakes have been repeated in state intervention on inshore fisheries.[64] External influence, however well intentioned, can have a negative impact on local communities if their autonomy, inclusion, genuine involvement, local knowledge, and interpretation of fairness are insufficiently considered.

The factors outlined above can move public diplomacy strategy toward engagement through effective collective action. The focus on collaborating with dispersed communities can allow public diplomacy strategy to change the odds of certain outcomes occurring. The ability to collaborate within multi-directional, multi-hub networks rests on a complex matrix of factors and behaviors.

CONCLUSION

This essay has introduced a four-pronged model of collaborative public diplomacy. In a world where many talk of common challenges, mutual understanding, and trust, it is important for public diplomacy practitioners and scholars to consider a range of approaches beyond models of competitive assertion and leviathan-like images of government centrality. The dynamic approach to working in collaboration requires ongoing negotiation, and is often contingent on a shift in behavior *on both sides*. This form of collaboration should not to be confused with soft power as "the ability to get what you want by attracting and persuading others *to adopt your goals*."[65] Rather than attempting to assert a predetermined answer through payment, coercion, or attraction, the collaborative public diplomat facilitates connection between others, allowing them to find their own locally relevant approaches to complex problems.

These considerations cut to the heart of redefining the diplomatic mission. A collaborative ethic will have to flow right through from strategy to evaluation, with appropriate processes used to analyze the impact of an initiative and the role of a diplomat within it. Organizational expectations will have to shift the emphasis away from audiences or customers, to collaborators and network members. Diplomats would not be the suppliers of knowledge and content, but rather receivers and distributors. Staff would become network facilitators, mapmakers, and network weavers, not information officers and program managers.

Developing a collaborative public diplomacy approach echoes Robert Axelrod's observations about strategies for the evolution of cooperation: "It succeeds by eliciting cooperation from others, not by defeating them."[66] The start and endpoint for strategies of a collaborative public diplomacy is working with, not controlling or even necessarily leading, others.

NOTES

1. Manuel Castells, *The Rise of the Network Society* (New York: Blackwell, 1996).
2. Larry Wall, "Open Sources: Voices from the Open Source Revolution," *O'Reilly Online Catalogue* (1999), accessed December 13, 2010, http://oreilly.com/catalog/opensources/book/larry.html
3. Chris DiBona, Mark Stone, Danese Cooper, eds., *Open Sources 2.0: The Continuing Evolution* (New York: O'Reilly Media, 2005).
4. "Occupy Together," http://www.occupytogether.org/
5. Elinor Ostrom, *Governing the Commons: The Evolution of Institutions for Collective Action* (Cambridge: Cambridge University Press, 1990), 5.
6. A number of studies have shown reported perception or even reported intention of action can fall a long way short of an individual actually adopting that behavior change. See Doug McKenzie-Mohr and William Smith, *Fostering Sustainable Behaviour: An Introduction to Community-Based Social Marketing* (Gabriola Island, BC: New Society Publishers, 2000).
7. Ali Fisher, "Music for the Jilted Generation; Open Source Public Diplomacy," *The Hague Journal of Diplomacy* 3 (2008): 2.
8. Larsen and Hill's 1954 research into the diffusion of news found that 35% of people heard of Senator Taft's death through interpersonal communication. A similar study showed that 50% of people found out about the terrorist attacks on 9/11 from interpersonal contact (rather than TV or radio). From B.S. Greenberg, L. Hofschire, and K. Lachlan, "Crisis Communication in Natural Disasters," *Journal of Black Studies* 37 (2002): 539–54.
9. M. W. Seeger, T. L. Sellnow, and R. R. Ulmer, "Communication, Organization, and Crisis," *Communication Yearbook* 21 (1998): 231–75.
10. Leysia Palen and Sophia Liu, "Citizen Communications in Crisis: Anticipating a Future of ICT-Supported Participation," Proceedings of the ACM Conference on Computer Human Interaction (CHI 2007), 727–36.
11. R. L. Heath, S. Liao, and W. Douglas, "Effects of Perceived Economic Harms and Benefits on Issue Involvement, Use of Information Sources, and Actions: A Study in Risk Communication," *Journal of Public Relations Research* 7 (1995): 89–109. Patrick Bracken, Elisabeth Kvarnström, Alberto Ysunza, Erik Kärrman, Anders Finnson, and Darren Saywell, "Making Sustainable Choices—The Development and Use of Sustainability-Oriented Criteria in Sanitary Decision Making," Third International Ecological Sanitation Conference, Durban, South Africa, May 26, 2005, http://conference2005.ecosan.org/presentations/bracken.pdf
12. Palen and Liu, "Citizen Communications in Crisis."
13. B. E. Aguirre, "Review of Social Science Research on Warning, Evacuation, and Search and Rescue" (College Station: Hazard and Recovery Center, Texas A&M 1993); Christian Reuter, Oliver Heger, and Volkmar Pipek, *Social Media for Supporting Emergent Groups in Crisis Management* (Seattle: CSCW, 2012).
14. G. F. Lanzara, "Ephemeral Organizations in Extreme Environments: Emergence, Strategy, Extinction," *Journal of Management Studies* 20 (1983): 71–95.
15. P. Law and Y. Peng, "Cellphone, Internet, and the SARS Epidemic," *International Workshop on Mobile Technologies: Health: Benefits and Risk,* Udine, Italy, June 7–8, 2004.
16. Sammy Zahran, Grover Himanshu, Samuel D. Brody, and Arnold Vedlitz, "Risk, Stress, and Capacity: Explaining Metropolitan Commitment to

Climate Protection," *Urban Affairs Review* 43 (2008): 447–74; R. W. Perry and M. K. Lindell, "The Effects of Ethnicity on Evacuation Decision-Making," *International Journal of Mass Emergencies and Disasters* 9 (1991): 47–68.

17. For a longer examination of this distinction, see Fisher, "Music for the Jilted Generation."
18. R. S. Zaharna, *Battles to Bridges* (Basingstokes: Palgrave Macmillan, 2010); R. S. Zaharna, "The Soft Power Differential: Network Communication and Mass Communication in Public Diplomacy," *Hague Journal of Diplomacy* 2 (2007): 213–28.
19. T. Wachtendorf, and J. M. Kendra, "Community Innovation and Disasters," in *The Handbook on Disaster Research* (New York: Springer, 2006); P. J. Camp, J. M. Hudson, R. B. Keldorph, S. Lewis, and E. D. Mynatt, "Supporting Communication and Collaboration Practices in Safety-Critical Situations," *Proceedings of the Conference on Computer-Human Interactions* (2000), 149–50.
20. Craig W. Reynolds, "Flocks, Herds and Schools: A Distributed Behavioral Model," *Computer Graphics* 21 (July 1987): 25–34.
21. Ibid.
22. B. Lemasson, J.J. Anderson, R.A. Goodwin, and T.S. Bridges, "Discerning Properties of a Self-Organizing Network (Swarm) Shaping Its Structure, Function, and Resilience," *Proceedings of the Army Science Conference* (26th), Orlando, Florida, December 2008, http://www.dtic.mil/cgi-bin/GetTRDoc?AD=ADA505781
23. Michael R. Frater, Michael J. Ryan, and Robin M. Dunbar, "Electromagnetic Communications within Swarms of Autonomous Underwater Vehicles." *WUWNet'06*, September 26, 2006: 64–70.,http://wuwnet.engr.uconn.edu/papers/p064-frater.pdf
24. Thomas C Schelling, *Micromotives and Macrobehavior*, rev ed. (New York: W.W. Norton, 2006), 17.
25. Ibid.
26. Yahya R. Kamalipour, "Bullets with Butterfly Wings: Tweets, Protest Networks and the Iranian Election" in *Media, Power, and Politics in the Digital Age: The 2009 Presidential Election Uprising in Iran* (Lanham, MD: Rowman & Littlefield, 2010)
27. Ushahidi products, http://www.ushahidi.com/products/ushahidi-platform
28. "About the Software," FrontLineSMS, http://www.frontlinesms.com/aboutthesoftware/about-the-software/
29. "Case Studies," FrontlineSMS, http://www.frontlinesms.com/aboutthesoftware/case-studies/
30. GitHub can be found at https://github.com/
31. Ali Fisher, "Music for the Jilted Generation."
32. "It's Buggered Mate," *Mashupaustralia*, http://mashupaustralia.org/mashups/its-buggered-mate/
33. Ali Fisher, "Looking at the Man in the Mirror: Understanding of Power and Influence in Public Diplomacy," in *Trials of Engagement: The Future of U.S. Public Diplomacy* (The Hague: Martinus Nijhoff, 2010).
34. Valente and Davis, "Accelerating the Diffusion of Innovations Using Opinion Leaders," *Annals of the American Academy of Political and Social Science* 566 (1999): 62–64.
35. Ibid., 62.
36. Barbara Wejnert, "Integrating Models of Diffusion of Innovations: A Conceptual Framework," *Annual Review of Sociology* 28 (2002): 297–326;

C. Baerveldt and T. Snijders, "Influence on and from the Segmentation of Networks: Hypotheses and Tests," *Social Networks* 16 (1994): 213–32.
37. Valente and Davis, "Accelerating the Diffusion of Innovations."
38. Richard M. Emerson, "Power-Dependence Relations," *American Sociological Review* 27 (1962): 31–41; P. Blau, *Exchange and Power in Social Life* (New York: Free Press, 1964).
39. R. S. Burt, *Structural Holes: The Social Structure of Competition* (Cambridge, MA: Harvard University Press, 1992); J. S. Coleman, "Social Capital in the Creation of Human Capital," *American Journal of Sociology* 94 (1988): 95–120.
40. R. S. Burt, "The Network Structure of Social Capital," in *Research in Organizational Behavior*, eds. B. M. Staw and R. I. Sutton (New York: Elsevier, 2000), 345–423.
41. Ibid., 347.
42. Reuben Abraham, "Mobile Phones and Economic Development: Evidence from the Fishing Industry in India," *Information Technologies and International Development* 4 (2007): 5–17.
43. Herminia Ibarra, "Network Centrality, Power, and Innovation Involvement: Determinants of Technical and Administrative Roles," *The Academy of Management Journal* 36 (1993): 471–501.
44. Sun-Ki Chai and Mooweon Rhee, "Confucian Capitalism and the Paradox of Closure and Structural Holes in East Asian Firms," *Management and Organization Review* 6 (2009): 5–29.
45. Z. Xiao, and A.S. Tsui, "When Brokers May Not Work: The Cultural Contingency of Social Capital in Chinese High-Tech Firms," *Administrative Science Quarterly* 52 (2007): 1–31; Yanjie Bian, "Bringing Strong Ties Back In: Indirect Ties, Network Bridges, and Job Searches in China," *American Sociological Review* 62 (1997): 366–85.
46. Y. Benkler, "Law, Policy and Cooperation," E. Balleisen & D. Moss (Eds.), *Government and Markets: Toward a New Theory of Regulation* (New York: Cambridge University Press, 2008): 1–34, http://www.benkler.org/Benkler_Law%20Policy%20Cooperation%2004.pdf
Larry Wall, "Diligence, Patience, and Humility," *Open Sources: Voices from the Open Source Revolution* (O'Reilly, January 1999), accessed 12 December 2010, http://oreilly.com/catalog/opensources/book/larry.html
47. Edward L. Deci and Richard M. Ryan, "Self-Determination Theory: A Macrotheory of Human Motivation, Development, and Health," *Canadian Psychology* 49 (2008): 182–85.
48. I. Bohnet and B. Frey, "The Sound of Silence in Prisoner's Dilemma and Dictator Games," *Journal of Economic Behaviour and Organization* 38 (1999): 43–57.
49. Ostrom, *Governing the Commons.*
50. I. Ozernoy, "Ears Wide Shut," *The Atlantic* (November 1, 2006).
51. Deci and Ryan, "Self-Determination Theory," 182–85.
52. W. Blomquist, E. Schlager, S. Tang, and E. Ostrom, "Regularities from the Field and Possible Explanations," in E. Ostrom, R. Gardner, and J. Walker (eds.), *Rules, Games and Common-Pool Resources* (Ann Arbor: University of Michigan Press, 1994), 305.
53. Valdis Krebs and June Holley, "Building Sustainable Communities through Network Building," *Supporting Advancement* (2002), http://www.supportingadvancement.com/web_sightings/community_building/community_building.pdf
54. Deci and Ryan, "Self-Determination Theory," 182–85.

226   *Ali Fisher*

55. Ostrom, *Governing the Commons.*
56. E. Ostrom, "Crowding Out Citizenship," *Scandinavian Political Studies* 23 (2000): 3–16.
57. S. Han and G. Northoff, "Culture-Sensitive Neural Substrates of Human Cognition: A Transcultural Neuroimaging Approach," *Nature Reviews Neuroscience* 9 (2008): 646–54; Bohnet and Frey, "The Sound of Silence."
58. J. Henrich et al. "'Economic Man' in Cross-cultural Perspective: Behavioral Experiments in 15 Small-Scale Societies," *Behavioural and Brain Sciences* 28 (2005): 795–855; M. R. Delgado, R. H. Frank, and E. A. Phelps, "Perceptions of Moral Character Modulate the Neural Systems of Reward during the Trust Game," *Nature Neuroscience* 8 (2005): 1611–18; M. Fenwick, R. Edwards, and P. J. Buckley, "Is Cultural Similarity Misleading? Experience of Australian manufacturers in Britain," *International Business Review* 12 (2003): 297–309.
59. J. Elster quoted in Ostrom, *Governing the Commons,* 95.
60. Ostrom, Governing the Commons," 45.
61. Ibid.
62. Ostrom, "Crowding Out Citizenship," 3–16.
63. Benkler, "Law, Policy and Cooperation," 1–34.
64. Ostrom, *Governing the Commons,* 23.
65. J. Nye, "Propaganda Isn't the Way: Soft Power," *International Herald Tribune* (January 28, 2003). Emphasis added.
66. Robert Axelrod, "The Evolution of Cooperation," in *Breakthrough: Emerging New Thinking,* eds. I. Gromyko and Anatolii Andreevich (New York: Walker Publishing Company, 1988).

Contributors

Amelia Arsenault is Assistant Professor of Communication at Georgia State University. She also serves as a research fellow at the USC Center on Public Diplomacy and as the Media and Democracy Research Fellow at the Center for Global Communication Studies at the Annenberg School for Communication, University of Pennsylvania. She received her PhD from the Annenberg School for Communication at the University of Southern California (2009). Dr. Arsenault's previous scholarly work on networks and public diplomacy has appeared in edited volumes and journals such as the *ANNALS of the American Academy of Political and Social Science* and *Information, Communication, and Society*.

Robin Brown is a Senior Lecturer in International Communications at the Institute of Communications Studies, University of Leeds. He has written several book chapters and articles and is currently completing a book manuscript on *Public Diplomacy: Communications, Organization, Politics*. Brown explores the implications of social network thought for both the theory and practice of public diplomacy on his blog *Public Diplomacy, Networks and Influence* (PDNetworks.wordpress.com). Brown holds a PhD from University College of Wales, Aberystwyth.

Charles Causey is a PhD candidate at the University of Washington. His focus is on the Middle East, especially Arabic language and political communication. His recent publications include "The Battle for Bystanders: Information, Meaning Contests, and Collective Action in the Egyptian Uprising of 2011," "Anti-Foreigner Sentiment: State of the Art" (2012), and "Religion and Comparative Political Sociology" (2010). He received his MA in Sociology from the University of Washington.

Daryl Copeland, Senior Fellow at the Canadian Defence and Foreign Affairs Institute, is a Canadian analyst, author, educator, and consultant specializing in diplomacy, international policy, global issues, and public management. From 1981 to 2011, Mr. Copeland served as a Canadian diplomat, with postings in Thailand, Ethiopia, New Zealand, and Malaysia. His headquarters assignments included Senior Advisor: Public Diplomacy; Strategic Policy and Planning. He is the author of *Guerrilla Diplomacy: Rethinking International Relations* (2009) and more than 100 articles for the scholarly and popular press. Professor Copeland holds teaching appointments at Ottawa, Otago (NZ), and East Anglia (London Academy of Diplomacy) universities.

Ali Fisher is the Associate Director of Digital Media Research at Intermedia, where he moved from Mappa Mundi Consulting in 2011. He specializes in providing insight to enhance public diplomacy strategy and evaluation through network analysis. He has previously worked as Director of Counterpoint, the cultural relations think-tank of the British Council. He received his PhD at the University of Birmingham and has worked as a lecturer in International Relations at Exeter University. His publications include *Trails of Engagement* (2010) and *Collaborative Public Diplomacy* (2013).

Kathy R. Fitzpatrick is Professor and Director of Graduate Studies in Public Relations at the Quinnipiac University School of Communications in Hamden, Connecticut. She is a senior public relations advisor and an attorney and focuses her research on U.S. public diplomacy and legal and ethical issues in public relations. Her recent books include *The Future of U.S. Public Diplomacy: An Uncertain Fate* (2009) and *Ethics in Public Relations: Responsible Advocacy* (2006). Fitzpatrick is coeditor of the Palgrave Macmillan Book Series on Global Public Diplomacy. Fitzpatrick received her juris doctor degree from Southern Methodist University.

Philip N. Howard is a fellow at Princeton University in its Center for Technology Policy. He is also a member of the faculty at the Jackson School for International Studies and the Information School at the University of Washington. A Canadian sociologist and communication researcher, he is the director of the Project on Information Technology and Political Islam at the University of Washington. His latest book is *Digital Media and the Arab Spring* (forthcoming from Oxford University Press). He earned his PhD in sociology at Northwestern University.

Michael L. Kent is Associate Professor of Public Relations at the University of Oklahoma. An active technology researcher and theorist, Dr. Kent studies dialogue, social media, technology and web communication, and international and intercultural communication. Dr. Kent consults on research methods, message design, mediated communication, journalism, and public relations. He has published dozens of journal articles and books, including books on public relations writing and public speaking textbooks. Most recently, Dr. Kent conducted a Delphi study of technology professionals and academics, examining issues in social media and new technology. He received his PhD from Purdue University.

Tadashi Ogawa is Regional Director for the Southeast Asia Japan Foundation. He has worked with the foundation for more than thirty years, as Assistant Director of the Japan Culture Center in Jakarta, Indonesia, and as Director of the Japan Foundation New Delhi, India. His recent publications include *Emergence of Hindu Nationalism* (2000, Asian Pacific Award); *Fundamentalism: Twisted Terror and Salvation* (2007), a coauthored work; and a new book, *The University of the Ryukyus: American Public Diplomacy toward Okinawa from 1945 to 1968*. He earned his PhD in public diplomacy from the Graduate School of Asia-Pacific Studies, Waseda University.

Ambassador **Kishan S. Rana,** who served in the Indian Foreign Service from 1960 to 1995, was Ambassador/High Commissioner to Algeria, Czechoslovakia, Kenya, Mauritius, and Germany and worked on the staff of Prime Minister Indira Gandhi from 1981 to 1982. He is a Professor Emeritus at the DiploFoundation and Honorary Fellow at the Institute of Chinese Studies in Delhi. His recent works include *Bilateral Diplomacy* (2002), *The 21st Century Ambassador* (2004), *Asian Diplomacy* (2007), and *Diplomacy of the 21st Century* (2011). Ambassador Rana coedited *Foreign Ministries* (2007) and *Economic Diplomacy* (2011). He received his MA from St. Stephens College in Delhi.

Ambassador **Harold H. Saunders** is Chairman and President of the International Institute for Sustained Dialogue and Director of International Affairs at the Kettering Foundation. He served as advisor to five U.S. presidents and was U.S. Assistant Secretary of State for Near Eastern and South Asian Affairs during the Carter administration. In addition to his numerous articles and lectures, Dr. Saunders's books include *A Public Peace Process: Sustained Dialogue to Transform Racial and Ethnic Conflicts* (1999), *Politics Is about Relationship: A Blueprint for the Citizens' Century* (2005), and *Sustained Dialogue in Conflicts: Transformation and Change* (2012). He holds a PhD from Yale University.

Hyunjin Seo is Assistant Professor of Strategic Communication in the School of Journalism and Mass Communications at the University of Kansas. Dr. Seo's research lies at the intersection of digital media, network analysis, and strategic communication. She has conducted research on identifying emerging properties of communications in the information age and their implications for public diplomacy, activism, and nation branding. Dr. Seo was a foreign affairs correspondent for South Korean and international media outlets. She has also consulted to U.S.- and Korea-based nongovernmental organizations regarding social media and international media strategies. She received her PhD from Syracuse University.

Maureen Taylor is Professor and Gaylord Family Chair of Strategic Communication in the Gaylord College of Journalism and Mass Communication,

University of Oklahoma. Her research is focused on international public relations, nation-building and civil society campaigns, and new communication technologies. She has conducted research and consulted for the U.S. Agency for International Development (USAID), U.S. Department of State, and the British Department for International Development (DFID) in Asia, Africa, Europe, and the Middle East. She received her MA and PhD from Purdue University.

Peter van Ham is Director of Global Governance Research at Clingendael Institute in The Hague and a professor at the College of Europe in Bruges, Belgium. He has authored more than seventy articles, studies, and books, including his most recent book, *Social Power in International Politics* (2010). Dr. van Ham is a member of the Advisory Council for International Affairs for the Netherlands government. His research investigates European defense policy, transatlantic relations, and place branding. He received his doctorate in Political Science from Leiden University.

Yiwei Wang is Distinguished Professor at Renmin University of China and Tongji University, Director of China-European Academic Network (CEAN), and a Senior Research Fellow at the Charhar Institute, the leading think tank on public diplomacy in China. Dr. Wang recently completed a three-year Scholar-in-Residence post at the Mission of the People's Republic of China to the European Union (2008–2010). He has published more than one hundred academic articles and ten books, including his most recent: *On Chinese-European Civilization G2* (2012) and *Beyond International Relations: A Chinese Cultural Understanding of International Relations Theories* (2007).

R. S. Zaharna is Associate Professor in the School of Communication at American University in Washington, D.C. She is a former Fulbright Scholar and a research fellow at the University of Southern California Center on Public Diplomacy. Dr. Zaharna specializes in intercultural and international strategic communication, has testified before the U.S. Congress, and has addressed diplomatic audiences and military personnel in the United States and Europe on cross-cultural communication and public diplomacy. She is author of *Battles to Bridges: US Strategic Communication and Public Diplomacy after 9/11* (2010). She received her doctorate in Communication from Columbia University.

Index

Note: page numbers with *f* indicate figures; those with *t* indicate tables.